The Police
and Pretrial
Release

The Police and Pretrial Release

Floyd Feeney
University of California, Davis

Foreword by
Edward L. Barrett, Jr.

LexingtonBooks
D.C. Heath and Company
Lexington, Massachusetts
Toronto

Library of Congress Cataloging in Publication Data

Feeney, Floyd.
   The police and pretrial release.

   Includes index.
   1. Pre-trial release—United States. 2. Police questioning. I. Title.
HV9304.F43   345.73′072   79-9629
ISBN 0-669-03597-1   347.30572   AACR2

Published simultaneously in Canada

Printed in the United States of America

International Standard Book Number: 0-669-03597-1

Library of Congress Catalog Card Number: 79-9629

To Peggy, Elizabeth, and Linda

Contents

Contents

List of Figures
and Tables

Foreword

The bail-reform movement in the United States flowered during the 1960s. The Manhattan Bail Project, the Federal Bail Reform Act of 1966, and the infusion of federal money to support bail projects at the local level all led to a national effort directed at reducing pretrial detention. The story of this period is recounted in W. Thomas, *Bail Reform in America* (1976).

The major focus of bail reform in the 1960s was securing release on their own recognizance of persons arrested for felonies. The Manhattan Bail Project provided the common model: an agency was established to secure the information necessary to assure the judge that the defendant, if released, would appear for trial.

Relatively little attention was paid to misdemeanor cases. Although the total number of individuals and the total detention time involved in such cases are large, individual detention times are low. With average periods of pretrial detention perhaps lower than a day per case, it is not feasible to invest time and money in investigations designed to determine if the defendant will appear, because in most instances the case will be disposed of before such investigation can occur.

Again, the Vera Institute of Justice led the way with the Manhattan Summons Project in 1964, showing the feasibility of increasing the use of station-house releases of misdemeanants. Gradually, police also began the use of citations and releases in the field for selected misdemeanor cases, other than the traffic cases in which such citations had long been used. A number of studies since have suggested increased use of police citations, but it is nevertheless fair to say that major attention has not been focused on this aspect of bail reform.

In the pages that follow, Floyd Feeney has created the bible for use in establishing and managing police release procedures. He recounts the history of the movement toward the use of citations and makes a convincing case that the human and social costs involved in unnecessary detention of misdemeanants can be substantially eliminated, and police costs markedly reduced, at the price of only minor increases in nonappearance rates. Finally, he devotes a major portion of the book to a how-to-do-it manual for the implementation and management of police-citation programs.

This book should provide the impetus for a national program directed toward expanding the use of police citations. In these days of fiscal constraints and taxpayer revolts, a program that reduces both the human and the monetary costs of our criminal-justice system should have wide appeal.

Professor Feeney's book is must reading for all persons concerned with the administration of criminal justice.

Edward L. Barrett, Jr.
Professor of Law
University of California, Davis

Acknowledgments

Many people and organizations have contributed to this book. I am particularly indebted to the Police Foundation, which funded the field work; to its president, Patrick Murphy, who has done so much to improve the work of the police in America; and to John Greacen, its former staff director, who originated the idea for a more extensive study of the police role in pretrial release. The views expressed are of course solely mine and do not represent the views of the Police Foundation.

Edward L. Barrett, Jr., professor of law at the University of California, Davis, and codirector of the Center on Administration of Criminal Justice, also contributed significantly to the book. His knowledge of police practices, practical wisdom concerning the operation of the criminal-justice system, and willingness to read and comment endlessly on material were enormously helpful.

Adrianne Weir, senior research associate at Davis, assisted in the design, pretesting, and analysis of the survey, in the writing of chapter 10, and with the book in many other ways. Without her assistance the book could not have been completed.

Others also helped in important ways. Professor Daniel Freed of the Yale Law School offered thoughtful advice and insight; Michael Farrell of the Vera Institute of Justice gave generously of his time and his copious knowledge; and Wayne Thomas provided many helpful comments.

Special appreciation is also due to the over two hundred police agencies that took the time to contribute survey information and to the dozens of other agencies and officials who hosted site visits or answered particular queries. Especially helpful in this connection were Chief Biagio Dilieto, Assistant Chief William Farrell, and Sergeant Walter Northrop of the New Haven Police Department; Sergeant Robert Hafvenstein of the Minneapolis Police Department; Chief George Hart and Robert Couzens of the Oakland Police Department; Chief John Kearns, Lieutenant Robert Austin, and Officer Robert Gillis of the Sacramento Police Department; Inspector James Moran of the New York City Police Department; and Captain Buford Quisenberry of the Duval County (Jacksonville, Florida) Sheriff's Office. Judge Peter Bakakos of the Cook County, Illinois, Circuit Court, Bruce Beaudin, director of the District of Columbia Pretrial Services Agency, and Marian Gewirtz, director of research for the New York City Criminal Justice Agency, also provided invaluable aid.

The information needed for the section on police practices in Denmark was kindly provided by Judge Else Mols of Copenhagen, and Charity Kenyon graciously assisted with the translations.

I would also like to express my appreciation to Irwin Feinberg, Victoria Pynchon, Denise Russell, and Ken Turner, former students at Davis, for their fine research assistance; to Barbara Glaser and Donarae Kincanon for typing the manuscript; and to the staff of Lexington Books for their professional help and advice.

Part I
Overview

1 Police Citations for Misdemeanor Offenses: A Procedure Whose Time Has Arrived

Each community should establish procedures to enable and encourage police departments to release in appropriate classes of cases, as many arrested persons as possible promptly after arrest upon issuance of a citation or summons requiring subsequent appearance.

—President's Commission on Law Enforcement and Administration of Justice, *The Challenge of Crime in a Free Society* (1967), p. 133.

Every police agency [should] immediately . . . make maximum effective use of State statutes permitting police agencies to issue written summonses and citations in lieu of physical arrest or prearraignment confinement.

—National Advisory Commission on Criminal Justice Standards and Goals, *Police* (1973), p. 83.

Quietly and without great fanfare, a major revolution is taking place today in the way minor criminal offenders are handled before trial. Instead of arresting and detaining defendants for hours or days prior to their appearance in court, a large and increasing number of police agencies are now releasing defendants on a citation or promise to appear.

Nearly zero twenty years ago, police use of citations now involves perhaps as many as one-third of the more than 6 million misdemeanor cases handled annually across the nation. Within the next decade use of citations will increase to perhaps 75 percent of all misdemeanors.

Of obvious advantage to defendants, the citation procedure also saves considerable police time and money. In a time of stringent budgets, the citation procedure enables officers to go back on the street quickly, saves the community unnecessary detention costs, helps reduce jail overcrowding and the need for bigger and more expensive jails, and saves court time. By putting the responsibility for the initial detention decision in the hands of the police—the agency that initially knows the most about the situation—the procedure operates both faster and less expensively than any other method of pretrial release. Thus, in addition to saving defendants both time and the cost of a bail bond, police citations also enable the community to devote whatever court investigative resources it has to felonies and those few misdemeanors that require extensive pretrial investigation and monitoring.

3

What is happening today with minor criminal offenses is similar to what happened seventy years ago when the automobile and the traffic infraction were first becoming common. Police departments at that time found it necessary to make physical arrests in the case of each traffic violation. As the number of cars and violations mounted, however, making a physical arrest in each case proved too cumbersome and demanding. Although the law had relied on the use of physical arrest as the principal way to begin criminal cases for hundreds of years, a new procedure, the police citation, was invented. In addition, the police were delegated authority widely to admit defendants to bail under preset bail schedules. The convenience and practicability of these new procedures were so great that they quickly became the standard way of handling ordinary traffic offenses, and the older arrest procedure was discarded except for the more serious cases. Since then, the new invention—the traffic citation—has slowly but relentlessly been replacing the police bail procedure, which came into being at the same time.

Somewhat surprisingly, the invention of the traffic citation a generation ago did not lead to a rethinking of the need to arrest and detain in the case of minor crimes. Physical arrest continued to be the almost exclusive method of beginning cases, and virtually no thought was given to whether detention was necessary to ensure appearance before the court.

Although the potential for use was pointed out by a number of observers and study groups, it was not until the 1960s that the citation procedure came into significant use for criminal cases. Strongly endorsed by every major, national criminal-justice study group in the past decade and a half, the procedure has proved to be both highly practical and widely applicable.

Under the procedure police agencies issue citations or promise-to-appear notices to defendants in lieu of jail detention, and in many instances in lieu of physical arrest, for misdemeanors and other minor offenses. Two basic types of release are used. One takes place on the street and works in much the same way as a traffic ticket. The arresting officer gathers the necessary information and releases the suspect on the spot with his promise to appear in court. In this book this kind of release is referred to as a *field citation*. The other kind of release takes place after booking, generally at the station house or the jail. This kind of release will be referred to in this book as a *station-house citation*.

While it is easy enough to describe the terminology used in this book, the terminology actually used around the country to describe the procedure is incredibly confusing. In some jurisdictions a release is referred to as a *citation*. In others, however, it is called a *summons*, an *I-bond*, or a *desk-appearance ticket*. In one jurisdiction the traffic-ticket-type release is called a *citation*, and the release after booking a *promise to appear*. Still other names exist in other jurisdictions. Whatever the name, however, the practice is becoming more frequent and is encompassing a much wider range of criminal offenses than has previously been the case.

Some thirty-eight states have adopted legislation or court rules authorizing and encouraging use of the procedure, and over three-fourths of the nation's major police agencies have adopted the procedure itself. Many states and police agencies still lag behind, however. Some have not seriously considered using the procedure, while others are not yet taking full advantage of it.

Because development of the citation procedure has been extremely rapid, relatively little information about its use in practice has been available. The purpose of this book is to help fill this gap. The book draws heavily on a study of field practices commissioned by the Police Foundation and conducted in 1976 by the Center on Administration of Criminal Justice of the University of California, Davis. The study included a mail survey of over 200 police agencies, telephone contacts with over 40 agencies, and direct observation and discussion in more than 20 jurisdictions.

This book seeks to bring together what is known about the citation practice, including both its successes and its failures, and to provide some indications of the likely directions of future development. Part I (chapters 1 through 6) provides an overview of the procedure, including current use, historical development, extent, results, and benefits of use, and legal framework. Part II (chapters 7 through 11) concerns methods for instituting and using the procedure and covers some case examples, specific implementation steps, the citation form, and the relationship to other agencies. Part III (chapters 12 through 19) deals with likely future directions and other issues. It includes discussions on the use of the citation procedure for felonies, juveniles, and warrants; the role of the individual officer; police bail-setting authority; the possibility of a constitutional right to citation release; use in other countries; the need for more research and statistics; and conclusions and recommendations.

2

Current Use of Citations

Almost three-fourths of the 217 agencies that responded to the Police Foundation-Center on Administration of Criminal Justice survey in the summer of 1976 indicated that they were currently using the citation procedure for some kind of nontraffic offense. This figure includes 81 percent of the large metropolitan agencies responding, 62 percent of the cities under 100,000 population, over three-fourths of the state police agencies, and over two-thirds of the sheriff's offices, as shown in table 2-1.

Eighty-seven percent of the agencies that used the procedure for some kind of nontraffic offense used it for both ordinance violations and misdemeanors, as shown in table 2-2.

Satisfaction

Over 80 percent of the agencies using the procedure indicated that they were satisfied with it, and another 6 percent indicated that their only dissatisfaction was that they would like to expand its use. Eight percent indicated that they were not satisfied with some aspect of current usage, as shown in table 2-3. Three agencies in this group were concerned that their citation procedure was not producing fingerprints or an adequate record of offenders. Several were disappointed that the procedure did not appear to be saving officer time. One indicated the lack of a deterrent effect on offenders, and another resistance by stores as a problem. Several cited mechanical problems of one kind or another. Five agencies were sufficiently dissatisfied that they had discontinued use of the citation procedure.

Nonuse

Sixty agencies, one-quarter of those responding, indicated that they did not use citations for nontraffic offenses. Five agencies, mentioned above, had tried the procedure and decided that it did not work. Of the remainder, about a third had considered using the procedure but decided not to, while almost two-thirds indicated that they had not considered the practice, as shown in table 2-4.

Table 2-1
Current Nontraffic Use of Citations
(percent of agencies responding)

	Use	Do Not Use
Cities over 100,000	81	19
Cities under 100,000	62	38
State police agencies	78	22
Sheriff's offices	69	31
All agencies	72	28
Number of agencies responding	(157)	(60)

Source: Police Foundation-Center on Administration of Criminal Justice survey, 1976.

Table 2-2
Citation Use for Misdemeanors and Regulatory and Ordinance Violations
(percent of using agencies)

	Regulatory and Ordinance Violations Only	Misdemeanor Offenses Only	Both
Cities over 100,000	6	4	90
Cities under 100,000	15	2	83
State police agencies	0	7	93
Sheriff's offices	18	9	73
All agencies	10	4	87
Number of agencies responding	(15)	(6)	(136)

Source: Police Foundation-Center on Administration of Criminal Justice survey, 1976.

Table 2-3
Satisfaction with Procedure
(percent of using agencies)

		Not Satisfied		
	Satisfied	Want More Use	Problems with Procedure	Discontinued
Cities over 100,000	78	8	11	3
Cities under 100,000	85	5	4	5
State police agencies	93	0	7	0
Sheriff's offices	82	9	9	0
All agencies	82	6	8	3
Number of agencies responding	(131)	(10)	(13)	(5)

Source: Police Foundation-Center on Administration of Criminal Justice survey, 1976.

Table 2-4
Nonuse by Type of Agency
(percent of nonusing agencies)

	Considered	Not Considered	Discontinued
Cities over 100,000	26	63	11
Cities under 100,000	38	53	9
State police agencies	0	100	0
Sheriff's offices	20	80	0
All agencies	30	62	8
Number of agencies responding	(18)	(37)	(5)

Source: Police Foundation-Center on Administration of Criminal Justice survey, 1976.

In addition to the 60 agencies that were not using the citation procedure and the 157 that were using it, 8 of the responding agencies indicated that they were in the process of implementing the use of citations.

The most frequent reasons given for not adopting the citation procedure, as shown in table 2-5, were that it would not permit adequate identification of the person involved and that the procedure was not lawful in the jurisdiction concerned. Interestingly, in most of the states in which agencies indicated that it would be unlawful to use the procedure, some other agency was already using nontraffic citations.

Table 2-5
Reasons for Nonuse of Citation Procedure
(percent of nonusing agencies)

	Considered	Not Considered	Discontinued	All Agencies
Not lawful in our jurisdiction	33	56	0	44
Would not permit adequate identification	50	44	20	42
Too many defendants will not appear	33	22	40	24
System doing too much for criminals already	11	17	0	14
Tried and didn't work out	0	0	60	5
Would restrict officer's ability to search	17	17	20	15
Our district attorney or court opposes such use	28	3	40	10
Number of agencies responding	(18)	(36)	(5)	(59)

Source: Police Foundation-Center on Administration of Criminal Justice survey, 1976.
Note: Multiple responses given.

3 Historical Development

In England summons, rather than arrest, is used regularly for minor prose-cutions. . . . [This practice] should be introduced [in the United States] wherever it is not provided for, and its use should be extended everywhere. Indiscriminate exercise of the power of arrest is one of the most reprehensible features of American criminal justice.
—National Commission of Law Observance and Enforcement, *Report on Criminal Procedures* (1931), p. 14.

Two hundred years ago there was much less need for a citation procedure than there is today. There were many fewer minor crimes than at present and no organized police departments to enforce them in any event. Detailed rules governed when arrests could be made without a warrant and when a warrant was required. For the most minor crimes, however—those which could be tried by a single magistrate—the English law did not authorize arrest at all (except by the magistrate himself).[1] A summons issued by the magistrate was the normal method of proceeding and was often used for most major crimes as well.

Today the restraints that were once built into the law of arrest are for the most part no longer present. With the advent of the modern police in the first half of the nineteenth century the law changed, and many additional defendants were made subject to custodial arrest.[2] Although this change appears to have been aimed primarily at eliminating the warrant requirement that made arrest for common misdemeanors cumbersome, its effect was much more sweeping; it resulted in authorizing custodial arrests for many offenses, such as ordinance and regulatory violations, that had previously not been subject to arrest at all.

Despite its obvious importance in the history of law enforcement, this change in the processing of petty offenses has gone largely unnoticed both by legal writers and by historians of the police.[3] This change has also been exactly opposite to the trend of other developments concerning the law of arrest. Many civil cases once began with arrest, and witnesses, in both civil and criminal cases, were also often subject to arrest. Today arrest as a method of beginning civil suits and as a device for ensuring the presence of witnesses is largely a thing of the past.[4]

The Law of Arrest

From the beginning of the modern English criminal law, some 700 or 800 years ago, until today, most criminal cases have begun in the same way—with the arrest of the defendant and his presentation in court.[5] For the most petty offenses, however, the early rules were different. Prior to the middle 1800s prosecutions for most such offenses began not with an arrest, but with the issuance of a summons by a justice of the peace.[6]

The law of arrest in this earlier era was that peace officers (sheriffs, constables, bailiffs, and other forerunners of the police)[7] were permitted to arrest without a warrant for felonies that they had seen or had reason to believe the defendant had committed.[8] Peace officers could also arrest without warrant for misdemeanors, but only for those involving a breach of the peace committed in the officer's presence.[9] Warrantless arrests for misdemeanors were allowed, it was said, not to apprehend the offender but to restore the peace.[10] Private citizens were allowed to arrest for felonies and for the same misdemeanors as officers, but only if the offense was committed in their presence.[11]

Other arrests required a warrant based on probable cause and issued by a magistrate.[12] To be sure, the magistrate in those days was not the neutral, detached judicial figure of today, but rather something of a cross between a judge and a chief detective.[13] The warrant requirement was a real limitation, however, because it meant the involvement of a number of people in the decision to arrest. For the most minor offenses—those which could be tried by a magistrate without a jury—the magistrate was not permitted to issue a warrant and could proceed only by summons.[14] Thus, for these offenses, arrest was not permitted at all.[15]

As there are no statistics for this period, the number of offenses of this kind is unknown. It must have been large, however, as the original reason for creating the summary offense in the 1600s was probably that there were too many such crimes to make it feasible to give each defendant a jury trial.[16] Single judges were consequently authorized to try these cases without juries. Despite this shift, however, by the late 1700s, Blackstone was complaining that the summary cases created a major work-load burden.[17] Among the offenses considered summary at this time were violations of law relating to liquor, trade and manufacture, labor, smuggling, traffic on the highway, the Sabbath, cheats, gambling, swearing, and dozens of others.[18]

Even for misdemeanors—for which warrants could be issued—the normal practice when arrests were not made on the spot was apparently for the magistrate to issue a summons rather than a warrant.[19] At times, even when a warrant was issued, the defendant was simply notified rather than arrested. Lord Mansfield mentioned one such instance in 1806, and it seems likely from his language that this was not an isolated occurrence.[20]

In the mid-1800s, as police departments were first being formed and new minor crimes began to be created, the arrest rules for misdemeanors and minor crimes began to change. Statutes and ordinances establishing the new minor crimes often specifically authorized arrest without warrant.[21] In addition, many U.S. jurisdictions adopted more general statutes authorizing police officers to arrest without warrant for any misdemeanor committed in their presence. One of the first such statutes was an 1848 Maine enactment that directed law enforcement officers "to arrest . . . every person found violating any law of the state or any legal ordinance or by-law" of a city or town.[22] Another early provision was that developed by the drafters of the Field Code of Criminal Procedure. This was adopted in California in 1851 and in New York, its state of origin, in 1878.[23]

Although the legislatures were persistent in passing these new laws, the courts did not like them, and a number of those extending arrest powers without warrant to misdemeanors were held unconstitutional.[24] Ultimately, however, the courts began to accept the laws, and today they are not thought to present any significant legal issue.[25] There is no indication that, in adopting these new statutes, any significant attention was given to the practical need of bringing these additional defendants into custody to begin the criminal proceedings or to any possible alternatives to arrest.[26]

The Field Code draftsmen talked primarily of the need to simplify the complicated law relating to misdemeanor arrests, although part of the intent of the changes was almost surely to avoid the necessity for getting a warrant for each arrest.[27] Whether intended or not, however, one effect of these statutes was that in many states virtually all minor cases came to be initiated in the same way as the more serious cases—by arrest.[28]

Further Development of the Judicial Summons

Around the same time that the power of the police to arrest without warrant for minor offenses was being extended in the United States, the authority of the magistrate to begin cases without arrest through use of the judicial summons was being expanded in England. While justices of the peace had long used the judicial summons instead of a warrant for misdemeanors, this practice rested on no specific provision of law.

In 1848, Parliament adopted a statute that confirmed the authority of magistrates to issue a summons instead of an arrest warrant for misdemeanors and authorized issuance for felonies as well. Under this statute the offender was to be notified of his obligation to appear, rather than physically arrested, if the magistrate was satisfied that the person summoned would appear.[29] Much more clearly than before, this new practice required the magistrate to consider the need for physical arrest when judicial intervention was called into play.

After the creation of this new statutory authority in England, U.S. jurisdictions began to provide for similar authority.[30] By 1930 this kind of legislation existed to some extent in thirteen American jurisdictions[31], and numerous groups and individuals were calling for its further extension.[32]

This new summons authority might have been expected to result in a great decrease in the number of defendants in custody, and this may have happened to a degree in England.[33] In the United States, however, most cases are initiated by physical arrest without warrant and without prior judicial contact.[34] Consequently, although the authority to issue judicial summonses has reduced unnecessary custody, it has not had great impact.

First Development of the Police Citation

When an arrest without warrant is made, the law requires that the officer bring the arrested offender before a magistrate as soon as practicable.[35] This requirement dates back to the time when there were no police forces and the justice of the peace was as much law-enforcement officer as judge.[36]

> The justices (of the peace) were first established in England in 1326 with the primary duty to "keep the peace." By 1360 they were empowered "to take and arrest all those that they may find by indictment, or by suspicion and to put them in prison." Under the governing statutes the justices "were, in fact, the overriding police authority in each county."[37]

Because little delay was contemplated at this time in bringing the defendant before the magistrate and the magistrate was empowered to grant bail immediately, it is not surprising that little thought was given to providing the constable with some alternative to arrest.

Nonetheless, the constable was, from at least the 1600s, authorized to release the defendant outright if he concluded that the defendant was innocent or that the reasons that necessitated the arrest no longer existed.[38] This authority has continued and is now codified in a number of state statutes.[39]

The common-law authority to release the defendant outright did not extend to releasing the defendant on a promise to appear before the magistrate. It seems likely that defendants were released on promises to appear from time to time, particularly in small communities, but the first formal authority was adopted in England in 1867.[40] By statute the desk sergeant was authorized to release defendants on a promise to appear in minor cases without judicial approval. For reasons that are unclear, this procedure does not appear to have been copied in the United States at this time, and the first widespread use of the citation procedure in the United States seems to have been for traffic violations.[41]

The Traffic Citation

The exact history of the traffic citation is not clear. It seems likely, however, that the early practice in traffic cases was physical arrest and that at a fairly early date a variety of noncustody procedures evolved. Thus the first comprehensive Pennsylvania motor-vehicle act, enacted in 1903, provided that:

> It shall be the duty of the constables and police officers of . . . this Commonwealth to arrest upon view and without a warrant, any person or persons violating [this act].[42]

Under this kind of statute the procedure was for the police officer to make a physical arrest and then to bring the defendant before the judge or the justice of the peace. The case would then be adjudicated summarily, or, if the defendant chose to contest the issue, bail would be set. Not too long thereafter, informal procedures were developed under which defendants were no longer taken into custody, or at least no longer detained for any length of time.

In some jurisdictions the procedure was citationlike from the start. Defendants were released under a threat that a warrant would be issued if they failed to appear in court or under a promise to appear.[43]

In other jurisdictions the first procedure to develop involved delegation of bail-setting authority, long thought to be a judicial function, to the police.[44] Instead of taking the defendant to court, the police set the bail according to a predetermined schedule and accepted the defendant's money. As with criminal cases, if the defendant did not have any money, he stayed in jail. Gradually—at least for in-state or in-community motorists—most of these jurisdictions began to switch over to the citation system, releasing defendants not on money bail but on their promise to appear.[45]

In most instances these new procedures lacked specific statutory authorization at the outset. Although the procedures were not illegal, citizens were not legally obligated to follow them. Citations were therefore unenforceable. As one court indicated, "while it may be true that such a procedure has about all the binding force of a 'royal invitation'," it does not amount "to an arrest" and the defendant in essence appears "voluntarily."[46]

Considerable confusion also existed at this time as to the true legal nature of the citation. Some jurisdictions showed the close relationship to arrest by creating a fictitious arrest. They simply issued a piece of paper to the motorist entitled "arrest notice" or "arrest notification."[47] This method is similar to the way in which the summons began to replace physical arrest in certain civil suits 300 years earlier.[48] Other jurisdictions issued a document called a "summons," a "warrant," a "writ," or a "recognizance," each of these being a wholly separate legal concept and each having somewhat different consequences.[49] One jurisdiction even went so far as to issue a citation that required the defendant to plead guilty to the offense.

Gradually the new procedures were taken over into the statutes. In California a statute authorizing the use of citations for traffic offenses was in effect by 1915, and this probably was not the earliest such provision.[50] By 1926 the need for procedures of this kind was sufficiently great that a uniform state law on the subject was proposed by the Commissioners on Uniform State Laws.[51] By 1942 some seventeen states had adopted this provision and thirteen other states had created statutory provisions authorizing the use of citations for traffic offenses.[52] Even at this late date, however, agencies in many states continued to handle traffic offenses by arrest. A survey by the National Committee on Traffic Law Enforcement in 1941 found that about 40 percent of the cities surveyed used tickets only for parking or for minor traffic offenses, as shown in table 3-1. A few city agencies and ten state highway patrols still relied almost wholly on arrest as the basic method for handling traffic offenses.[53]

Other Early Citation Uses

The use of citations for criminal offenses involving juveniles also developed quite early in some departments. Such a procedure existed in New York City as early as 1913 and was developed in Oakland, California, in 1938.[54] The use of citations for criminal offenses was also developed at a fairly early point by a few district attorney's offices. One such office was that of the Alameda County district attorney, which began to use the procedure in 1921 for neighborhood disputes and other minor crimes.[55]

The Citation for Criminal Offenses
Develops in the United States

One of the first to suggest that these noncustody or limited-custody methods of handling traffic and juvenile offenders might be used by the police for nontraffic criminal cases involving adults was Arthur Beeley, in his landmark study of the bail system in Chicago in 1927.[56] This theme was picked up to a limited extent in the American Law Institute's proposed Code of Criminal Procedure in 1930 and by the Wickersham Commission, the first great national commission on crime, in 1931.[57] Both of these bodies, however, while raising questions about the need for physical arrest, emphasized the use of the judicial summons rather than the police citation.

The first statute specifically authorizing the use of the citation procedure by the police for offenses other than traffic offenses appears to have

Table 3-1
Cities Using Traffic Tickets in 1941

	Tickets Not Used	Tickets Used for Parking Offenses Only	Tickets Used for Minor Offenses Only	Tickets Used for All Offenses below Reckless Driving
76 cities visited	1%	17%	25%	57%
60 cities by questionnaire	2	20	17	61

Source: G. Warren, *Traffic Courts* 37 (1942). Reprinted with permission from the National Conference of Judicial Councils.

been that adopted by New York in 1932.[58] This statute required judicial concurrence in the procedure, however, and initially was applied only to regulatory offenses.[59] It remained therefore for the Interstate Commission on Crime to propose in 1941 in clear and simple terms that police officers be given the authority to release minor offenders on their promise to appear. This proposal, called the Uniform Arrest Act, was later endorsed by the Commissioners on Uniform State Laws and by the International Association of Chiefs of Police. The draftsman of the act, Samuel Warner, explained the provision:

> Even guilty people should often be released without being brought into court. For example, a police officer sees a man lying in the street dead-drunk. Though the drunkard must be taken to the station for his own protection, by six in the morning he will be sober and ready to go to work. If the officers hold him for court, he is likely to lose his job and to join those on relief.

> Even though the person arrested ought to appear in court for trial and punishment, often he should not be held in jail pending trial. Most people arrested for misdemeanors are local residents who will be placed on probation or given a small fine by the judge. They will not desert their homes and jobs simply because released without bail. To require them to furnish bail adds needlessly to their punishment and often increases the impoverishment of their families and the cost of relief. Besides being expensive to the county or state, detention in jail pending trial causes them similar hardships, and justifies the adage that there is one law for the rich and another for the poor.[60]

The new provision was adopted almost immediately in New Hampshire and Rhode Island, and a decade later in 1951 in Delaware.[61] Comments also began to appear in the literature.[62]

The extent to which police agencies in the states that adopted the citation procedure at an early date actually began to use the procedure is not known. It is clear, however, that there was some use in New York state as early as 1942,[63] and that a few other departments began to use the procedure around this time, if not before. Two of the cities responding to the Police Foundation-Center on Administration of Criminal Justice survey indicated that they began use prior to 1940; several others indicated that they began prior to 1950.[64] Use in the beginning tended to be sporadic and was much more common for regulatory than for criminal offenses.[65]

The first major use of citations for nontraffic criminal cases appears to have been in New York in the spring of 1964, when the New York City Police Department joining with the Vera Institute of Justice in developing the Manhattan Summons Project as an experiment to "test the hypothesis that persons charged with minor offenses who possess verifiable roots in the community can be relied upon to appear in court voluntarily and need not be held in custody until arraignment."[66] This experiment was a direct outgrowth of the tremendous success of the Manhattan Bail Project, an earlier experiment in which the courts had released defendants with strong community ties on their own recognizance. The summons project, which is discussed further in chapter 7, rapidly proved so successful in the pilot precincts that it was extended to all of Manhattan in 1966, and throughout the entire city in 1967.[67]

At about the same time that the Manhattan Summons Project was getting under way, several California police departments began experimenting with similar procedures. Perhaps the most widespread experience was developed in Contra Costa County, where a county-wide committee under the leadership of district attorney John Nejedly, and including members of the judiciary, was formed in 1964 to look into the matter and where a number of police departments developed citation programs at that time.[68]

The National Bail Conferences in 1964 and 1965 gave a great deal of publicity to the Manhattan Summons Project and indicated that a few other departments were using the procedure.[69] Agencies listed in the 1965 report included Contra Costa County, Glendale, and Sunnyvale in California; Denver, Colorado; Jersey City, Newark, Passaic, and Trenton, New Jersey; Nassau County, New York; and Toledo, Ohio, in addition to New York City.[70]

In 1966 the President's Commission on Crime in the District of Columbia recommended that the police and the courts develop practices permitting "more extensive release at the precinct station without bail." The commission indicated that:

[R]elease at the precinct relieves the police of housing, feeding and transporting thousands of arrested people. Insofar as collateral forfeitures dispose of cases, court congestion is relieved. Most importantly, release at the precinct avoids the adverse personal effects of needless incarceration where the prosecutor decides not to proceed against a person who has been arrested and held in jail overnight or where the court immediately grants him release on bail.[71]

The first draft of the American Law Institute's Model Code of Pre-Arraignment Procedure was also issued in 1966. This draft, which was widely circulated, endorsed the procedure and suggested both new statutory language and the development of police regulations concerning citations.[72]

In 1967 the President's Commission on Law Enforcement and Administration of Justice urged "each community" to:

> establish procedures to enable and encourage police departments to release, in appropriate classes of cases, as many arrested persons as possible promptly after arrest upon issuance of a citation or summons requiring subsequent appearance.[73]

In 1968 the American Bar Association Project on Standards for Criminal Justice also endorsed the concept, saying that:

> It should be the policy of every law enforcement agency to issue citations in lieu of arrest or continued custody to the maximum extent consistent with the effective enforcement of the law.[74]

A staff report to the National Violence Commission in 1970 also commented favorably on the procedure,[75] although the commission itself did not make any new recommendations.

In 1973 the National Advisory Commission on Criminal Justice Standards and Goals addressed the subject more fully. It recommended that:

> [E]very police agency issue, where legal and practical, written summons and citations in lieu of physical arrest. Police should establish procedures to seek out expeditiously and take into custody individuals participating in these programs who fail to appear in court.[76]

The commission task forces addressed the issues in even greater detail. The police task force emphasized the development of departmental guidelines:

> Every police agency immediately should make maximum effective use of State statutes permitting police agencies to issue written summonses and citations in lieu of physical arrest or prearraignment confinement. . . .

> Every police agency should adopt policies and procedures that provide guidelines for the exercise of individual officer's discretion in the implementation of State statutes that permit issuance of citations and summonses, in lieu of physical arrest or prearraignment confinement.[77]

The courts task force envisioned the use of police citations in a wide range of circumstances:

> Upon the apprehension, or following the charging, of a person for a misdemeanor or certain less serious felonies, citation or summons should be used in lieu of taking the person into custody.

All law enforcement officers should be authorized to issue a citation in lieu
of continued custody following a lawful arrest for such offenses.[78]

The corrections task force made even more detailed recommendations,
adopting in effect the recommendations of the American Bar Association's
Standards for Criminal Justice Project, which is discussed in greater detail
in chapter 6.[79]

In 1974 the International Association of Chiefs of Police developed a
set of Model Rules for Law Enforcement Officers for the Texas Council on
Criminal Justice.[80] Included within the rules suggested was a set of proposed
rules concerning release on citation. The proposed rules mandated the use of
a field release for misdemeanor offenders except for eight specific situations:

1. Where there is an outstanding arrest warrant.
2. Refusal or failure to offer satisfactory proof of name and address.
3. Refusal to sign notice to appear.
4. Where a records check indicates a previous refusal to appear.
5. Insufficient ties to the jurisdiction to insure appearance in court.
6. Where physical arrest is necessary to prevent imminent bodily harm to
   the offender or another or prevent continuation of the offense.
7. Where there is reason to believe the violator might be involved in past
   felony crimes.
8. Where the arrest was made by a citizen and the offender is being turned
   over to the officer.

If a physical arrest is made pursuant to one of these provisions, the rules
authorize a station-house release after fingerprints and a photograph are
taken if the violator has not been arrested for a felony within the last three
years.[81]

In 1974 the procedure was also endorsed by the Commissioners on Uniform State Laws in their Model Code of Criminal Procedure. In 1975 the
American Law Institute gave final approval to the Model Code of Pre-
arraignment Procedure, and in 1977 the National District Attorneys Association adopted its National Prosecution Standards, which also recommend
such use. Other groups that have endorsed the procedure include the National Association of Pretrial Services Agencies (1978) and the American
Bar Association, in the second edition of the American Bar Association
Standards for Criminal Justice (1980).[82]

Statutory Development

In 1981 there were thirty-eight states that had a statute or a court rule
authorizing the use of citations for at least some nontraffic offenses. The

oldest of these are the New Hampshire and Rhode Island statutes, adopted in 1941. These were followed by the Delaware statute, adopted in 1951, and California statutes, adopted in 1955 and 1957. A few other states followed suit in the early sixties, and by the end of the sixties the list had begun to grow rapidly, as shown in table 3-2.

The first acts, those of New Hampshire and Rhode Island, were clearly patterned after the Uniform Arrest Act and were adopted at about the time it was first unveiled in 1941.[83] The 1951 Delaware statute also followed this model.[84]

The next statute developed was that of California. After an attorney general's opinion in 1953[85] that the existing California traffic-citation procedure could not be used for nontraffic offenses, the legislature adopted a statute, modeled after the state's traffic citation, permitting use for county regulatory offenses.[86] In 1957 a new statute, based on the Uniform Arrest Act, was adopted to permit use for misdemeanors as well.[87]

In 1963, Illinois followed suit, patterning its actions, as had the other states, on the Uniform Arrest Act.[88] From 1967 on the statutes clearly show the influence of the Manhattan Summons Project.[89] A number also show the influence of the American Bar Association Standards on Pretrial Release.[90]

Although it has been known for some time that a growing number of states were adopting statutes or rules relating to citations, the extent to which these laws had been implemented by local police agencies was not known.

Table 3-2
Statutes and Court Rules

Year of Adoption	State
1941	New Hampshire, Rhode Island
1951	Delaware
1957	California
1963	Alaska, Colorado, Illinois
1966	Arizona
1967	Connecticut, Montana, Oklahoma
1968	Michigan
1969	Oregon, Tennessee
1970	District of Columbia, New York Pennsylvania
1972	Hawaii
1973	Florida, Nevada, New Mexico, North Carolina, Ohio, Virginia
1974	Nebraska, Vermont
1975	Kansas, Louisiana, Utah
1976	Arkansas, Kentucky, Maine, Minnesota, New Jersey, Wisconsin
1977	Massachusetts, South Dakota
1978	Indiana

The Police Foundation-Center on Administration of Criminal Justice survey provides important new information in this area. It shows that, along with the increase in the number of statutes and study-commission recommendations, there has been a sizable increase in the number of police agencies using the citation procedure. From the trickle of pioneering agencies in the early years, the number of agencies adding the procedure has now become a steady stream, as shown in table 3-3.[91]

The survey also shows that in every state with a statute or rule authorizing the citation procedure, at least one agency has adopted the procedure. In addition, the survey shows that in states that do not have a statute or court rules authorizing the citation procedure, many agencies have nonetheless adopted the use of citations. This use is so extensive that some agency has adopted the procedure in at least forty-five states. Although some agencies in jurisdictions without statutes or court rules feel that it would be illegal for them to issue citations, it is clear that many others do not.

Table 3-3
Year Citation Use Begun for Nontraffic Offenders
(number of agencies responding)

1940 or before	2
1940-1949	0
1950-1959	1
1960-1965	5
1966-1970	27
1971	14
1972	10
1973	12
1974	15
1975	28
1976 (8 months)	10
In planning stage in 1976	8
Total agencies responding	(132)

Source: Police Foundation-Center on Administration of Criminal Justice survey, 1976.

Notes

1. See notes 5-18 infra.

2. The police department in London was first created in 1829, and the Boston police department in 1838. See 4 L. Radzinowicz, *A History of English Criminal Law and its Administration from 1750,* at 158-207 (1956); S. Walker, *A Critical History of Police Reform* (1977).

3. Major writers who do not discuss the effects of these statutes on summary offenses include Wilgus, "Arrest Without a Warrant" (pts. 1-3), 22 *Mich. L. Rev.* 541, 673, 798 (1924); W. LaFave, *Arrest* (1965); and E. Fisher, *Laws of Arrest* (1967). All of these writers, however, discuss changes in the limitations concerning breach of the peace.

4. Morris and Wiener, "Civil Arrest: A Medieval Anachronism," 43 *Brooklyn L. Rev.* 383 (1977); Carlson, "Jailing the Innocent: The Plight of the Material Witness," 55 *Iowa L. Rev.* 1 (1969).

5. See 1 J. Stephen, *A History of the Criminal Law of England* (1883). For this purpose the modern English criminal law can be said to have begun when the era of self-help began to fade away.

6. See J. Goebel and T. Naughton, *Law Enforcement in Colonial New York* 415-419 (1944); W. Paley, *The Law and Practice of Summary Convictions* 19 (1st ed. 1814).

7. See 1 J. Stephen, *A History of the Criminal Law of England* 184-216 (1883); J. Crocker, *The Duties of Sheriffs, Coroners and Constables* (1855).

8. See Wilgus, "Arrest Without a Warrant" (pts. 1-3), 22 *Mich. L. Rev.* 541, 673, 798, at 703-709 (1924); 4 W. Blackstone, *Commentaries on the Laws of England* 289 (1769).

9. See note 8 supra. The rules indicated in *United States* v. *Watson,* 423 U.S. 411, 418 (1976) are not wholly correct as to the power to arrest for misdemeanors. Prior to the mid-1800s or later peace officers had no general authority to arrest for misdemeanors not involving a breach of the peace. Some offenses were exceptions to this rule, but there is uncertainty as to what these offenses were. There is also considerable uncertainty as to what constituted a breach of the peace. See American Law Institute, *Code of Criminal Procedure with Commentaries* 231 (1931); Wilgus, "Arrest Without a Warrant" (pts. 1-3), 22 *Mich. L. Rev.* 541, 673, 798, at 573 (1924).

10. 1 J. Stephen, *A History of the Criminal Law of England* 193 (1883).

11. Id.

12. At one time there was a serious question as to whether a magistrate could issue a warrant for a felony based on probable cause. Coke, for example, would have limited the issuance to cases in which there had already been an indictment. This issue was apparently resolved in the early 1700s when it was decided that a magistrate could issue a warrant on probable cause. See J. Goebel and T. Naughton, *Law Enforcement in Colonial New*

York 419-431 (1944); 1 J. Stephen, *A History of the Criminal Law of England* 191-193 (1883). Goebel and Naughton indicate that *warrant* was a generic name for writs prior to indictment and suggest that there were various forms of warrants—some for arrest and some for other actions. Thus even the warrant may sometimes not have called for custody. P. 387.

13. See note 37 infra and accompanying text.

14. See note 6 supra.

15. See W. Paley, *The Law and Practice of Summary Convictions* 19 (1st ed. 1814) ("For offenses merely arising by penal statutes, and not connected with any breach of the peace, a justice has no authority . . . to apprehend the accused in the first instance."). The summons was apparently also used for minor offenses during the Dutch days of the New York colony. See J. Goebel and T. Naughton, *Law Enforcement in Colonial New York* 392 n. 40 (1944).

16. See Paley, note 15 supra, introduction at xx-xxix.

17. See 4 W. Blackstone, *Commentaries on the Laws of England* 278-279 (1769). See also Frankfurter and Corcoran, "Petty Federal Offenses and the Constitutional Guaranty of Trial By Jury," 39 *Harv. L. Rev.* 917, 928-930 (1926); *Duncan* v. *Louisiana*, 391 U.S. 145 (1968).

18. See Frankfurter and Corcoran, note 17 supra. Some summary offenses were breaches of the peace (assaults, etc.) and some, such as vagrancy, even though not breaches of the peace, could be the subject of arrest.

19. The authorities are not altogether clear as to whether a warrant or a summons (venire facias) was the preferred procedure. It is probable that the older procedure was to issue a venire, but that by Blackstone's time the custom had changed to prefer an arrest warrant (capias). Compare M. Hale, *Summary of the Pleas of the Crown* 93-94 (1678) with W. Blackstone, *Commentaries on the Laws of England* 313 (1769). See also J. Goebel and T. Naughton, *Law Enforcement in Colonial New York* 419-442 (1944); T. Starkie, *Criminal Pleading* 317 (1824). It does seem clear, however, that at minimum the magistrate could issue a summons instead of a warrant after an indictment had been found.

20. *Arrowsmith* v. *LeMesurier*, 127 Eng. Rep. 606, 2 Box Pul. (N.R.) 210 (C.P. 1806) ("The warrant was made no other use of than as a summons.") See also *Berry* v. *Bass*, 157 La. 81, 102 So. 76 (1924).

21. See Wilgus, "Arrest Without a Warrant" (pts. 1-3), 22 *Mich. L. Rev.* 541, 673, 798, at 703-709 (1924). A list of English statutes of this kind is given in 9 H. Halsbury, *Laws of England* 89-95, particularly notes (f)-(h) (2d ed., 1933). See also Warner, "Modern Trends in the American Law of Arrest," 21 *Can. Bar Review* 192, 201-202 (1943).

22. Laws of Maine, 1848, c. 71, §1. The proposed Field Code of Criminal Procedure, which was published in 1850, included a provision authorizing a peace officer to arrest without warrant for any "public offense, committed or

attempted in his presence." New York (State) Commissioners on Practice and Pleadings, *The Code of Criminal Procedure of the State of New York* §175 (1850).

23. This code was not adopted in New York until 1878 but was adopted in California in 1851. See T. Hittell, *General Laws of California 1850-1864,* at 272 (1865). The code was also adopted in Montana and undoubtedly had influence elsewhere. Other areas with early statutes of this kind include the District of Columbia, Maine, Ohio, and Wisconsin. By 1931 thirty-eight states had adopted such provisions. American Law Institute, *Code of Criminal Procedure* 232-233 (Official Draft, 1931).

24. See discussion in Wilgus, "Arrest Without a Warrant" (pts. 1-3), 22 *Mich. L. Rev.* 541, 673, 798, at 550-552, 706 (1924).

25. Id.

26. If limited to the nineteenth and twentieth centuries, it is largely accurate to say, as the author of one major work on the law of arrest has stated, that "The law which defines when a peace officer can make an arrest has developed with almost no concern with whether the taking of immediate custody is necessary." See W. LaFave, *Arrest* 168 (1965).

27. See, for example, New York (State) Commissioners on Practice and Pleadings, *The Code of Criminal Procedure of the State of New York* 76-78 (1850). This commentary to the proposed Field Code of Criminal Procedure indicates clearly that one purpose of the proposals as to arrest was to compress the vast extent of the common law authority "into a few plain and intelligible directions" because of "the utter impossibility of its being brought within the reach of the officer and the citizen."

28. See, for example, R. Pound and F. Frankfurter, *Criminal Justice in Cleveland* 203 (1922).

29. Indictable Offenses Act of 1848, 11 & 12 Vict., c. 42, §1.

30. An early state to adopt this procedure was Massachusetts. See 1890 Mass. Acts, ch. 225.

31. See American Law Institute, *Code of Criminal Procedure with Commentaries* 218-219 (1931). See also §§12-14, at pp. 25-26. W. LaFave, *Arrest* 203 (1965) indicates that about a third of the states had adopted provisions of this kind by 1965.

32. One early call for the adoption of the summons in the United States was that by Lawson and Keedy, "Criminal Procedure in England," 1 *Am. Inst. of Crim. L. and Criminology,* 748, 778 (1910). Others who advocated introduction of this procedure included Bettman and Burns, "Prosecution," in R. Pound and F. Frankfurter, *Criminal Justice in Cleveland* 203 (1922); National Commission on Law Observance and Enforcement, Report on Criminal Procedure, at 14 (Report No. 8, 1931); American Law Institute, *Code of Criminal Procedure* §§12-14 (Official Draft, 1930). See also S. Warner and H. Cabot, *Judges and Law Reform* 25 (1936).

33. See Foote, "Safeguards in the Law of Arrest," 52 *N. L. Rev.* 16, 32-33 (1957), discussing the English practice. The English seem to take the summons authority more seriously, perhaps because their law has changed less from the common law than has the American law.

34. See, for example, D. McIntire, *Law Enforcement in the Metropolis* 50-54 (1967). See also Barrett, "Police Practices and the Law—From Arrest to Release or Charge," 50 *Cal. L. Rev.* 11, 20-21 n. 53 (1962). The law apparently does make some difference as to the number of arrests made with and without warrant. The number of arrests indicated with warrant by Warner and Cabot in Boston in the 1930s is far greater than would be true in U.S. jurisdictions today. *Judges and Law Reform* 143 (1936). Many minor arrests are crimes "without victims" in which there is no citizen complainant. See, for example, Hall, "The Law of Arrest in Relation to Contemporary Social Problems," 3 *U. Chi. L. Rev.* 345, 363 (1936).

35. See, for example, Warner, "The Uniform Arrest Act," 28 *Va. L. Rev.* 315, 339 (1942); Federal Rules of Criminal Procedure 5(a). See also W. LaFave, *Arrest* 206 (1965).

36. See 3 L. Radzinowicz, *A History of English Criminal Law* (1956); M. Hale, *Summary of the Pleas of the Crown* 89-95, 165-169 (1678).

37. Barrett, "Police Practices and the Law—From Arrest to Release or Charge," 50 *Calif. L. Rev.* 11, 16 (1962). Copyright © 1962, California Law Review, Inc. Reprinted with permission.

38. See J. Bishop, *New Criminal Procedure* 156 (2d ed., 1913). See 1 C. Alexander, *The Law of Arrest in Criminal and Other Proceedings* 637 (1949) ("[I]n most states he has no discretion at all; as, a person once arrested must be arraigned as the law commands."). See also W. LaFave, *Arrest* 403 (1965).

39. See, for example, Cal. Penal Code §849(b)(1) (West Cum. Supp. 1981); Del. Code Ann. Tit. 11, §1908 (1979); N.H. Rev. Stat. Ann. §594:18 (1975); R.I. Gen. Laws Ann. §12-7-12 (1970). See also Uniform Arrest Act §10, in Warner, "The Uniform Arrest Act," 28 *Va. L. Rev.* 315, 336-339, 346 (1942).

40. Summary Jurisdiction Act, 1879, 42 & 43 Vict., c. 49, §38. See also *Lewis* v. *Time*, (1952) All E.R. 1203.

41. See W. LaFave, *Arrest* 171 n.10 (1965).

42. 1903 Pa. Laws, ch. 202, §10, p. 270.

43. See, for example, Baker, "Traffic Tickets," 30 *J. Crim. L. C. and P.S.* 386 (1939).

44. See, for example, G. Warren, *Traffic Courts* 56-58 (1942). The use of the bail schedule was sometimes authorized by the judge and was sometimes simply an informal police procedure.

45. Id. at 36-38. See also note 51 infra.

46. *People* v. *Yerman*, 138 Misc. 272, 246 N.Y. 665, 667 (Oneida County Ct. 1930). See also E. Fisher, *Laws of Arrest* 84-86 (1967).

47. See Baker, "Traffic Tickets," 30 *J. Crim. L. C. and P.S.* 386, 396 (1939). See also A. Beeley, *The Bail System in Chicago* 13-16 (1927).

48. See, for example, B. Sellon, *The Practice of the Courts of King's Bench and Common Pleas* 110 (1792); R. Sutton, *Personal Actions at Common Law* 43-44 (1929). It should be remembered that not all civil cases began with an arrest even under the early common law.

49. A summons is an order from a court to a defendant to appear; a warrant is a court order that a defendant be arrested; a writ is a written method of requesting a court ruling; and a recognizance is a surety bond. For a critique of the confusion that existed see Baker, "Traffic Tickets," 30 *J. Crim. L.C. and P.S.* 386 (1939).

50. 1915 Cal. Stats. ch. 188, §22c, at p. 409. See also 1923 Cal. Stats. at 566.

51. Section 66, Uniform Act Regulating the Operation of Vehicles on Highways. See *Handbook of the National Conference of Commissioners on State Laws and Proceedings of the Thirty-sixth Annual Meeting* 565 (1926). See also Warner, "The Uniform Arrest Act," 28 *Va. L. Rev.* 315, 335 (1942).

52. See Warner, "The Uniform Arrest Act," 28 *Va. L. Rev.* 315, 335 (1942).

53. G. Warren, *Traffic Courts* 37 (1942).

54. E. Coulter, *The Children in the Shadow* (1913); Alameda County Probation Department, Citation System (1966). The California procedure was not specifically authorized by statute until 1961. See Cal. Welf. and Inst. Code §626 (West Cum. Supp. 1981).

55. Hederman and Dahlinger, "Citation Hearing System," 12 *Hastings L. J.* 275 (1961). A more recent example is the Columbus Night Prosecutor Project. See National Institute of Law Enforcement and Criminal Justice, U.S. Department of Justice, Citizen Dispute Settlement (1974).

56. A. Beeley, *The Bail System of Chicago* 13-18 (1927).

57. National Commission on Law Observance and Enforcement, Report on Criminal Procedure, at 14 (Report No. 8, 1931); American Law Institute, *Code of Criminal Procedure* §§12-14 (Official Draft, 1930).

58. 1932 N.Y. Laws, ch. 537, §§82h, 84, at p. 1145. Warner, "The Uniform Arrest Act," 28 *Va. L. Rev.* 315, 335 n. 35 (1942), citing W. Va. Code Ann. (Michie and Sublett, 1937) §6182, also indicates that West Virginia had an early statute authorizing the issuance of citations in non-traffic matters. The statute cited, however, conferred police bail setting rather than citation authority. See chapter 14 infra. It has since been repealed. 1965 W. Va. Acts, ch. 38.

59. See chapter 7 infra.

60. Warner, "The Uniform Arrest Act," 28 *Va. L. Rev.* 315, 337 (1942). See also Warner, "Investigating the Law of Arrest," 26 *A.B.A.J.* 151 (1940); Warner, "Modern Trends in the American Law of Arrest," 21 *Can. Bar Rev.* 192, 201-202 (1943).

61. 1941 N.H. Laws, ch. 163; 1941 R.I. Pub. Laws, ch. 982; 48 Del. Laws, ch. 304 (1951).

62. See Comment, "Some Proposals for Modernizing the Law of Ar-

rest," 39 *Calif. L. Rev.* 96, 107-108 (1951). See also Foote, "Compelling Appearance in Court: Administration of Bail in Philadelphia," 102 *U. Pa. L. Rev.* 1031, 1074 (1954).

63. See *Mormon* v. *Baran*, 35 N.Y.S.2d 906, 909 (Sup. Ct. 1942) (indicating no penalty for failure to appear); 1 C. Alexander, *The Law of Arrest in Criminal and Other Proceedings* 259 (1949), says that judicial summonses are sometimes issued in blank and given to officers for use.

64. A questionnaire sent to cities in 1964 indicated that even in jurisdictions authorized to issue citations and court summonses these procedures were often used for traffic offenses only. D. Freed and P. Wald, *Bail in the United States: 1964*, at 71 n.4 (1964).

65. 44 *Calif. L. Rev.* 561, 565 (1956) indicates that the practice was "widely used" in the 1950s in California.

66. Criminal Justice Coordinating Council for New York City and Vera Institute of Justice, The Manhattan Summons Project (1969).

67. Id. at 4.

68. See Feeney, "Citation in Lieu of Arrest: The New California Law," 25 *Vand. L. J.* 367 (1972). A program in Sunnyvale began even earlier—November 6, 1963. See *Bail and Summons: 1965*, at 145 (August 1966). See also Comment, "An Alternative to the Bail System: Penal Code Section 853.6," 18 *Hastings L. J.* 643 (1967).

69. National Conference on Bail and Criminal Justice, Washington, D.C., *Proceedings and Interim Report* (April 1965); *Bail and Summons: 1965* (August 1966).

70. *Bail and Summons: 1965*, at 182-183 (August 1966). The state of Connecticut was also listed, but this appears to have been a court rather than a police program. The extent to which the police were involved in the New Jersey programs is also not clear.

71. President's Commission on Crime in the District of Columbia, *Report*, at 512 (1966). The commission also endorsed the creation of a judicial conference committee to consider this problem. *Report*, at 984 n.33.

72. *Model Code of Pre-Arraignment Procedure* §3.02, at 14-16 (Tent. Draft No. 1, 1966). This draft was approved in 1972 and in 1975.

73. President's Commission on Law Enforcement and Administration of Justice, *The Challenge of Crime in a Free Society* 133 (1967).

74. American Bar Association Project on Standards for Criminal Justice, *Standards Relating to Pretrial Release* 31 (1968).

75. J. Campbell, J. Sahid, and D. Starg, *Law and Order Reconsidered* 440-442 (1970).

76. National Advisory Commission on Criminal Justice Standards and Goals, *A National Strategy to Reduce Crime* 90 (1973).

77. *Police*, standard 4.4, at 83 (1973). See id. at 83-85.

78. *Courts*, standard 4.2, at 70 (1973). See id. at 70-72.

79. *Corrections*, standard 4.3, at 116 (1973). See id. at 116-119.

80. International Association of Chiefs of Police, *Model Rules for Law Enforcement Officers: A Manual on Police Discretion*, ch. 2 (1974). Several other recent major efforts to develop model rules did not address the use of citations as an issue. See Arizona State University College of Law and Police Foundation, *Model Rules for Law Enforcement* (1974); American Bar Association Project on Standards for Criminal Justice, *Standards Relating to the Police Function* (1973).

81. Ch. 2, §§3.01, 3.03. See also commentary at 113-128.

82. Ch. 2, §3.02. This rule also requires that the offense be a "property crime, crime against the person, or vice offense." This would seem to include most offenses and therefore does not appear to be an additional limitation.

83. See Warner, "The Uniform Arrest Act," 28 *Va. L. Rev.* 315, 317 n. 4 (1942), for the history of the New Hampshire and Rhode Island Acts.

84. The patterning of the Delaware Act on the Uniform Arrest Act is easily seen from the text of the statute. Del. Code tit. 11, §§1907-1908 (1979).

85. 18 *Cal. Op. Att'y Gen.* 167 (1951).

86. In 1955 the California Legislature instituted a procedure entitled Citations for the Violations of County Ordinances, 1955 Cal. Stats. ch. 537, §1, at p. 1006 (repealed 1967). The procedure was later incorporated into the more broadly worded penal code sections that allow for the release by citation of all misdemeanants, Act of Sept. 18, 1967, 1967 Cal. Stats. ch. 816, §1, at p. 2240. The history of the 1955 provision is given in 44 *Calif. L. Rev.* 561 (1956). This account indicates that the legislation was modeled after the traffic citation and that it was aimed at permitting citations for violations of county dog and other ordinances.

87. Act of July 8, 1957, 1957 Cal. Stats. ch. 2147, §6, at 3806 (repealed 1969). See Act of July 3, 1959, 1959 Cal. Stats., ch. 1558, at 3888 (amended 1969). See 32 *Cal. S.B.J.* 607, 609 (1957). See also Coakley, "Restrictions in the Law of Arrest," 52 *Nw. L. R.* 2, 6-8 (1957).

88. See Ill. Ann. Stat. ch. 38 §107-112, comments of draftsman (Smith-Hurd 1980).

89. The language often speaks of community ties or factors, such as residence or jobs, that are encompassed in the Manhattan Summons Project point scale.

90. See, for example, Ariz. Rev. Stat. §13-3903 (1978).

91. As might be expected, earlier surveys indicated a much smaller proportion of agencies using the citation procedure. See 2 J. Galvin, W. Busher et al., *Instead of Jail: Pre- and Post-Trial Alternatives to Jail Incarceration* 20-21 (National Institute of Law Enforcement and Criminal Justice, Oct.

1977); P. Wice, *Freedom for Sale* 109 (1974). Some of the surveys discussed were based on contacts with *OR* programs rather than police agencies.

4 Extent of Use

In 1979 almost 8 million adults were arrested in the United States for offenses other than minor traffic violations. Nearly 7 million of these arrests were for misdemeanors, rather than felonies, as shown in table 4-1. The largest single categories were driving under the influence (16 percent of all criminal arrests), drunkenness (14 percent), disorderly conduct (8 percent), theft (6 percent), and assault (5 percent).

To show how these figures would appear in a medium-sized city, table 4-2 gives the breakdown for Jacksonville, Florida, a combined city-county of around 540,000 people. In 1979 the number of adult arrests in this jurisdiction was over 23,000, with over 80 percent of these for misdemeanors. As in the national statistics the most frequent offense was driving under the influence. In Jacksonville this offense accounted for 19 percent of all adult arrests. Other important categories were drunkenness (15 percent), larceny (15 percent), and drugs (8 percent).

Most of the misdemeanor arrestees in the national totals are given some form of pretrial release. At least half are released in virtually all jurisdictions, and the release rate in many jurisdictions is 80 percent or higher.[1] Of those detained, the cases of 50 percent or more are disposed of at their first appearance in court.[2] In most instances the detainees are held not because anyone thinks they are dangerous or has decided that they need to be jailed, but because there is no mechanism in the jurisdiction for release prior to appearance in court. As the citation is introduced more broadly, more and more of these defendants can be released prior to court.

Unfortunately, almost no statistics are available to show the extent to which the releases given are releases on police citations. Neither the number of releases, the percentage of defendants released in particular categories, nor the specific trends in citation releases are known. What information there is, however, suggests that perhaps as many as one-third of all misdemeanor releases involve the use of police citations and that the use of citations is increasing rapidly.

One indication both of the extent of use and of increasing use is data collected by the Uniform Crime Reports concerning persons summoned. Although these data cover court summonses as well as police citations, are no longer collected, and have some serious statistical shortcomings,[3] they show, nevertheless, that the percentage of arrestees summoned increased from 12 percent in 1969 to 30 percent in 1977.[4]

Table 4-1

1979 Adult Arrests—United States

Felony		Misdemeanor	
Criminal homicide	17,768	Larceny	495,000
Forcible rape	26,466	Assault	394,000
Robbery	96,338	Forgery and	
Aggravated assault	233,220	counterfeiting	65,000
Burglary	258,850	Fraud	252,000
Larceny	174,635	Embezzlement	7,000
Motor vehicle theft	78,486	Stolen property	77,000
Felony drug	108,927	Vandalism	117,000
Arson	10,098	Weapons	137,000
Other	40,000	Prostitution	85,000
		Other sex offenses	55,000
Felony arrest total	1,044,788	Drug laws	326,000
		Gambling	52,000
		Offenses against	
		the family	54,000
		Driving under the	
		influence	1,290,000
		Liquor laws	266,000
		Disorderly conduct	630,000
		Vagrancy	30,000
		Drunkenness	1,123,000
		Other	1,350,000
		Misdemeanor	
		arrest total	6,805,000
		Total adult arrests	7,849,778

Source: Formulated from W. Webster, *Crime in the United States, 1979.* The basic figures are from table 24, p. 188. These are adjusted by the age figures in table 33, p. 198; by the offense-analysis figures in table 18, p. 176; and by drug-offense data obtained from several states. The felony-misdemeanor distinction used here is approximate, as the distinction differs considerably from state to state.

Much of this increase is undoubtedly the result of the increasing number of agencies using the citation procedure. Some, however, also seems clearly attributable to increasing use by agencies that had previously adopted the procedure. In New York City, for example, even though a few offenses, such as prostitution and drugs, are by department policy not eligible for citation release, citations are now issued for over 50 percent of all nontraffic misdemeanor cases.[5]

In other jurisdictions use of the procedure varies enormously from agency to agency. A few examples are given in table 4-3.

These figures suggest that use of the citation procedure is likely to increase even more rapidly in the next decade than in the last, particularly in view of the great amount of jail overcrowding that now exists. Many de-

Table 4-2
1979 Adult Arrests—Jacksonville, Florida

Felony		Misdemeanor	
Murder	67	Assault	696
Manslaughter	16	Larceny	2,928
Forcible rape	124	Forgery	207
Robbery	406	Fraud	199
Aggravated assault	1,025	Stolen property	341
Burglary	1,319	Vandalism	21
Larceny	705	Weapons	438
Auto theft	221	Prostitution	572
Drugs	103	Other sex offenses	681
Other	24	Drugs	1,781
		Gambling	186
Felony total	4,010	Offenses against family	235
		Driving under the influence	4,497
		Liquor laws	76
		Drunkenness	3,465
		Disorderly conduct	120
		Other	3,031
		Misdemeanor total	19,474
		Total adult arrests	23,484

Source: Estimated from data in Jacksonville, Florida, Office of the Sheriff, Annual Report 1978-1979, p. 28.

partments and many jailing authorities are still in the process of learning that they can release most misdemeanants with a reasonable likelihood of appearance in court and with relative safety in terms of future crimes.

Although situations vary from agency to agency, the extent to which misdemeanor citations could be increased with acceptable failure-to-appear

Table 4-3
Adult Nontraffic Misdemeanor Defendants Released on Police Citation
(includes both field and station-house releases)

Agency	Year	Percentage Released
Baton Rouge, Louisiana	1973	20
Bethlehem, Pennsylvania	1975	44
Cincinnati, Ohio	1974	51
New Haven, Connecticut	1973	44
Reno, Nevada	1975	27
Oakland, California	1976	45

Source: Information supplied by agencies concerned and 2 J. Galvin, W. Busher et al., *Instead of Jail: Pre- and Post-Trial Alternatives to Jail Incarceration,* 20-21 (National Institute of Law Enforcement and Criminal Justice, Oct. 1977).

rates is suggested by data from California's Contra Costa County. In this county in 1969 the police issued citations for about 47 percent of all misdemeanor defendants.[6] Counting bailed defendants, the total release rate for the county was 78 percent. Even with this high rate of release, however, the failure-to-appear rate was a low 6 percent, as shown in table 4-4.

Even more dramatic was an experiment carried out in the Santa Clara County, California, jail for a one-month period in 1971. With the approval of the judiciary and the sheriff, virtually all misdemeanor defendants, with the exception of drunkenness defendants, were released prior to trial in order to test a point scale then being used for making releases in the county.

> The procedure was to interview each offender as ordinarily done, and release those that qualified under the [ordinary] criteria. . . . Those that did not qualify and who did not appear to be in danger to themselves or others were also released. During the month 98.4% of all misdemeanants, excluding drunks, booked into the Sheriff's custody at Main Jail were released from custody.[7]

The defendants who would not normally have been released were tracked to determine how often they failed to appear:

> [A]pproximately 14% or 28 out of 205 non-qualifying releases failed to appear. These results suggest, in the Project Director's opinion, that it would be more economically sound for law enforcement agencies to cite all misdemeanants who do not appear to be a danger to themselves or others at the time of apprehension.[8]

Analysis by Offense

The citation procedure is used more extensively for some offenses than for others. In the 1976 survey the criminal offenses for which use was most frequent were petty theft and minor assaults, as shown in table 4-5.

Table 4-4
Rate of Appearance, Contra Costa County, California, for All Forms of Release
(one-month sample, 1969)

Agency	Percent Released	Failure-to-Appear Rate
Richmond	83.4	8%
Contra Costa Sheriff	84.4	6
San Pablo	75.4	0
Concord	81.5	6
Pittsburg	55.8	4
Walnut Creek	71.4	0
All departments	78.3	6

Source: Center on Administration of Criminal Justice, University of California, Davis, *Citation in Lieu of Arrest for Misdemeanor Defendants* (1972).

Table 4-5
Nontraffic Offenses Eligible for Citation
(percent of using agencies)

Offense	Misdemeanors and Ordinance or Regulatory Violations	Ordinance or Regulatory Violations Only
Petty theft or shoplifting	79	0
Misdemeanor assaults	70	0
Other misdemeanors	86	0
Public drunkenness[a]	30	0
Nonfelony marijuana possession	49	0
Nonfelony marijuana sale	15	0
Other nonfelony drug offenses	32	0
Municipal and county ordinances	87	93
Nontraffic regulatory violations	79	33
Number of agencies responding	(142)	(15)

Source: Police Foundation-Center on Administration of Criminal Justice survey, 1976.
[a]Many agencies indicated that public drunkenness is not a crime in their jurisdiction.

Petty Theft and Shoplifting. As indicated in the survey, the citation procedure is widely used for this offense. In many agencies more nontraffic citations are issued for this offense than for any other. A few departments appear to have encountered some resistance on the part of stores to the use of the citation procedure for shoplifting, and some departments do not use the procedure because they anticipate problems of this kind.

In some states shoplifting after a previous conviction or several convictions for shoplifting is a felony rather than a misdemeanor.[9] No particular problem arises for agencies using a station-house or jail-release procedure because any prior shoplifting convictions can usually be identified at the time of booking. Use of the field citation, however, does create something of a problem. Some departments have addressed this by requiring the defendant to place a thumbprint on the citation; others have relied on other methods. In general, this problem does not seem to have created a great deal of difficulty among agencies using the procedure.

Many shoplifting arrests are made by store security officers. In a number of jurisdictions the citation procedure has also proved useful to these officers as a way to cut down on the time involved in processing arrest cases. In New York City many store security personnel are appointed as special patrolmen by the police commissioner and as such may issue a desk-appearance ticket for shoplifting, in much the same way as the police.[10] In Tucson, Arizona, store security officers do not have citation authority, but some have worked out innovative procedures with the police department. The department has supplied these security officers with police forms, which are usually completed by the time the police arrive. Some stores have gone so far as to supply polaroid cameras so that stolen merchandise may be photographed instead of held as evidence. These procedures conserve police manpower by reducing forms-preparation time, eliminating the wait for the sergeant on patrol to bring the police-department camera, and eliminating the need for the police property clerk to hold store property as evidence.[11]

Minor Assaults. Departmental practices as to when to arrest for minor assaults differ considerably. Many departments do not arrest if the situation can be cooled off without an arrest. Physical arrests in these departments are made only when there is a need to separate the parties involved for some longer time. In such instances there is little opportunity for use of the field citation. The station-house citation, however, is appropriate in many cases because the trip to jail serves the purpose of separating the parties and reducing the level of anger.

Some departments go beyond the cooling off idea, using newer techniques, such as crisis intervention, both as a method for reducing officer injuries in handling disputes and as a way of helping the parties to deal with, or at least begin to deal with, the dispute itself. These techniques rely primarily on the use of persuasion and communication, as opposed to legal authority for handling this kind of situation.[12] At times, however, these crisis-intervention techniques fail, and some authority must be used. Although experience in some departments suggests that the citation is useful in situations in which crisis techniques fail,[13] further exploration of the best ways to mesh the use of the citation with that of crisis-intervention techniques is needed.

In the case of domestic disputes the use of crisis intervention has been criticized as insensitive to the needs of battered women. In New York and elsewhere women's groups have brought lawsuits seeking to force the use of physical arrest.

The New York suit was settled in 1978. Under the agreement the city will not attempt to mediate if there is reasonable cause to believe that a crime has been committed or an order of protection violated; in addition, the city will arrest the husband if there is reason to believe that an order of protection has been violated.[14] The agreement does not discuss citations but presumably leaves officers free to use station citations in all cases.

Driving under the Influence of Alcohol. Some departments do not consider the use of citations appropriate for drunk drivers, probably because they think that the drunk driver will not fully realize the extent to which he could have hurt himself or others unless he wakes up in jail the next morning.

A growing number of agencies do consider the use of citations for drunk drivers appropriate, however. Most use citations only as jail releases after the driver has sobered up. This permits the completion of a breathalyzer or other intoxication tests that the agency may require and ensures that the driver is able to comprehend the notice to appear. A few agencies release the driver on a citation if someone, such as a member of the family, will assume responsibility for him. An experimental program in Twin Falls, Idaho, operated in this fashion in 1976. Under the program approximately 44 percent of all persons arrested for driving under the influence were released on condition that a friend or family member agree in writing to keep the defendant from driving for six hours. The failure-to-appear rate for these releases was around 2 percent.[15]

A few agencies have found the field citation useful for driving under the influence. In Minneapolis, if another person in the car is sober, the arresting officer may cite the driver and release him to the custody of the sober party. The department requires the citation to be signed by the driver, and has had no particular problem with drivers claiming that they did not receive the notice or that they did not understand it.

Drunkenness. In many jurisdictions drunkenness is no longer an offense, but is handled on a voluntary basis or through detoxification facilities. In other jurisdictions, however, drunkenness continues to be handled through the criminal-justice system. In these jurisdictions a person will not usually be arrested for drunkenness unless his condition is such that he would not qualify for a field release under any test. In fact, many departmental procedures prohibit the release of anyone who is intoxicated. The drunk's inability to care for himself ordinarily passes with time, however, and, as the individual usually is not dangerous, some departments find these cases appropriate for a jail release. Where this is done the rate of nonappearance for this kind of case may be high. Generally, however, this is not a matter of great concern, as there is a belief that the court can do little for the drunkenness offender and that, in any event, the drunkenness offender is likely to be picked up again soon.[16]

Prostitution and Gambling. Many agencies prohibit the use of citations for prostitution, gambling, or other vice offenses. In some instances the agency does not want to create a misleading or improper public appearance; in other instances the exclusion is made because of a concern as to whether this kind of defendant will appear in court; and in other instances the agency is seeking to remove any possible temptation to use the citation for improper purposes, physical arrest being seen as a more open and accountable procedure. One agency responding to the survey, however, indicated that it issued citations for more than half its gambling-law violations (350 of 633 violations in the year reported). No problems were indicated.

Warrants. In most jurisdictions a substantial number of defendants are arrested on misdemeanor, parking, or traffic warrants. In Cincinnati, for example, this group constitutes about 30 percent of all misdemeanor arrests; in the area served by the Los Angeles County sheriff's office, it constitutes around 20 percent.[17]

In most instances defendants arrested on misdemeanor, traffic, or parking warrants are arrested after being stopped for a traffic infraction or arrested for another offense rather than as the result of an apprehension effort directed specifically at the warrant violation. The existence of the warrant, however, becomes the reason for nonrelease.

Many warrant arrests are for minor crimes or infractions that would be considered for citation release if no warrant were involved. Often, however, the warrant is considered a command from the court to arrest the defendant and bring him before the judge. Little discretion is seen in this situation. If the warrant itself makes a provision for bail, as most do, the defendant may be released on bail. Few warrants authorize citation release, however, and many departments interpret the statutes authorizing release on citation as not extending to the warrant situation.

It can be argued that many of these defendants should not be released at all, or at least not given an easy release, since they are being arrested primarily for their previous failure to appear or respond in court. This argument is clearly valid for some defendants, particularly those who have had multiple opportunities and have totally ignored their responsibilities. Many others are now released on money bail, however, or in some agencies by citation. It seems likely that even more would be released through citation if there was clear legal authority to do so.

About two-thirds of the agencies surveyed indicated that this kind of case is not eligible for citation, as shown in table 4-6. In most instances this was for policy reasons, but in a considerable number of agencies release on citation for this kind of case was considered unlawful.

Use of Citations for Marijuana Possession

Nearly every state has eliminated felony penalties for the possession of small quantities of marijuana. Consequently, in virtually every state that authorizes the use of citations, police officers may issue citations for marijuana possession. In addition, eleven states have eliminated incarceration as a penalty for this offense.[18] Five of the ten specifically mandate the use of citations for marijuana possession, and a sixth has mandatory features in its general-citation statute.[19] At the time of the study survey in 1976, incarceration had been eliminated in seven states (Alaska, California, Colorado, Maine, Minnesota, Ohio, and Oregon). For these seven states a special questionnaire asked about the use of citations for marijuana possession.

Table 4-6

Eligibility of Parking, Traffic, and Misdemeanor Warrant Cases for Citation Releases

(percent of agencies responding)

	Agencies Issuing Citations for:	
	Misdemeanors and Ordinance or Regulatory Violations	Ordinance or Regulatory Violations Only
Generally eligible	13	7
Eligible if the warrant so states[a]	12	0
Eligible if defendant voluntarily appears at the police station after finding out he is wanted on a warrant[a]	4	7
Not eligible, this is against our policy[b]	39	67
Not eligible, this would be illegal[b]	19	14
Other	13	7
Number of agencies responding	(134)	(15)

Source: Police Foundation-Center on Administration of Criminal Justice survey, 1976.

[a]Includes one department checking each of these answers.

[b]If checked both policy and illegal, answer was coded as illegal.

Of the thirty-five departments answering the questionnaire, almost one-third indicated that the use of a citation was mandatory for all marijuana-possession offenses under a specific amount. Six additional departments said that a citation was generally required. (One indicated that an officer could arrest if he had reason to believe that the defendant would not appear in court, for example.) Half of the departments said that the use of a citation was not mandatory.

Most departments (66 percent) reported that persons cited for marijuana possession were expected to appear in court, as for other nontraffic offenses. One-quarter indicated, however, that defendants could post and forfeit "bail-fines" similar to the procedure used when traffic tickets are issued.

The departments were also asked if they were using the same citation procedures and forms for marijuana possession as those used for other nontraffic offenses. As seen in table 4-7, most said they were. Generally, departments have not created new citation procedures for marijuana possession but have simply integrated this offense into already existing systems.

When asked if they had experienced any particular problems with the use of citations for marijuana possession, five departments responded affirmatively. Two (both in California) said there were problems with require-

Table 4-7

Comparison of Marijuana Citation Procedures with Procedures for Other Misdemeanor Offenses

(percent of using agencies)

Use same form and procedure as for other nontraffic citations	63
Use same form and procedure as for traffic tickets	11
Use same form and procedure for traffic and nontraffic tickets	7
Same form as other nontraffic citations, but different procedure	15
Separate form and procedure for marijuana possession	4
Number of agencies responding	(27)

Source: Police Foundation-Center on Administration of Criminal Justice survey, 1976.

ments for purging records, particularly when other charges were included on the same citation. Problems mentioned by the other three departments were the inability to search for larger amounts of marijuana or for more serious drugs; false or misleading identifications; and a high failure-to-appear rate. When asked specifically if failure to appear had been a problem with marijuana citations, three additional departments said that it had been.

Departments were also asked if the payment of fines had been a problem. Over two-thirds (twenty-one) said that this was not a problem. Six said they did not know, that payment of fines was a court rather than a police problem. Three departments felt that it was a problem. One said that many defendants did not have the funds to pay the fines so must "lag it out in jail" instead. A second department reported problems with a deferred-payment plan, and a third said that the fines were not consistent.

Some observers have theorized that the downgrading of penalties for marijuana possession in general and the problems involved in determining exact amounts possessed would lead to a decline in police enforcement of laws against marijuana possession. Departments were asked if they thought this was actually happening. Over half (nineteen) said that enforcement actions within their departments had not declined. Nine departments thought they had, including one that said that law-enforcement actions had declined by over 50 percent. As the laws of six of the seven states surveyed had been in effect for a year or less at the time of the survey, the survey should be taken as only suggestive of the law's ultimate effect.

When asked if they would recommend revising their state's marijuana citation law in any way, seven agencies indicated that they would. Several of these, however, mentioned changes having nothing to do with citations—one California department, for example, wanted a mandatory jail sentence, and a department in Maine wanted possession of marijuana to be a criminal rather than a civil offense.

A 1977 study for the National Governors' Conference indicated that enforcement of laws against marijuana possession has decreased nationally and that there have been particularly sharp drops in some of the citation states. California, for example, is reported to have had a 47 percent decrease in enforcement actions in the first year after enactment of its citation provision, and Minnesota a 43 percent drop. Major police agencies in Colorado, Maine, and Ohio also reported fewer enforcement actions than under the old law. Oregon officials, on the other hand, reported no major changes in enforcement actions during the first year of their new law.[20]

These declines in enforcement actions do not appear to be caused by any decrease in marijuana usage, and probably have more to do with the decrease in penalties involved than with use of the citation procedure. Law-enforcement agencies in the states involved report substantial cost savings, as do prosecutors and the courts. Savings were greater in states that mandated the use of citations.[21] Since 1977 the number of arrests nationally has continued to decline.[22]

Notes

1. See W. Thomas, *Bail Reform in America* 65-70 (1976).
2. Id.
3. See chapter 17, note 10.
4. See chapter 17, table 17-1.
5. See chapter 7, table 7-5.
6. Center on Administration of Criminal Justice, University of California, Davis, *Citation in Lieu of Arrest for Misdemeanor Defendants: Implementing the New California Law*, table 5 (1972).
7. Santa Clara County Pretrial Release Program, *Pretrial Release Program in an Urban Area, Final Report*, at 17 (Aug. 1, 1973).
8. Id.
9. See, for example, Cal. Penal Code §666 (West Cum. Supp. 1981); Conn. Gen. Stat. Ann. §53a-40 (West Cum. Supp. 1981).
10. The appointment procedure is authorized by the New York City Administrative Code.
11. See Vera Institute of Justice, Tucson Police Department Arrest Alternative Project, at 11 (Oct. 1, 1976) (unpublished report to the Police Foundation).

12. See, for example, Bard, *The Function of the Police in Crisis Intervention and Conflict Management: A Training Guide* (U.S. Dept. of Justice, 1975).

13. See Comment, "Pretrial Release Under California Penal Code Section 853.6: An Examination of Citation Release," 60 *Calif. L. Rev.* 1339, 1351 (1972).

14. See, for example, *Bruno* v. *Codd*, 90 Misc. 2d 1047, 396 N.Y.S. 2d 974 (1977). The settlement is described in the *New York Law Journal*, June 27, 1978, p. 1, col. 7.

15. See Sinclair, "A Proposal for An 'Own Recognizance Release' Bail Program, With Focus on the DWI Arrest," 13 *Idaho L. Rev.* 81 (1976).

16. Houston is apparently an exception to this general lack of concern as the high rate of nonappearance for drunkenness offenders is cited as one reason for discontinuing use of the citation for misdemeanor offenses. This contrasts sharply with California practice. See Woods, of "Pretrial Release of Public Drunkenness Offenders in California," 15 *Santa Clara Law.* 81 (1974).

17. Criminal Justice Section, Cincinnati Police Department, "Stationhouse Release Program Results, Second Year of Operation," at 6 (March 1975); Los Angeles County Sheriff's Department, "Fiscal Year 1975-1976 Statistical Summary," at 8.

18. Alaska Stat. §17.12.110(e)(1979); Cal. Health & Safety Code §11,357 (West Cum. Supp. 1981); Colo. Rev. Stat. §12-22 412 (12)(1978); Me. Rev. Stat. tit. 22, §2383 (1980); Minn. Stat. Ann. §152.15, subdiv. 2(5)(West Cum. Supp. 1981); Miss. Code Ann. §41-29-149 (Supp. 1980); Neb. Rev. Stat. §28-416(6)(a)(Cum. Supp. 1980); N.Y. Crim. Proc. Law §150.75 (McKinney Supp. 1980-81); N.C. Gen. Stat. §90-95(d)(4)(Cum. Supp. 1979); Ohio Rev. Code Ann. §2925.11 (Page Cum. Supp. 1980); Or. Rev. Stat. §475.992(2), (4)(f)(1979). A twelfth state eliminated incarceration in 1976 but later amended its law. See 1976 S.D. Sess. Laws, ch. 158, §42-6; 1977 S.D. Sess. Laws, ch. 189, §92.

19. The five states which specifically mandate use of the citation are California, Colorado, Mississippi, Nebraska, and New York. The sixth state is Minnesota.

20. 2 National Governors' Conference, *Marijuana: A Study of State Policies and Penalties* 40-44 (Peat, Marwick, Mitchell and Co., March 1977).

21. Id. at 42.

22. W. Webster, *Crime in the United States—1979*, at 188.

5 Results and Benefits of Use

The use of citations for misdemeanor cases has grown rapidly because the procedure provides significant benefits to police agencies, defendants, and the community. Perhaps the most significant benefit for most police agencies has been the savings in time and money that the procedure affords. Other important benefits include the additional measure of control created by the availability of a new option for handling minor criminal problems and a strengthening of relationships with the community.

The citation procedure has clear benefits for defendants. It respects the right of the defendant not to be punished until proven guilty and minimizes the harm to job and family relationships that is often caused by pretrial detention.

From the beginning it has also been demonstrated that large numbers of misdemeanor defendants can be released with a safe expectation that the overwhelming majority will appear in court as promised. There are in addition strong indications, however, that as the proportion of defendants released increases, the number of failure-to-appear cases goes up.

Court-Appearance Rates

One of the most important findings of the Manhattan Summons Project was that a high percentage of the defendants appeared in court as promised. In the first six months of the project the appearance rate was nearly 98 percent, and for the first year of city-wide operation, around 94 percent.[1]

Early data from California were equally encouraging. A 1966 *Hastings Law Journal* study of citation programs in several of the Contra Costa County communities experimenting with the procedure showed an appearance rate, excluding public drunkenness, of 96 percent or better in each of the three departments surveyed,[2] as shown in table 5-1. A similar rate was shown for the Sunnyvale department.

During the summer of 1969 the Center on Administration of Criminal Justice, University of California, Davis, made another survey of some of the same communities to determine how well the procedure had held up over a longer period and to collect more detailed information about how it worked. This survey showed that for a one-month period less than 9 percent of the defendants released through the use of jail citations had failed to

Table 5-1
Rate of Appearance for Citation Releases

	Release on Citation	Failures to Appear	Rate of Appearance
Contra Costa Sheriff	92	1	99%
Pittsburg	530	23	96
Richmond	69	3	96
Sunnyvale	50	1	98

Source: Note, "An Alternative to the Bail System: Penal Code Section 853.6," 18 *Hastings Law Journal* 643, 655, 657-658 (1967). Reprinted with permission. Taken from 1966 Contra Costa County survey.

appear,[3] as shown in table 5-2. The appearance rate would have been higher if certain drunk cases, in which there was some doubt as to whether an appearance was really wanted, had been excluded.

Field releases were then used by fewer departments in Contra Costa County, but generally produced results that were similar to those for departments using jail releases. In the one-month sample only about 7 percent failed to appear.[4]

Other departments showed similar results. In San Francisco, which instituted a field-citation program in July 1969, the results for the first several months of operation showed a total of 496 releases on citation, 53 cases of failure to appear, and an appearance rate of 89.3 percent.[5] In Sacramento County, where the sheriff's office used field citations for shoplifting and some regualtory offenses, analysis of a five-month period in 1969 showed a total of 94 field releases for shoplifting, with an appearance rate of 97 percent.[6]

Table 5-2
Rate of Appearance for Jail Citation Releases
(one-month sample, 1969)

	Jail Citation Releases	Failures to Appear	Rate of Appearance
Concord	1	0	100%
Contra Costa Sheriff	15	2	87
Pittsburg	15	1	93
Richmond	76	9	88
San Pablo	17	0	100
Walnut Creek	12	0	100
Total	136	12	91

Source: Feeney, "Citation in Lieu of Arrest: The New California Law," 25 *Vanderbilt Law Review* 367, 375 (1972). Reprinted with permission.

Early results in Washington, D.C., and Miami were similar.[7] The rate of nonappearance for station releases in Washington was less than 1 percent in 1971 and less than 3 percent in 1973. The rate in Miami, primarily for field releases, was around 6 percent.

The experience in Oakland, California, another of the early programs, was quite different. During the program's first six months (March-September 1970) the failure-to-appear rate was over 20 percent. The rate began to drop almost immediately, however, and after a year of operation had settled to around 12 percent.[8]

In New Haven, Connecticut, the nonappearance rate for field citations in 1970-1971, the first year of operation, was 20.5 percent. Many of the nonappearances were in motor-vehicle cases, however, and the rate for non-motor-vehicle cases was 14.5 percent.[9]

Some more recent programs have been plagued with even higher failure-to-appear rates. In Minneapolis, where an extensive field-citation procedure began in 1975 without much preparation, the initial failure-to-appear rate was nearly 50 percent. This rate has subsequently come down to 30 percent, but is still quite high by earlier standards.[10]

Although the failure-to-appear rates in Oakland and Minneapolis decreased from what they were initially, the rates in other cities have shown some tendency to increase. The rates in Washington, D.C., have increased,[11] and the 1975 rate in Tucson was around 18 percent.[12] In New York City the failure-to-appear rate has also climbed, from 5 percent in 1972 to over 20 percent in 1975 and over 30 percent in 1981.[13]

Failure-to-appear rates continue to be low in many other jurisdictions, however. In Cincinnati, for example, the rate for 1973 and 1974 was only 7 percent.[14] Moreover, over half of the agencies responding to the Police Foundation-Center on Administration of Criminal Justice survey indicated that the number of persons failing to appear in their jurisdictions was less than 6 percent of all cited defendants, as shown in table 5-3. Another fourth of the agencies responding reported a failure-to-appear rate of 10 percent or less. Only 7 percent reported rates greater than 20 percent, and only two agencies reported a rate greater than 30 percent.

Over half the agencies using the citation procedure for nontraffic offenses indicated that they did not consider the number of persons failing to appear in court to be a problem, as shown in table 5-4. Slightly over a third indicated that failure-to-appear cases were a minor problem. Most of those indicating a serious problem had failure-to-appear rates greater than 20 percent.

When asked how high the rate of failure-to-appear cases could rise before they would cancel or curtail issuing citations for nontraffic offenses, over a fourth of the agencies using the procedure indicated that they would continue to use the procedure regardless of the number of defendants fail-

Table 5-3
Current Failure-to-Appear Rate (Estimated)
(percent of agencies responding)

	Agencies Issuing Citations for:	
Percent of Cited Defendants Failing to Appear	*Misdemeanors and Ordinance or Regulatory Violations*	*Ordinance or Regulatory Violations Only*
0-5	54	73
6-10	27	13
11-20	11	0
21-30	6	7
Over 30	1	7
Number of agencies responding	(125)	(15)

Source: Police Foundation-Center on Administration of Criminal Justice survey, 1976.

ing to appear, as shown in table 5-5. About a fifth said they would cancel or curtail use if the number of defendants not appearing rose to 11 to 20 percent of those released, and another 15 percent of the agencies said that they would cancel or curtail use if the number of defendants not appearing rose to 6 to 10 percent of those released.

Almost half the agencies indicated that they kept regular statistics on the number of citations issued, but very few kept any data at all concerning the number of defendants failing to appear. One of the major difficulties in determining the extent to which there is a failure-to-appear problem is the general lack of data and the lack of comparability of data that do exist.

Computing and comparing failure-to-appear rates is a treacherous undertaking, as one recent study of pretrial release programs indicates.[15] According to this study the problem stems in part from the need to use court records. It indicates that:

Table 5-4
Are Failure-to-Appear Cases a Problem
(percent of using agencies)

	Agencies Issuing Citations for:	
	Misdemeanors and Ordinance or Regulatory Violations	*Ordinance or Regulatory Violations Only*
A serious problem	5	7
A minor problem	38	33
Not a problem	56	60
Number of agencies responding	(133)	(15)

Source: Police Foundation-Center on Administration of Criminal Justice survey, 1976.

Table 5-5

Rate of Nonappearance at Which Agency Would Cancel or Curtail Use of Citations

(percent of using agencies)

	Agencies Issuing Citations for:	
Percent of Cited Defendants Failing to Appear	*Misdemeanors and Ordinance or Regulatory Violations*	*Ordinance or Regulatory Violations Only*
0-5	1	0
6-10	14	21
11-20	24	7
21-30	17	21
Over 30	11	14
Would continue to use regardless of rate	28	21
Other	5	14
Number of agencies responding	(129)	(14)

Source: Police Foundation-Center on Administration of Criminal Justice survey, 1976.

While in some courts the records were quite complete, in others the minutes were very sketchy. Thus, while in some courts we could be quite confident that every time the defendant was not in court this fact would be noted, in other courts this was not the case. This difficulty is encountered not only in comparing failure to appear rates from one city to another, but also in comparing the rates in the same city from one year to another.[16]

Another factor in the differences in failure-to-appear rates is that the kinds of offenses covered by the citation procedure differ from one jurisdiction to another. Although relatively little information concerning failure-to-appear rates by different offenses exists, what evidence there is suggests considerable variation, as indicated in table 5-6.

Use of the citation procedure for drunkenness offenders is particularly likely to cause a relatively high rate of nonappearance. In one department contacted in an earlier survey, the rate of nonappearance for this offense was over 50 percent.[17]

Probably the most important factor in the increase in failure-to-appear rates in most departments has been increased usage of the procedure. When used in a limited way and with a select group of defendants, the failure-to-appear rate is almost always very low. As the procedure is used with more and more defendants, however, it eventually reaches the poorer risks, and the failure-to-appear rate increases.[18] This increase seems to relate more to the type of defendant released than to whether the defendant is released on citation, under a bail bond, or through some other method. The few comparisons of the appearance rates of defendants released on citation with those of defendants released through other methods suggest that those

Table 5-6
Field and Jail Citation Releases, Contra Costa County
(one-month sample, 1969)

	Total Charged	Field and Jail Citation Releases	Failures to Appear	Rate of Appearance
Assault and battery	31	8	1	87.5%
Petty theft	54	36	2	94
Drunkenness	123	46	5	89
Disturbing the peace	11	5	1	80
Drunk driving	43	19	3	84
Other traffic custody	32	14	1	93
Drugs	15	10	1	90
All other	56	31	1	97
Total	365	169	15	91

Source: Data from Center on Administration of Criminal Justice, University of California, Davis.

released on citation do as well or better than those released through other methods. In Cincinnati, where such a comparison was made in 1973, the citation failure-to-appear rate was 6 percent lower than the bond release rate for a comparable group of defendants in the six months prior to the beginning of the citation procedure in Cincinnati.[19]

In many areas the failure-to-appear rate for traffic citations is about 20 percent.[20] What appears to have happened in a number of jurisdictions is that as the number of nontraffic misdemeanor citations has increased, the failure-to-appear rate for the nontraffic citation has grown to about the same level as the failure-to-appear rate for the traffic citation.

As might be expected, departments have reacted differently to this situation. A few (Houston, St. Petersburg, Florida) have seen the growth of the failure-to-appear rate as a major problem and have discontinued the whole procedure of citing for misdemeanor offenses. Some others have seen the issue more as one of management, tightening their procedures and lowering the number of releases so as to reduce the failure-to-appear rate to an acceptable level.

A third group of agencies has largely accepted the increased failure-to-appear rate as a part of the price for an increased level of releases. These agencies are not pleased about the failure-to-appear rate, and would like to have it lower, but feel that it is undesirable to attempt to reduce the rate by reducing the number of releases. Officials in some of these agencies indicate that most of the defendants involved will eventually appear voluntarily, be apprehended for another offense, or be identified through some kind of traffic violation. The limited data available suggest that these officials are correct and that about 90 percent of the failure-to-appear violators will eventually turn up in the ways suggested.[21]

Concern for the Defendant

The American Bar Association (ABA) Project on Standards for Criminal Justice states that:

> The bare fact that a person has been charged with a crime does not justify his detention before conviction. Only if some legitimate purpose of the criminal process, such as prevention of flight, requires it, should the defendant be deprived of pretrial liberty.[22]

Finding that the history of the bail system and the constitutional prohibition against excessive bail indicate a principle that defendants are not to be locked up simply because of a criminal charge,[23] the ABA Standards continue:

> History aside, however, it is now clear that unnecessary pretrial detention involves unconscionable costs both to individual defendants and their families and to the public which must pay the financial price of detention.[24]

If the misdemeanor defendant has the funds, he can, of course, be released prior to trial simply by posting bail, but if he lacks funds for bail, he usually must remain incarcerated. His ability to get out of jail, therefore, is based solely on his financial means—a clearly inequitable result.[25] In addition, the defendant who posts bond is often using already limited funds and may be pushing his family over the poverty line or onto the welfare rolls. Moreover, even when the defendant can post bond, it seems undesirable for the system of justice to depend on money bail any more than necessary. If a person can be released safely, the release should be based on that fact rather than on the payment of a fee. Even in the jurisdictions in which there are organized release-on-own-recognizance programs, these systems often do not operate effectively for misdemeanor defendants because the time span between arrest and initial disposition is too short to permit necessary investigation at the court level.

The ABA Standards state:

> The defendant has not yet been convicted and, while the presumption of innocence surely does not preclude all pretrial detention, something akin to it does prevent the use of pretrial detention as a sort of anticipatory form of punishment.[26]

Simply stated, the purpose of the citation procedure is to ensure that, whenever possible, misdemeanor defendants who are not likely to flee the jurisdiction be released without the payment of money bail.

Costs

In an era of tight budgets and many demands, one of the most attractive aspects of the citation procedure for many administrators has been the opportunity to cut costs and save manpower. Most police administrators today are looking for ways to keep officers on the street.

This possibility was clearly one of the considerations leading to the New York City experiment and an even greater factor in its rapid expansion throughout the city. During the second full year of city-wide operation, the department released 22,685 persons, for an estimated net savings of $1,587,950, or more than 28,000 eight-hour tours of duty. In later years the estimates of savings were even higher.[27]

Use of field citations generally produces greater savings than use of station-house citations. In Oakland, California, for example, the saving in 1971 for each field citation was estimated at $20.37, and for each station-house release at $11.72.[28] Station-house release normally results in some saving on jail costs and transportation to court. Field release saves the additional expense of transporting the defendant to the station and, in many cases, the expense of booking. In both instances the savings produced by the use of citations must be reduced by the costs of apprehending and prosecuting or otherwise handling defendants who fail to appear in court.

In the case of the field citation one early estimate of time savings based on experience in California was:

30 to 40 minutes transportation and booking time on the part of the arresting officer

1 to 2 days jail-detention costs

15 to 30 minutes officer time for transportation to court

15 to 30 minutes time to complete the complaint if the citation itself was used as the complaint [29]

A more recent "minimum-cost" estimate used by the American Bar Association in a cost analysis of alternatives to arrest broke down the savings for field citations somewhat differently:

13 minutes transportation time to station house

47 minutes booking time

7.5 minutes transportation to court

6 hours detention costs[30]

The American Bar Association study is helpful in showing how the prosecution and apprehension costs for defendants who fail to appear in court can cut into the savings from station-house releases, particularly if defendants not released stay in jail only a short time before reaching court. The study also shows that, under almost any assumptions, use of the field citation produces substantial savings.[31]

The cost picture is actually more complicated than the studies indicate. In many jurisdictions the alternatives are not limited to citation or jail in the period prior to appearance in court; they also include release on money bail. In cases in which a defendant released on citation would have been able to secure release on bail, no additional cost results from a citation failure-to-appear because the defendant would also presumably have failed to appear if released on bail.

A more precise determination of the savings attributable to citations therefore requires an analysis of the extent to which the defendants released on citation would have been released on bail prior to appearance in court. Making this determination is difficult and is even more difficult in jurisdictions that have release-on-own-recognizance projects, which are involved in pretrial release prior to first appearance. In addition, the presence of these agencies adds other cost considerations to the picture because they are generally funded from tax sources.

Complicating matters further is the fact that in many jurisdictions the agency that runs the jail is different from the agency that has general police responsibility. In these jurisdictions the taxpayers, who support both agencies, generally benefit from the savings generated through the use of citations. Some of the savings accrue to the agency that runs the jail, however, and the agency giving the citation may not receive any budgetary benefit.

With so many factors involved it should be obvious that any realistic detailed calculation of savings for a particular jurisdiction must be based on the practice and procedures of that jurisdiction. These factors differ greatly from place to place and must be examined carefully. In New York City, for example, the saving of officer time is clearly substantial, even though release normally occurs at the station house after booking rather than in the field. In New Haven, Connecticut, on the other hand, even field releases do not seem to generate large cost savings.[32]

For most agencies, however, it may not be necessary to go into detailed, sophisticated cost calculations. A good minimum estimate of the value of the procedure can be determined simply by calculating the amount of officer time saved. This calculation almost always underestimates the total savings, as the savings in jail costs will almost always be greater, and usually considerably greater, than the costs associated with defendants failing to appear, even if the impact of release on money bail and release-through-own-recognizance projects is taken into account.

To get some idea of differing amounts of officer time saved in different jurisdictions, the agencies responding to the mail survey were asked to estimate how much time the citation procedure saved over the procedure previously followed. About 45 percent indicated a saving of thirty-one to fifty-nine minutes per case; 20 percent of the agencies indicated savings of one to two hours per case; and only 4 percent indicated no saving, as shown in table 5-7.

Observations and discussions in individual jurisdictions tended to confirm the estimates of patrol-officer savings given in the survey.

The time savings appeared to depend in part on the jurisdiction's requirements concerning appearance of the arresting officer. The savings tended to be higher in jurisdictions in which the arresting officer was required to appear in court each time the defendant did. This situation occurred in nearly 20 percent of the agencies responding to the survey, as shown in table 5-8.

Other Benefits

Benefits to the police departments, in addition to manpower and cost savings, are not easy to catalog. Some departments, however, feel that there are other benefits, as indicated in the following statements taken from the files of the district attorney of Contra Costa County. Each statement is from a chief of a department within the county.

Table 5-7
Time Savings per Citation
(percent of using agencies)

| | Agencies Issuing Citations for: | |
	Misdemeanors and Ordinance or Regulatory Violations	Ordinance or Regulatory Violations Only
No saving	3	13
0-15 minutes	3	7
16-30 minutes	21	40
31-59 minutes	48	13
1-2 hours	21	27
More than 2 hours	4	0
Number of agencies responding	(136)	(15)

Source: Police Foundation-Center on Administration of Criminal Justice survey, 1976.

Table 5-8
When Arresting Officer Appears in Court
(percent of agencies responding)

	Agencies Issuing Citations for:		
	Misdemeanors and Ordinance or Regulatory Violations	*Ordinance or Regulatory Violations Only*	*All Agencies*
Only if defendant has pled not guilty	68	93	71
When the defendant first appears and at various times afterwards	7	0	6
Every time defendant appears	19	7	18
Other	7	0	6
Number of agencies responding	(138)	(15)	(153)

Source: Police Foundation-Center on Administration of Criminal Justice survey, 1976.

In addition to the savings of actual output of dollars for meals, we feel that we have saved many hours of jailers' time. We have practically eliminated all complaints emitting from the jail, i.e., police brutality, refusal to make telephone calls, and so on.

I am especially pleased with the result of this program . . . I see no reason why a ranking officer of a police agency is not just as well qualified to authorize physical releases by citation or under the Penal Code section, which of course does not require the added burden of bail bond costs.

The use of Section 849(3)P.C. affords my staff with the necessary latitude to effect an intelligent and sound arrest release. Unless there are extenuating circumstances prohibiting an arrested person's release, the person is not incarcerated in our city jail. We have experienced an appreciable savings in cost for prisoners' meals. We have reduced drastically the man hours devoted to prisoner inspection and care, transporting to court, handling of visitors and attorney interviews and the processing and safeguarding of prisoners' property. There is an additional savings in reduced costs in lighting, heating, laundry and janitorial duties in our jail facilities. I believe our use of this method of release has been highly successful.[33]

Some other benefits were indicated in a study made by the New Haven, Connecticut department:

Officers reported greater ease in performing their duties when not forced to remove suspects from their homes. Moreover, there were no injuries whatsoever in citation arrest cases, nor was there any physical violence. Finally, there was a sense of improved police-community relations stemming from the citation program which, while not quantifiable, nevertheless seemed to help ease local tensions. Of course, the citation program did not eliminate the police-community relations problem; rather the process was apparently viewed as a positive step by the police to improve the treatment of arrestees, and was accepted and appreciated on that level.[34]

Just as some agencies see benefits beyond those relating to costs and manpower, some agencies have also expressed concerns other than failure-to-appear rates. A proposal to begin citation use in Boston, for example, was criticized by some officers because the use of citations would give offenders a second chance to avoid prosecution by creating the possibility that a clerk's hearing would "wash out" the arrests made by officers. The use of citations was also criticized because it would introduce more discretion into police work, thereby allowing more bias to enter. The belief was that a citation system would have to be monitored and regulated to see that it was being applied equitably in different districts.[35]

Benefits to Courts, Prosecutors, and Pretrial-Release Agencies

In addition to its effect on police agencies the citation procedure also has direct effects on the courts and the prosecution and pretrial-release agencies. In general, the effects on these agencies have also been quite positive.

The citation procedure enables courts to better regularize their calendars, gives the prosecutor the opportunity to screen misdemeanor complaints if he cares to, and allows pretrial-release agencies to concentrate on more serious cases, where the cost of their services is better justified. The procedure may also bring some problems, such as court delay caused by an increased number of failure-to-appear cases. Most courts, prosecutors, and pretrial-release agencies contacted, however, clearly saw the procedure as a net gain. The relationship between the procedure and these agencies is discussed further in chapter 11.

Notes

1. See chapter 7, at table 7-3.
2. Note, "An Alternative to the Bail System: Penal Code Section 853.6," 18 *Hastings L.J.* 643, 655, 657-658 (1967).
3. Feeney, "Citation in Lieu of Arrest: The New California Law," 25 *Vand. L.J.* 367, 375 (1972).
4. Id.
5. Id. at 376.

6. Id.

7. See chapter 8 for the Washington data. The Miami program is described in National Advisory Commission on Criminal Justice Standards and Goals, *Police* 84 (U.S. Government Printing Office, 1973).

8. See chapter 8 concerning the Oakland experience.

9. See chapter 8. Evanston, Illinois, experienced a failure-to-appear rate of 22 percent in its first year of operation. See "An Analysis of the Citation System in Evanston, Illinois: Its Value, Constitutionality and Viability," 65 *J. Crim. L. & Criminology* 75, 84 (1974).

10. See chapter 8.

11. See chapter 8.

12. Vera Institute of Justice, Tucson Police Department Arrest Alternative Project (Oct. 1, 1976) (unpublished report to the Police Foundation).

13. See chapter 7.

14. Criminal Justice Section, Cincinnati Police Department, Stationhouse Release Program Results, Second Year of Operations (March 1975).

15. W. Thomas, *Bail Reform in America* 87 (1976).

16. Id. at 88. Reprinted with permission of the University of California Press.

17. R. Bachman, "Misdemeanor Citation Release: A Study After Three Years of Trial in California" (1973) (unpublished study, Center on Administration of Criminal Justice, University of California, Davis).

18. This would be similar to what has happened with pretrial release generally where much better data exist. According to Thomas, supra note 15, at 87-88, the average nonappearance rate for misdemeanor defendants, not including drunks, for twenty large cities increased from 6 percent in 1962 to 10 percent in 1971, "due at least in part to the increased release rates." P. 88.

19. See note 14 supra. The much smaller Evanston program, supra note 9, showed a 7 percent advantage for bailed defendants.

20. Estimates given by various offices interviewed.

21. There are no data available based solely on citation releases. W. Thomas, *Bail Reform in America* 104 (1976) reports that about 90 percent of all releases are eventually accounted for through one of the methods listed. There is no reason to think that persons released on citation are more likely to flee permanently than are those released by other methods.

22. ABA Project on Standards for Criminal Justice, *Standards Relating to Pretrial Release*, at 23 (1968). Reprinted with permission.

23. Id. See generally Foote, "The Coming Constitutional Crisis in Bail" (pts. 1-2), 113 *U. Pa. L. Rev.* 959, 1125 (1965); Note, "Compelling Appearance in Court: Administration of Bail in Philadelphia," 102 *U. Pa. L. Rev.* 1031, 1038 (1954). For a discussion of bail and alternatives to bail see D. Freed and P. Wald, *Bail in the United States: 1964* (May 1964).

24. See note 22.

25. A further result of the defendant's inability to purchase his freedom may be an increased likelihood that he will receive an unfavorable disposition of his case. See Wald, "Pretrial Detention and Ultimate Freedom: A Statistical Study," 39 *N.Y.U.L. Rev.* 631 (1964). See also Fabricant, "Bail as a Preferred Freedom and the Failures of New York's Revision," 18 *Buffalo L. Rev.* 303 (1968-1969).

On the impact of jail on the life of the individual and his family, see Langsley, Pittman, and Swank, "Family Crisis in Schizophrenics and Other Mental Patients," 149 *J. Nervous and Mental Disease* 270, 271-276 (1969).

26. See note 22.

27. Vera Institute of Justice, Manhattan Summons Project—Activity Report for the Second Year of City-Wide Operation—July 1, 1968 through June 30, 1969, at 2, 6 (Aug. 25, 1969). See also R. Molleur, *Bail Reform in the Nation's Capital* 89 (1966); ABA Project on Standards for Criminal Justice, *Standards Relating to Pretrial Release* 24 (1968).

28. See Comment, "Pretrial Release Under California Penal Code Section 853.6: An Examination of Citation Release," 60 *Calif. L. Rev.* 1339, 1361 (1972).

29. Feeney, "Citation in Lieu of Arrest: The New California Law," 25 *Vand. L.J.* 367, 371 (1972).

30. 2 S. Weisberg, *Cost Analysis of Correctional Standards: Alternatives to Arrest*, 29, 33, 36 and 41 (Oct. 1975) (Standards and Goals Project, ABA Correctional Economics Center) (based on expert opinion rather than empirical observations).

31. Id. at 44-45. This study showed that, under some assumptions, apprehension and prosecution costs could eat up most of the savings from station-house releases, particularly if defendants averaged only a short stay in jail before reaching court. The major assumptions used, however, are contrary to current practice in most jurisdictions.

32. Berger, "Police Field Citations in New Haven," 1972 *Wisc. L. Rev.* 382, 408.

33. Each of these statements was made by a chief of police in Contra Costa County during the first several years of citation use in that county.

34. Berger, supra note 32, at 411.

35. Boston University Center for Criminal Justice, "Police Policymaking to Structure Discretion: The Boston Experience" 123 (Oct. 1978).

6 The Legal Framework

The statutes and court rules concerning citations thus far adopted fall into two general groups: (1) those which simply authorize the use of cititations as the agency or the officer sees fit, and (2) those which mandate or encourage the use of the procedure in some way.

The Statutes and Rules

Most statutes and rules fall into the authorization category. Over twenty-five states have provisions of this kind. The Delaware statute is typical:

> In any case in which it is lawful for a peace officer to arrest without a warrant a person for a misdemeanor, he may, but need not, give him a written summons.[1]

At least eight states have gone further, however.[2] In six, the law clearly mandates the use of a citation or a promise to appear in some situations. In the other two, the law encourages their use. In three of the mandatory states (Minnesota, Vermont, and Virginia) the mandate applies to all or most misdemeanors. In the other three (Kentucky, Nebraska, and Pennsylvania) the mandatory features are applicable only to infractions or summary offenses.

The Minnesota rule is perhaps the strongest. Entitled "Mandatory Issuance of Citation," it states:

> Law enforcement officers acting without a warrant, who have decided to proceed with prosecution, *shall issue citations* to persons subject to lawful arrest for misdemeanors, unless it reasonably appears to the officer that arrest or detention is necessary to prevent bodily harm to the accused or another or further criminal conduct, or that there is substantial likelihood that the accused will fail to respond to a citation. (Emphasis added.)[3]

The Minnesota rule also mandates the use of jail citations for misdemeanors. The officer in charge is instructed that he "*shall* issue a citation in lieu of continued detention" unless one of the exceptions applies.[4]

The Vermont rule is also entitled "Mandatory Issuance," and provides that law enforcement officers "*shall* . . . issue" citations for misdemeanors.[5]

57

The exceptions listed are similar to those in the Minnesota law but are somewhat broader. Arrest is specifically authorized when necessary to prevent harm to property or to obtain nontestimonial evidence that is on or within reach of the arrested person. If the passage of time causes the reasons for an exception to cease to apply, however, the statute mandates release at that point. Similarly, if the arrest is initially for a felony but the charge is later reduced to a misdemeanor, release is mandated.

The Virginia statute provides that for ordinance violations and most misdemeanors "the arresting officer *shall* take the name and address of such person and *issue* a summons. . . . ."[6] The officer is empowered to make a physical arrest, however, if the suspect refuses to give a written promise to appear, is likely to disregard a summons, or is likely to cause harm to himself or another. The statutes in Kentucky, Nebraska, and Pennsylvania are similar but limited to infractions or summary offenses.[7]

For misdemeanors not punishable by incarceration, both the Virginia and the Minnesota statutes are even more directory than the provisions already discussed. The exceptions do not apply, and a citation must be issued if the accused signs the form agreeing to appear.[8]

The Florida law is weaker. It does not explicitly require the use of citations, but does require that rules governing the use of citations be adopted. Originally, these rules were to be promulgated by "the chiefs of the respective law enforcement agencies" in order to "effectively implement" the citation law. Under amendments adopted in 1977, however, the regulations are to be issued by the chief judge of the circuit.[9] While this provision leaves a great deal of leeway as to how the statute is implemented, it seems to require that there be some kind of implementation.

The California statute falls somewhere between the requirement for rules in Florida and the mandatory-use provisions in the other six states. It requires that police officers and agencies consider the use of citations in each instance. After authorizing use of the citation for any misdemeanor, the statute states that if the arrested person is not released "prior to being booked," the person in charge

> *shall* make an immediate investigation into the background of the person to determine whether he should be released . . . [on citation]. Such investigation shall include, but need not be limited to, the person's name, address, length of residence at that address, length of residence within this state, marital and family status, employment, length of that employment, prior arrest record, and such other facts relating to the person's arrest which would bear on the question of his release . . . [under citation].[10]

If the person is not released, the statute also requires the arresting officer to indicate whether or not one of the following was a reason for nonrelease:

1. The person arrested was so intoxicated that he could have been a danger to himself or others.
2. The person arrested required medical examination or medical care or was otherwise unable to care for his own safety.
3. The person was arrested . . . [driving under the influence of alcohol or drugs].
4. There were one or more outstanding arrest warrants for the person.
5. The person could not provide satisfactory evidence of personal identification.
6. The prosecution of the [arrest] offense or any other offense . . . would be jeopardized by immediate release of the person arrested.
7. There was reasonable likelihood that the offense or offenses would continue or resume, or that the safety of persons or property would be imminently endangered by release of the person arrested.
8. The person arrested demanded to be taken before a magistrate or refused to sign the notice to appear.
9. Any other reason.[11]

If the reason for not releasing the person arrested is not one of the reasons listed, the arresting officer is required to type on the form "the reason for the nonrelease."

Although some of these statutes and court rules have been in effect for nearly a decade, they have not been extensively interpreted by the courts. The few opinions that have been rendered take the mandatory features seriously.[12]

Development of the Mandatory Concept

Viewed historically there is a clear trend toward the more mandatory-type legislation. Initially, the effort was simply to create authority for the use of a summonslike procedure by the police. Thus in 1932, in addition to heeding the call of the Wickersham Commission to create judicial authority to issue summonses as well as warrants, the New York legislature

> empowered and directed [the New York City board of City magistrates] to prepare and issue summons in blank . . . to members of the city police force . . . which summons when filled in and countersigned by such officer . . . shall have the same force and effect as if individually and directly issued by the chief city magistrate. . . .[13]

The reference to the city magistrates and other provisions of the law indicated that the function was still viewed as having a judicial character.

By 1942, when the Uniform Arrest Act was proposed, the function was no longer viewed as wholly judicial. This act contained two provisions relating to release on summons (the term used for citation). The first related to the issuance of a summons in lieu of arrest:

In any case in which it is lawful for a peace officer to arrest without a warrant a person for a misdemeanor, he may, but need not, give him a written summons in substantially the following form. . . . [14]

The other provision concerned the release of persons already arrested:

Any officer in charge of a police department or any officer delegated by him may release, instead of taking before a magistrate, any person who has been arrested without a warrant . . . whenever the person was arrested for a misdemeanor . . . has signed an agreement to appear in court . . . [and the] officer is satisfied that the person is a resident of the state and will appear in court at the time designated. [15]

As discussed in chapter 3, these procedures were promptly adopted in Rhode Island and New Hampshire, and, in 1951, in Delaware as well. [16] Citation legislation that soon followed in other states was also of the authorization type. [17]

Although the first draft of the American Law Institute's Model Code of Pre-Arraignment Procedure had suggested in 1966 that police agencies be required to adopt regulations governing citation usage, [18] it was not until 1968, when the American Bar Association's Standards for Criminal Justice Project issued its Pre-Trial Release Standards, that mandatory use was first advocated. [19] The standards recommended that legislatures and courts enumerate minor offenses "for which citations must be issued," and that use be required for all offenses for which total imprisonment does not exceed six months. The standards recognized, however, that even for these offenses arrest might be necessary in certain situations, such as failure of the accused to identify himself satisfactorily, refusal to sign the citation, the need to prevent imminent bodily harm to the accused or another, insufficient ties to the jurisdiction to assure the accused's appearance in court, and a previous failure to appear.

The standards also suggested that legislatures adopt statutes and that agencies adopt regulations authorizing the use of citations in other cases requiring

such inquiry as is practicable into the accused's place and length of residence, his family relationships, references, present and past employment, his criminal record, and any other facts relevant to appearance in response to a citation. [20]

The very next year (1969) California amended its statute and created the first citation provision with mandatory or semimandatory features. Although it rejected a requirement that reasons be given for each failure to issue a citation, the legislature included a requirement that there be an investigation in each instance.[21] In 1974 the law was again amended, this time requiring that reasons be given for nonissuance.[22]

In 1973 the National Advisory Commission on Criminal Justice Standards and Goals issued its report. Although the commission itself did not recommend new legislation, its corrections task force joined the American Bar Association in recommending legislation that would require the use of citations.[23]

In 1974 the International Association of Chiefs of Police developed a set of model rules for the Texas Council on Criminal Justice that recommended mandatory use,[24] and in 1975 the American Law Institute made final its Model Code of Pre-Arraignment Procedure, recommending the use of citations and the mandating of regulations governing such use.[25] In 1977 the National District Attorneys Association recommended mandatory use for "minor misdemeanors" as well as optional use for other misdemeanors.[26]

In 1978 the National Association of Pretrial Services Agencies added a new element by recommending that the type of citation mandated be the field citation.[27] In 1980 the American Bar Association, in the second edition of its Standards for Criminal Justice, expanded its previous recommendations by urging that the policy favoring use of citations be "implemented by statutes of statewide applicability."[28]

Going even further are the Uniform Rules of Criminal Procedure developed by the National Conference of Commissioners on Uniform State Laws in 1974. These rules treat the question more as a part of the law of arrest than as an issue concerning release. In effect, they require an officer to make a preliminary determination prior to making a full arrest. The officer is authorized to detain the offender for the purpose of making this preliminary determination. During the determination the officer must decide if

1. The offense or the manner in which it was committed involved violence to person or imminent and serious bodily injury or the risk or threat thereof;
2. The person is committing an offense in the officer's presence and will deliberately continue to commit the offense unless arrested;
3. The person committed an offense punishable by incarceration and would not respond to a citation; or
4. Arrest is necessary for the protection of the person arrested or to administer, or to bring him to a source of needed medical or other aid.[29]

Unless one of these conditions is met, the officer must issue a citation rather than complete the arrest. The provision would apply to felonies as well as misdemeanors.

By far the most important influence in the development of the idea of mandatory use has been the American Bar Association's Pre-Trial Release Standards. The standards were the first to articulate the idea of mandatory use and have clearly been the model for many of the other recommendations for mandatory use. In addition, a number of states have explicitly patterned their statutes on these standards.[30] The later endorsements of the idea of mandatory use have no doubt played a part in keeping the idea moving and have provided some useful innovations and suggestions.

Like many other aspects of misdemeanor citation practice this trend toward more mandatory use follows the earlier experience in the traffic area. Initially, the statutes authorizing use of citations for traffic offenses were also simply permissive.[31] At an early point, however, the idea of mandatory use was introduced into the Uniform Vehicle Code, and as time went on more and more states adopted either the Uniform Code or some other mandatory provision.[32]

Agency Views of the Mandatory Statutes

To what extent are the statutes that appear to be mandatory viewed as such by police agencies operating under their authority? To determine the answer to this question the 1976 Police Foundation-Center on Administration of Criminal Justice survey asked police agencies in five of the eight mandatory jurisdictions to indicate whether they considered their law to be mandatory.[33] In Virginia all but one of the agencies responding indicated a belief that the provisions were mandatory, as shown in table 6-1. In Minnesota most agencies also thought that issuance was required, while in Vermont and California the agencies were divided. In Florida agencies generally believed that issuance was not required.

Most agencies in the five states also indicated that use of the citation procedure had increased when their statute or court rule became somewhat more directory, as shown in table 6-2.

Very few problems were indicated by agencies operating under the mandatory or semimandatory statutes.

Thus, for states desiring to go beyond mere authorization, at least three models now exist:

1. The Model Code of Pre-Arraignment Procedure, which places the responsibility on local departments to develop rules for implementation.

Table 6-1
Whether Issuance Is Mandatory
(number of agencies responding)

	Up to Department	Consideration Required	Issuance Required
California	6	5	5
Florida	5	2	0
Minnesota	0	1	6
Vermont	0	1	1
Virginia	0	1	7

Source: Police Foundation-Center on Administration of Criminal Justice survey, 1976.

2. The California statute, which requires an investigation in each case and the giving of reasons for nonrelease.
3. The Uniform Rules of Criminal Procedure, which eliminate the authorization for physical arrest where a citation will do.

Each of these procedures has an advantage over a general authorization statute in that it provides greater specificity without eliminating the flexibility needed by local departments. As each approach has some advantages, and as the approaches are not mutually exclusive, it may well be that the future will see the best features of each plan combined into a single approach. Whether this occurs or not, however, it seems likely that the trend toward more mandatory legislation will continue.

Citations and the Law of Arrest

In the United States the law of arrest is a combination of constitutional and state law. The Constitution requires that there be probable cause to believe that the suspect has committed a crime.[34] Many states have additional requirements for misdemeanors. Generally, these are that arrests without a warrant may be made only for misdemeanors committed in the presence of the officer. A few states are even more restrictive, continuing remnants of the common-law rule that limited warrantless misdemeanor arrests to breaches of the peace committed in the presence of the officer.[35]

One set of questions that the use of citations poses is the extent to which these rules apply to citations. As a practical matter most states have applied the same restrictions to citations that they apply to physical arrests. The question as to whether states could relax the rules for citations nonetheless has some importance.

Table 6-2
Whether State Law Resulted in Increased Use of Citations
(number of agencies responding)

	Greatly	Some	None or a Little
California	9	3	5
Florida	0	6	1
Minnesota	5	2	0
Vermont	1	0	0
Virginia	4	3	0

Source: Police Foundation-Center on Administration of Criminal Justice survey, 1976.

Although the United States Supreme Court has never ruled on the validity of arrests for misdemeanors made outside the presence of the officer or where there is no breach of the peace, most authorities believe that arrests of this kind are constitutional.[36] Presumably, therefore, states could, if they chose, authorize the issuance of citations for offenses outside the officer's presence and for offenses not involving a breach of the peace.

The more difficult question is whether they could also eliminate the requirement of probable cause. In the case of station-house citations the answer to this question is almost surely no. These citations come after a substantial detention and presumably require the same justification as an arrest.[37]

It is not as clear, however, that the field citation requires the kind of probable cause necessary for an arrest. The fact that the defendant is not kept in custody and the intrusion is less than that for the typical arrest suggests that some lesser amount of cause might be permissible.[38] There is a detention, however, and the citation does begin the criminal case. Taken together, these may require the presence of classic probable cause.[39] At a minimum they would seem to require the reasonable suspicion necessary for a stop and frisk.[40]

As a policy matter it seems undesirable to relax the probable-cause requirement even if it is constitutional to do so. In most cases in which a citation would be appropriate there is no reason to start a criminal case unless there is enough evidence to prosecute. Generally if the investigation is to be delayed, it makes sense to delay the citation as well.

The policy considerations with respect to the in-presence limitation are more balanced. On the one hand, there are good reasons for making the citation rules the same as for arrests. Such a policy has the virtue of simplicity, which is important when the rules are already complicated and there are many people involved. Such a policy also makes it difficult to use the citation procedure to expand the scope of the criminal-justice system by bringing in defendants who would have been ignored in a system based on physical arrest.

On the other hand, the American Law Institute argues that an officer ought to be allowed to issue a citation in any case in which he has reasonable cause to believe that the suspect is involved in criminal activity. Officers, the institute suggests, often find themselves in situations in which a victim is seeking to have some action taken but in which they cannot make a misdemeanor arrest because the offense was not committed in their presence. Allowing officers to issue a citation in this situation would, the institute believes, reduce the pressure to characterize the situation as a felony in order to make an arrest.[41] At least one state has adopted this point of view.[42]

Collateral Consequences of Citation Use

An arrest generally has a number of collateral consequences. As a normal rule the suspect may be searched incident to the arrest, fingerprinted or placed in a lineup for identification purposes, and subjected to other investigative procedures. If interrogated concerning the crime, he becomes entitled to *Miranda* warnings. If the police arrest power is seriously misused, the officer becomes civilly liable to the arrestee. Conversely, if the suspect resists or abuses the officer during the arrest, he commits an additional offense. Usually the arrest is recorded and becomes part of the suspect's criminal record.

As the citation is a substitute for arrest, the question naturally occurs as to how use of a citation instead of arrest affects the collateral consequences.

One possible way of resolving these questions is in the legislation authorizing the use of citations. The legislation can be made to say that the citation either comes after arrest or that it comes in lieu of arrest. The Arizona statute, for example, clearly says that the citation comes after arrest:

> In any case in which a person is arrested for an offense that is a misdemeanor, the arresting officer may release the arrested person from custody in lieu of taking such person to the police station.[43]

Some other states and some of the model rules make it clear that a citation either is not an arrest or that it can be issued in a way that it will not be considered an arrest.[44] The Minnesota rules of criminal procedure, for example, state that "the citation may be issued in lieu of an arrest, or if an arrest has been made, in lieu of continued detention."[45]

Although some of the questions involved in the use of citations are state-law questions and can clearly be solved through statutory definition or case law at the state level, some are questions of federal constitutional law.

How far these questions can be resolved by statutory or case-law definitions is open to debate. The Supreme Court has in at least one instance relied on a state's definition of *arrest* in the determination of a constitutional question, finding that state law did not permit a traffic citation to be determined an arrest for purposes of a probation violation.[46] In other contexts, however, the Court has felt itself free to ignore the technicalities of local arrest law.[47]

The sections that follow discuss some of the more important collateral consequences of arrest. In order to simplify the discussion it is assumed that citations are issued only on probable cause.

Right to Search

Generally, a police officer who makes an arrest may make a full search of the person concerned incident to the arrest.[48] Such a search is constitutionally permitted both as a protection to the officer and as a method of preventing the destruction of evidence. And while most other kinds of search require specific reasons to believe that criminal activity is afoot, the search incident to arrest is automatic, requiring no justification other than that necessary to justify the arrest.

Suppose, however, that the officer decides to issue a citation instead of making a full custodial arrest? May he still search the defendant, either before or after the citation is issued? Does he have to have separate probable cause for the search? May he make a full search or only a pat down? Does it matter whether the citation is a field citation or one issued at the station house?

At least two separate questions are involved in these issues: whether such a search is valid as a matter of federal constitutional law, and whether the law of the state or jurisdiction permits a search to be made in the circumstances.

Searches and the Federal Constitution

Assuming that a state chooses to permit searches incident to a misdemeanor citation, may it constitutionally do so? If the citation is a station citation issued after booking, it seems virtually certain that a full search as part of the normal booking process would be found constitutional.[49] If the citation is a field citation, however, the question is much less clear.

The starting point for analysis is *Robinson* v. *United States* and *Gustafson* v. *Florida*, two 1973 cases in which the United States Supreme Court held that it was constitutionally permissible to search traffic offenders who were under "full custodial arrest."[50] The Court indicated that the primary purpose of searches incident to arrest is to protect the officer's safety and to preserve evidence of the offense. The Court rejected the argument that there was no need to allow searches of traffic offenders, however, because they are not normally armed or dangerous or in possession of any evidence of the offense. The Court reasoned that there is always danger to the officer in an enforcement action and concluded that this warrants a blanket authorization to search whenever there is a full custodial arrest, even if only for a traffic offense. The Court declined to "reach the question" as to whether such a search was permissible when the officer issued a citation instead of making a custodial arrest.[51]

The more recent case of *Pennsylvania* v. *Mimms* offered another opportunity to consider the permissibility of searches incident to a traffic citation.[52] In this case the police stopped a car in order to issue a citation for an expired traffic plate. The driver was asked to step outside and show his license and registration. When the driver got out, the officer noticed a bulge under the driver's jacket. Fearing that the bulge might be a weapon, the officer frisked the driver and found a loaded .38 caliber revolver. When later prosecuted for possession of a concealed weapon, the driver claimed the frisk was illegal because the police did not have authority to order him out of the car. In a six-to-three decision the Supreme Court upheld the frisk. The majority said that the officer was justified in ordering the driver out of the car to protect his own safety and that once out of the car the pat down was lawful under normal stop-and-frisk rules.

Although the Court in this case chose not to rule on whether a full search could be conducted as incident to any traffic citation or even whether a pat down could automatically be made as incident to a traffic citation, it did decide that an officer could automatically order a traffic offender out of his car as incident to a traffic citation. This decision leaves open the larger questions insofar as the United States Supreme Court is concerned.[53]

A number of lower courts, however, have considered these matters. The Arizona Supreme Court found that stops for traffic violations are arrests and that a full search may be made incident to the "arrest."[54] Another court ruled that, because the person stopped could be arrested, a search is valid.[55] Other courts, though, have taken the position that a stop for a traffic violation is not a custodial arrest and therefore that a full search may not constitutionally be made.[56]

These cases all concern searches incident to traffic citations. The concern in these cases is that automatically allowing a search would legitimate intrusions into the millions of routine and relatively harmless traffic stops that take place each year. In the case of criminal offenses, however, there are far fewer relatively innocent defendants, a much greater likelihood of danger from weapons, and a greater possibility that the offender will be in possession of evidence of the offense.

The case for the constitutionality of searches incident to citations for criminal offenses has been put by one author as follows:

> [A] persuasive argument can be made that a search incident to a citation will present no constitutional problems. The Fourth Amendment prohibits "unreasonable" searches and seizures. Is it unreasonable to search incident to a citation when the police officer could have arrested the accused and searched his person? Additionally, there is probably some danger to the police officer after he issues a citation to an incensed citizen, although admittedly not at the level of the danger inherent in the arrest process. Finally, there is the police argument that citations should be encouraged, and full use of the process will result only if law enforcement officers do not lose any investigative powers when the citation is employed.[57]

Another consideration is the desirability of using broad general rules as opposed to complicated justifications for each individual case.[58] Where the rules involved must be applied by thousands of officers in countless different situations, the attractiveness of a broad general rule is apparent and has been thought by some both to justify the search-incident-to-arrest doctrine and to explain its extension in *Robinson* to the custodial traffic arrest.

At least one case has clearly taken the position that a search incident to a nontraffic citation is constitutionally permissible. In this case a New York police officer was in the process of issuing citations to three young males who had been involved in an altercation. While moving to a quieter location to write the citation, he noticed a knife handle in one defendant's pocket and proceeded to search all three of the defendants. Finding that the situation involved was an arrest, the court upheld the search. The court said:

> Certainly, an arrest of the defendants *ab initio* for disorderly conduct, in the officer's discretion, would have been a greater intrusion of the defendant's person than the lesser intrusion of a search incident to the arrest.[59]

Search under State Law

Even if the U.S. Constitution permits searches incident to misdemeanor citations, the states are free to impose greater restrictions if they wish. Some states have done so with respect to searches incident to traffic arrests. Other states, however, have followed the lead of the United States Supreme Court in *Robinson* and *Gustafson* and allowed searches incident to arrest for traffic and minor offenses.[60]

As might be expected, the courts that allow searches incident to arrests for traffic offenses have been much more sympathetic to searches incident to traffic citations than have the courts that impose limitations on searches incident to traffic arrests. The courts that follow *Robinson* have sometimes upheld searches related to traffic citations on the theory that citations are arrests and sometimes on the theory that an arrest could have been made.[61] At least one court that follows *Robinson* has refused to uphold searches of this kind, however, insisting that the authority to search is limited to those situations in which a full custodial arrest is made.[62]

There have not been many cases involving searches related to traffic citations in states that restrict searches incident to traffic arrests, but the indications are, as might be expected, that such searches will not be permitted.[63]

No cases have been found in the states that follow *Robinson* ruling on the validity of searches incident to a misdemeanor citation. These states could be expected to be favorably disposed to allowing such searches, particularly if they have statutes that seek to make citation searches possible where arrest searches are possible.[64]

In the states that place restrictions on the right to arrest traffic offenders there have been two decisions ruling on the validity of searches incident to a criminal citation. These decisions reached sharply different results.

The California Supreme Court ruled that suspects who were being given citations for violating a county ordinance concerning open fires could not be fully searched even though the officers had to escort them on foot over difficult terrain for several miles.[65] Because of the traveling required, the court indicated that the officers could legitimately pat the suspects down for weapons. Had traveling not been involved, however, the court strongly implied that the officers could not even have patted the suspects down unless they had reasonable suspicion that the suspects were armed and dangerous. Essentially, the court applied the same rules that it had developed for handling traffic offenses.

There have been no subsequent California cases involving searches incident to citations. There have been several cases, however, in which the California courts refused to permit searches incident to arrests for public drunkenness offenses.[66] These cases strongly suggest that searches incident to citation for these offenses would not be permitted either.

A New York court has taken a different approach. Although New York refuses to allow searches incident to traffic arrests, the New York court indicated that a disorderly conduct charge was a different matter.[67] Because "public policy favors issuing citations rather than arresting citizens where minor offenses are involved," the court said that searches should be allowed. To rule that officers could not search would eliminate the incentive for an officer to issue citations "because to do so would require him to put his life on the line by holding an individual in custody pending the issuance of the ticket without knowledge regarding possible weapons possession by the defendant."[68]

The California and New York decisions both came in states that have imposed restrictions on searches incident to traffic arrests as a matter of state constitutional law.[69] A number of other states have created somewhat similar restrictions as the result of interpretations of state statutes, particularly statutes establishing bail schedules for traffic or minor offenses. These statutes have been found to prohibit a full station-house search until after the suspect has been notified of the bail amount and given an opportunity to post bail.[70] Several courts have even said that the suspect should have a reasonable time to try to obtain the bail amount.[71] Although these statutes are not directly applicable to citations, it is unlikely that searches would be allowed as incident to citations in situations in which they would not be allowed as incident to a physical arrest.

ABA Standards

The American Bar Association Standards of Criminal Justice Project considered the state-law question and suggested that state legislation in this area should explicitly permit searches in the citation situation to the same extent that they would be permitted if the defendant were arrested. The language suggested was:

> Nothing in these standards should be construed to affect a law enforcement officer's authority to conduct an otherwise lawful search even though a citation is issued.[72]

As the standards explained:

> [T]hese standards should not operate to hamper in any way the police officer's authority to make a lawful search, for otherwise he would properly elect to make the search rather than issue a citation.

The purpose of this language was not to say that searches either should be permitted or that searches should not be permitted in connection with offenses for which citations might be issued. Rather the purpose was to say that the legitimacy of the search should not depend on whether the offender was cited instead of arrested.

Several states have followed the recommendation and adopted language of this type in their citation statutes.[73] Some of these states also follow the *Robinson* doctrine, and the language can therefore reasonably be interpreted to authorize searches incident to the citation. No published court decisions to this effect have been found, however.

The only court that has considered the language is the Minnesota Supreme Court, and it has not done so fully.[74] It held that in a situation in which the officer was not allowed to arrest but was required to issue a citation, this language did not authorize a search. The court said that:

What Rule 6.01, subd. 4, arguably seeks to do is to extend the *Robinson-Gustafson* rule to situations where the police normally would have authority to subject the defendant to a custodial arrest but, exercising their discretion, issue a citation instead. Whether the officer in such a situation can issue a citation and still conduct a full search of the person without any independent justification for it is a matter we do not decide because the issue is not presented. This is a case where the officer had no discretion to subject defendant to a custodial arrest for a petty misdemeanor, and therefore, the *Robinson-Gustafson* rule clearly does not justify the search.[75]

In the second edition of the standards the recommended statutory language has been significantly changed. It reads as follows:

When an officer makes a lawful arrest, the defendant's subsequent release on citation should not affect the lawfulness of any search incident to the arrest.[76]

The purpose of this change is to indicate "that there must in fact be an arrest in order to justify a search incident to it." This is a quite different policy from that embodied in the first edition of the standards and is intended to indicate that:

A police officer who decides *ab initio* to issue a citation cannot justify a search of the accused on the ground that the officer could have, but did not, arrest the accused.[77]

The second edition appears to indicate that this change is legally compelled rather than made for policy reasons. As already discussed, however, this is probably an incorrect conclusion.[78]

On the merits of the policy there is much to be said for a statute that mandates the use of citations for minor offenses and that limits searches to dangerous situations and crimes for which there is evidence. To the extent that arrests are permitted for minor offenses, however, the policy of the first edition of the standards appears preferable to that of the second—it seems foolish to force the officer to arrest the offender in order to conduct a search.

Interrogation

Arrest is a threshold issue not only with respect to search, but also with respect to when the *Miranda* warnings must be given. Generally, suspects who are not in custody need not be given the warnings. Before questioning suspects who are in custody, however, the police must advise the suspect that he does not have to say anything, that anything he says may be used against him, that he is entitled to consult with counsel, and that if he cannot afford counsel counsel will be appointed.[79]

Although the *Miranda* opinion itself said that the test as to whether the warnings were required was whether the suspect was in custody "or otherwise deprived of his freedom by the authorities in any significant way,"[80] the line generally drawn has been whether the suspect was under arrest.[81] The courts have not usually required that the warnings be given for suspects detained for brief questioning of the stop-and-frisk variety.[82]

Applying these rules to the station-house citation, it would seem clear that the accused has been taken into custody and that any interrogation would have to follow the rules concerning interrogation of arrested persons. Once more, in the case of the field citation, the situation is not so clear. Physically, there is a detention akin to the stop and frisk. Legally, however, the situation may be characterized as an arrest or not as an arrest. Thus there are at least four possible alternatives as to whether the warnings should be given:

1. Whether the *Miranda* warnings must be given depends on the law of the state. If the state calls the field citation an arrest, the warnings must be given. If the state does not call the field citation an arrest, the warnings need not be given.
2. The citation is a substitute method of arrest, and regardless of whether state law calls the citation an arrest, the warnings must be given as a matter of federal law.
3. The field citation is not physically an arrest, and even if state law calls it an arrest, there is no federal duty to give the warnings.
4. The approach should be that taken by the Uniform Rules of Criminal Procedure. Under this approach there is a detention rather than an arrest, but the warnings must be given anyway as a matter of state law.

There has been little litigation concerning these questions, and the issues have not been clearly settled by the courts. The evil that the *Miranda* rules are designed to combat is that of oppressive interrogation. Certainly that is not present in its worst forms in the limited periods of detention generally involved in the field citation.[83] At the same time, citizens are likely to feel under some compulsion to cooperate, particularly when they are expected to sign the citation form itself. As the extent of this compulsion is not determined by the niceties of the arrest law in the jurisdiction concerned, courts should resolve these questions on the basis of their views of compulsion, rather than attempting to follow the law concerning arrests.

Some courts have finessed these questions altogether by deciding that the *Miranda* rules do not apply to traffic violations or minor offenses. They consequently do not require the warnings to be given even in situations in which there clearly is an arrest.[84] In these states obviously there is no requirement that the warnings be given for either field or station-house citations.

Although the legal issues concerning citations and questioning are important, they do not lead to any major conclusions concerning whether a police agency or a legislature should adopt a citation procedure.

Civil Liability

Although police officers are often sued for false arrest, there has been little litigation concerning the liability of police officers for the wrongful issuance of a citation. In some citation cases courts have held that there is no liability, because there was no arrest.[85] These cases suggest that states that describe the citation as an arrest would be likely to find officers subject to suit for false arrest.

One benefit suggested for the concept that a field citation is an action in lieu of arrest rather than an arrest is that it might expose officers to less potential civil liability, particularly in those instances in which it was issued in the field without any involuntary detention.[86] The desirability of limiting false-arrest liability in this way has been questioned, however, by one commentator. In his view citation issuance involves a serious use of power, and the individual "should therefore have full recourse to a civil action if official power is misused."[87]

Police Records

Practices vary in the extent to which citations are recorded as arrests in police records. Many agencies record citation offenses on the suspect's rap sheet just as they would record an arrest for a similar offense.

Another benefit suggested for the in-lieu-of-arrest concept is that suspects could truthfully say that they had not been arrested.[88] This is no doubt a logical consequence of the in-lieu-of-arrest concept; however, to the extent that there is a desire to protect the suspect from the consequences of a record, it seems preferable to address this issue specifically in the statute.[89]

Issues under Mandatory Statutes

In states mandating the use of citations there are some additional issues. If the citizen is arrested when he should be cited, the arrest is illegal. Does that mean that any search conducted is also illegal? In states that prohibit searches when citations are involved it seems clear that such a search would be illegal, and many states would exclude any evidence discovered.[90] In states that permit searches incident to citations it is still possible that the search would be found illegal, as the fruit of the illegal arrest.[91] Alternatively, it might be argued that the search is not a product of the arrest, since it could have been made in any event.

Another issue concerns the possible liability to citizens who are arrested when the statute says they should be cited. These citizens may well be able to sue for false arrest. The Canadian citation statute attempts to address this issue, specifying that officers who have reasonable cause to believe that the suspect has committed an offense are not subject to suit even if they arrest when they should have issued a citation.[92]

Equal Protection of the Law

Another concern that has sometimes surfaced is whether the citation authority itself raises constitutional problems. Three questions concerning equal protection of the law, for example, are mentioned in a 1974 article:

> First, does the delegation of extensive discretion to individual officers create the possibility that the system will be applied discriminatorily? Second, can eligibility for citation be limited to those individuals who possess adequate community roots? Third, can felons be excluded from the operation of the system?[93]

The article correctly points out that it would be clearly unconstitutional for an agency to systematically issue citations to persons of one race or creed while arresting persons of another race or creed for offenses of the same kind. The article indicates that proof of this kind of violation is likely to be difficult, however, because of the low visibility of discretionary practices, because police rarely admit to discretionary enforcement, because there is a presumption that police act in a regular and proper manner, and because anything less than an almost total focus on one class may be explained as a function of chance or laxity.[94]

Although the article recognizes that the issue of discretionary enforcement covers much more than the use of citations, it argues nonetheless that in jurisdictions not having clear guidelines the citation procedure is particularly susceptible to abuse.

The second constitutional problem raised relates to the use of the community-roots test for determining eligibility. Citing cases in which the United States Supreme Court invalidated residency requirements for receiving welfare and for voting, the article says that:

> Arguably, the requirement that an offender establish ties to a given com-
> munity before he is eligible for citation interferes with that offender's right
> to travel.[95]

The article points out, however, that the community-roots test serves to ensure the appearance of the defendant at trial and the release of poor defendants, and on this basis argues that it is constitutionally justified.

The third constitutional issue mentioned is the limitation of the citation
procedure to misdemeanor offenses. As to this issue, the article says:

> The potential for economic discrimination in the bail system is as great with
> respect to felons as it is with misdemeanants. Furthermore, the distinction
> between certain felonies and misdemeanors are inconsequential at least as
> far as the concerns underlying the citation system are involved. Assuming
> that the concerns reflected in the citation system focus on the cessation of
> the offense in point and the likelihood that the offender will honor his sum-
> mons to appear in court, felonies that differ from misdemeanors only with
> regard to the value of the merchandise stolen should be citable. . . . Fur-
> thermore, the distinction between felonies and misdemeanors is rendered
> less meaningful due to the practice of pleabargaining.[96]

The article rejects the argument that felonies as a group are more
serious offenses and that they should therefore be subjected to the safeguards of bail. Arguing that bail is a matter of right in noncapital cases,
the article in effect contends that the Constitution requires that citations be
as available for nonviolent felonies as for misdemeanors.

The questions raised in this article do not cast any serious doubt on the
constitutionality of the citation procedure. The distinction between felonies
and misdemeanors is well recognized in the law, and a holding that it was
unconstitutional would bring down much more than the citation procedure.
Similarly, the community-roots test has been widely used by the judiciary in
setting bail and granting release-on-own recognizance.[97] The article is clearly
correct, however, in stating that discriminatory use of citation authority
would violate the equal protection of the law.

One case in which the citation procedure was subjected to a constitutional attack occurred in the Washoe County District Court in Nevada in
1975.[98] A citizen arrested for driving under the influence of alcohol sued to
be released on citation rather than having to post $250 bail. The Reno police
defended on the ground that the defendant had not been an area resident
for one year and that he therefore did not qualify for release under their
policy for issuing citations.

The arrestee's principal claim was that the authority to release suspects
was a judicial power, that giving authority to the police to release suspects
on citation was therefore, in effect, the delegation of judicial authority to
the executive branch, and that this violated the doctrine of separation of

powers. The court concluded that the authority to grant releases "while primarily a judicial one," was "not exclusive" and that "concurrent use of power by other branches of the government" was therefore permitted.

> I see nothing unreasonable or prohibited by court rule in allowing the Police Chief to *release* individuals on their own recognizance before they are brought for consideration of bail.[99]

Notes

1. Del. Code tit. 11, §1907 (1979).

2. California, Florida, Kentucky, Minnesota, Nebraska, Pennsylvania, Vermont, Virginia.

3. Minn. R. Crim. P. 6.01, subd. 1(1)(a).

4. Minn. R. Crim. P. 6.01, subd. 1(1)(b) (Emphasis added.).

5. Vt. R. Crim. P. 3(c) (Emphasis added.).

6. Va. Code §19.2-74 (Cum. Supp. 1980) (Emphasis added.).

7. Ky. Rev. Stat. §431.015(2) (Cum. Supp. 1980); Neb. Rev. Stat. §29-435 (1979); Pa. R. Crim. P. 51(A)(3). There is some doubt as to whether the Kentucky statute is mandatory. See Ky. Op. Att'y Gen. 80-143 (1980).

8. Minn. R. Crim. P. 6.01, subd. 1(1)(b); Va. Code 319.2-74.1 (Cum. Supp. 1980).

9. Fla. R. Crim. P. 3.125(j), which supersedes Fla. Stat. Ann. §901.28 (West Cum. Supp. 1981). See also Yetter, "The Florida Rules of Criminal Procedure: 1977 Amendments," 5 *Fla. State U. L. Rev.* 243, 244 (1977).

10. Cal. Penal Code §853.6(i) (West Cum. Supp. 1981).

11. Id., subsection (j).

12. See *State* v. *Martin*, 253 N.W.2d 404 (Minn. 1977). See also *People* v. *Brisendine*, 13 C.3d 528, 119 Cal. Rptr. 315,531 P.2d 1009 (1975).

13. 1932 N.Y. Laws, ch. 537, §§82h, 84, at p. 1145.

14. See Warner, "The Uniform Arrest Act," 28 *Va. L. Rev.* 315, 346 (1942).

15. Id.

16. Id. at 317 n. 4. See also 1941 N.H. Laws, ch. 163; 1941 R.I. Laws, ch. 1.982; 48 Del. Laws, ch. 304 (1951).

17. See chapter 3.

18. *Model Code of Pre-Arraignment Procedure* §3.02 (Tent. Draft No. 1, 1966).

19. ABA Project on Standards for Criminal Justice, *Standards Relating to Pretrial Release* 11 (1968). The tentative draft was issued in March and approved in August.

20. Id. at 12.

21. 1969 Cal. Stats., ch. 1259, §2 at p. 2459.

22. 1974 Cal. Stats., ch. 1230, §1, at p. 2672.

23. See National Advisory Commission on Criminal Justice Standards and Goals, *Corrections* 116-119 (1973).

24. International Association of Chiefs of Police, *Model Rules for Law Enforcement Officers: A Manual on Police Discretion* 13-19 (1974).

25. *Model Code of Pre-Arraignment Procedure* §120.2 (1975).

26. National District Attorneys Association, *National Prosecution Standards* 136 (1977).

27. National Association of Pretrial Services Agencies, *Performance Standards and Goals for Pretrial Release and Diversion: Release* 9-14 (1978).

28. 2 ABA Standards for Criminal Justice, *Pretrial Release*, standard 10-2.1 (2d ed. 1980).

29. *Uniform Rules of Criminal Procedure* 211(c).

30. These include Arkansas, Arizona, California, Florida, Minnesota, and Vermont. The Nebraska law is apparently patterned after the Model Code of Pre-Arraignment Procedure.

31. See, for example, 1923 Cal. Stats., ch. 266, §154, at p. 566.

32. See Uniform Act Regulating the Operation of Vehicles on Highways §66, in *Handbook of the National Conference of Commissioners on Uniform State Laws and Proceedings of the Thirty-sixth Annual Meeting* 565 (1926). The current version of the Uniform Act is Uniform Vehicle Code §16-206(a) (Supp. 1979).

33. The Kentucky, Nebraska, and Pennsylvania laws were not then in effect.

34. *United States* v. *Watson*, 423 U.S. 411 (1976).

35. *Model Code of Pre-Arraignment Procedure* app. X (1975); E. Fisher, *Laws of Arrest* 180-189 (1967).

36. *Street* v. *Surdyka*, 492 F.2d 368 (4th Cir. 1974); *Diamond* v. *Marland*, 395 F. Supp. 432 (S.D.Ga. 1975); *Erickson* v. *City of Phoenix*, 105 Ariz. 19, 458 P.2d 953 (1969); *State* v. *Berber*, 391 A.2d 107 (R.I. 1978); E. Fisher, *Laws of Arrest* 128-132 (1967). But see *United States* v. *Watson*, 423 U.S. 411, 455 n. 21. (1976); *Ewing* v. *State*, 300 So. 2d 916 (Miss. 1974).

37. *Dunaway* v. *New York*, 442 U.S. 200 (1979).

38. In *Gerstein* v. *Pugh*, 420 U.S. 103, 125 n. 26 (1975), the Supreme Court said that a "probable cause determination" is "not a constitutional prerequisite to the charging decision." "[I]t is required," the Court said, "only for those suspects who suffer restraints on liberty other than the condition that they appear for trial." See also Barrett, "Personal Rights, Property and the Fourth Amendment," 1960 *Supreme Court Review* 46, for a discussion of the concept of variable probable cause.

39. *The Restatement (Second) of Torts* §112 (1965) defines an arrest as "the taking of another into custody . . . for the purpose of bringing the

other before a court. . . . '' By this definition the arrest is complete when the citation is issued. See also Gless, ''Arrest and Citation: Definition and Analysis,'' 59 *Neb. L. Rev.* 246, 321-322 (1980).

40. See *Terry* v. *Ohio*, 392 U.S. 1 (1968).

41. *Model Code of Pre-Arraignment Procedure* §120.2, commentary at 304 (1975). The *Uniform Rules of Criminal Procedure* authorize citations only where an arrest could be made. Rule 211, comment.

42. See Kirkpatrick, ''Arrest, Citation and Summons—The Supreme Court Takes a Great Leap Forward,'' 30 *Ark. L. Rev.* 137, 148-150 (1976).

43. Ariz. Rev. Stat. §13-3903 (1978).

44. ABA Project on Standards for Criminal Justice, *Standards Relating to Pretrial Release* 31-39 (1968); *Model Code of Pre-Arraignment Procedure* §120.2, commentary at 304 (1975); *Uniform Rules of Criminal Procedure* rule 211.

45. Minn. R. Crim. P. 601 subd. 1(1)(a).

46. *Douglas* v. *Buder*, 412 U.S. 430 (1973).

47. *Cupp* v. *Murphy*, 412 U.S. 291 (1973).

48. See, for example, *Chimel* v. *California*, 395 U.S 752 (1969). See also 2 W. LaFave, *Search and Seizure* 261-301 (1978).

49. *United States* v. *Edwards*, 415 U.S. 800 (1974); 2 W. LaFave, *Search and Seizure* 302-334 (1978).

50. 414 U.S. 218 (1973); 414 U.S. 260 (1973).

51. 414 U.S. 218, 236 n. 6.

52. 434 U.S. 106 (1977).

53. The conclusion in the second edition of the ABA Standards that the Supreme Court has decided that there must be an arrest to justify the search seems to be in clear conflict with the Court's own statement concerning citation situations. Compare ABA Standards for Criminal Justice, *Pretrial Release* standard 10-2.4 (2d ed. 1980) and commentary with *Robinson* v. *United States*, 414 U.S. 218, 236 n. 6. See also Folk, ''The Case for Constitutional Constraints upon the Power to Make Full Custody Arrests,'' 48 *U. Cinn. L. Rev.* 321, 328 (1979).

54. *State* v. *Susko*, 114 Ariz. 547, 562 P.2d 720 (1977). See also *United States* v. *Santangelo*, 411 F. Supp. 1248 (S.D.N.Y. 1975) (dictum).

55. *United States* v. *Ricard*, 563 F.2d 45 (2d Cir. 1977). See also Gless, ''Arrest and Citation: Definition and Analysis,'' 59 *Neb. L. Rev.* 279, 322 n. 269 (1980); Agata, ''Searches and Seizures Incident to Traffic Violations—A Reply to Professor Simeone,'' 7 *St. Louis U.L.J.* 1 (1962); Simeone, ''Search and Seizure Incident to Traffic Violations,'' 6 *St. Louis U.L.J.* 506 (1961).

56. *State* v. *Breaux*, 329 So.2d 696 (La. 1976); *United States* v. *Robinson*, 471 F.2d 1082, 1096-1097 (D.C. Cir. 1972) (en banc), rev'd on other grounds, 414 U.S. 218 (1973); *State* v. *Gustafson*, 258 So.2d 1, 3 (Fla. 1972)

(dictum), aff'd on other grounds, 414 U.S. 260 (1973); *Conn v. Commonwealth*, 387 S.W.2d 285 (Ky. 1965). See also *Luckett v. United States*, 484 F.2d 89 (9th Cir. 1973); E. Fisher, *Laws of Arrest* 87 (1978).

57. Kirkpatrick, "Arrest, Citation and Summons—The Supreme Court Takes a Giant Step Forward," 30 *Ark. L. Rev.* 137, 152 (1976). Reprinted with permission.

58. LaFave, " 'Case-by-Case Adjudication' versus 'Standardized Procedures': The Robinson Dilemma," 1974 *Sup. Ct. Rev.* 127.

59. *People v. Hazelwood*, 106 Misc. 2d 213, 429 N.Y.S.2d 1012, (1980), citing *United States v. Watson*, 423 U.S. 411 (1976).

60. States that have followed Robinson include Indiana, Maine, Missouri, Oklahoma, and Oregon. See, for example, *Sizemore v. State*, 159 Ind. App. 549, 308 N.E.2d 400 (1974); *State v. Cromwell*, 509 S.W.2d 144 (Mo. Ct. App. 1974); *State v. Dubay*, 338 A.2d 797 (Me. 1975); *Hughes v. State*, 522 P.2d 1331 (Okla. Crim. App. 1974); *State v. Florence*, 270 Ore. 169, 527 P.2d 1202 (1974). See also Howard, "State Courts and Constitutional Rights in the Day of the Burger Court," 62 *Va. L. Rev.* 873, 897-900 (1976).

61. *State v. Susko*, 114 Ariz. 547, 562 P.2d 720 (1977); *United States v. Ricard*, 563 F.2d 45 (2d Cir. 1977).

62. See *State v. Grady*, 548 S.W.2d 601 (Mo. Ct. App. 1977).

63. *People v. Brisendine*, 13 Cal.3d 528, 531 P.2d 1009, 119 Cal. Rptr. 315 (1975), reaffirming earlier traffic cases.

64. See notes 73 to 74 infra.

65. *People v. Brisendine*, 13 Cal.3d 528, 531 P.2d 1009, 119 Cal. Rptr. 315 (1975).

66. *People v. Longwill*, 14 Cal.3d 943, 538 P.2d 753, 123 Cal. Rptr. 297 (1975); *People v. Maher*, 17 Cal.3d 196, 550 P.2d 1044, 130 Cal. Rptr. 508 (1976). See also *People v. Rich*, 72 Cal. App.3d 115 (1977).

67. *People v. Hazelwood*, 106 Misc. 213, 429 N.Y.S.2d 1012 (1980).

68. Id. (Court approves "search" but also speaks of "pat down").

69. *Zehrung v. State*, 569 P.2d 189 (1977), modified on rehearing, 573 P.2d 858 (Alaska 1978); *People v. Brisendine*, 13 Cal.3d 528, 531 P.2d 1009, 119 Cal. Rptr. 315 (1975); *People v. Clyne*, 189 Colo. 412, 541 P.2d 71 (1975); *State v. Kaluna*, 55 Haw. 361, 520 P.2d 51 (1974); *People v. Palmer*, 62 Ill.2d 261, 342 N.E.2d 353 (1976); *People v. Erwin*, 42 N.Y.2d 1064, 369 N.E.2d 1170, 399 N.Y.S.2d 637 (1977).

70. *People v. Seymour*, 80 Ill. App.3d 221, 398 N.E.2d 1191 (1979). See also *People v. Garcia*, 81 Mich. App. 260, 265 N.W.2d 115 (1978) (per curiam).

71. *State v. Jetty*, 176 Mont. 519, 579 P.2d 1228 (1978); *State v. Gwinn*, 12 Or. App. 444, 506 P.2d 187 (1973). See also 2 W. LaFave, *Search and Seizure* 331-335 (1978).

72. ABA Project on Standards for Criminal Justice, *Standards Relating to Pretrial Release* 38 (1968). Reprinted with permission.

73. See, for example, Ark. R. Crim. P. 5.5; Ariz. Rev. Stat. §13-3903(F) (West 1978); Fla. R. Crim. P. 3.125; Minn. R. Crim. P. 6.01 subd. 4; Tenn. R. Crim. P. 3.5.

74. *State* v. *Martin*, 253 N.W.2d 404 (Minn. 1977) (per curiam).

75. Id. at 406.

76. 2 ABA Standards Relating to Criminal Justice, *Pretrial Release* standard 10-2.4 (2d ed. 1980).

77. Id., history of standard.

78. See notes 50 to 59 supra.

79. *Miranda* v. *Arizona*, 384 U.S. 436 (1966).

80. Id. at 478.

81. *Beckwith* v. *United States*, 425 U.S. 341 (1976); *Oregon* v. *Mathaison*, 429 U.S. 492 (1977).

82. *United States* v. *Tobin*, 429 F.2d 1261 (8th Cir. 1970); *United States* v. *Montos*, 421 F.2d 215 (5th Cir.), cert. denied, 397 U.S. 1022 (1970).

83. In recent years the Supreme Court has generally taken a very restrictive view of the *Miranda* requirements. See, for example, *Harris* v. *N.Y.*, 401 U.S. 222 (1971); *United States v. Mandujano*, 425 U.S. 564 (1976).

84. See, for example, *Clay* v. *Riddle*, 541 F.2d 456 (4th Cir. 1976); National District Attorneys Association, *Confessions and Interrogations after Miranda* 65-66 (rev. 6th ed. 1978); Broderick, "Interrogation and Confessions," in R. Cipes, *Criminal Defense Techniques* §3.06[5](1970) (and 1980 Supp.). See also Note, "The Applicability of *Miranda* to the Police Booking Process," 1976 *Duke L. J.* 574.

85. *Hart* v. *Zerzig*, 131 Colo. 458, 283 P.2d 177 (1955); *Berry* v. *Bass*, 157 La. 81, 102 So. 76 (1924).

86. *Model Code of Pre-Arraignment Procedure* §120.2, commentary at 304 (1975).

87. Berger, "Police Field Citations in New Haven," 1972 *Wisc. L. Rev.* 382, 391.

88. *Model Code of Pre-Arraignment Procedure* §120.2, commentary at 304 (1975).

89. See Berger, "Police Field Citations in New Haven," 1972 *Wisc. L. Rev.* 382, 391; Comment, "Criminal Procedure: Expungement of Arrest Records," 62 *Minn. L. Rev.* 229 (1978). Protective statutes are common in some fields. See Cal. Wel. & Inst. Code §781 (West 1980); Lab. Code §423.7 (West Cum. Supp. 1981).

90. See *People* v. *Superior Court*, 7 C.3d 186, 496 P.2d 1205, 101 Cal. Rptr. 837 (1972). Even though it is not clear that there is a constitutional requirement that states apply the exclusionary rule in this situation, many do. See 1 W. LaFave, *Search and Seizure* 144-150 (1978); 2 id. at 232-233.

91. This may be the rationale of *State* v. *Martin*, 253 N.W.2d 404 (Minn. 1977); *State* v. *Armstrong*, 291 N.W.2d 918 (Minn. 1980). Statutory provisions that seek to preserve the right of search in citation situations (see note 72 supra) are ambiguous in the states mandating citation use. Interpreted narrowly, they authorize searches only when the officer has discretion to arrest rather than cite. Interpreted broadly, they authorize searches whenever an arrest could have been made under the previous nonmandatory law.

92. See chapter 16, notes 35 to 36.

93. Comment, "An Analysis of the Citation System in Evanston, Illinois: Its Value, Constitutionality and Viability," 65 *J. Crim. Law and Criminology* 75, 80 (1974). Reprinted with permission. See also Sinclair, "A Proposal for an 'Own Recognizance Release' Bail Program, with Focus on the DWI Arrest," 13 *Idaho L. Rev.* 81, 88 (1976); *People* v. *Copeland*, 77 Misc. 2d 649, 354 N.Y.S.2d 399 (1974), rev'd on other grounds, 82 Misc. 2d 12, 370 N.Y.S.2d 775 (1975), aff'd mem., 39 N.Y.2d 986, 355 N.E.2d 288, 387 N.Y.S.2d 234 (1976); 2 W. LaFave, *Search and Seizure* 290 (1978).

94. Comment, "An Analysis of the Citation System in Evanston," 65 *J. Crim. Law and Criminology* 75, 80-81 (1974).

95. Id. at 81 (1974), citing *Shapiro* v. *Thompson*, 394 U.S. 618 (1969) and *Dunn* v. *Blumstein*, 405 U.S. 330 (1972). See also Kirkpatrick, "Arrest, Citation and Summons—The Supreme Court Takes a Great Leap Forward," 30 *Ark. L. Rev.* 137, 153 n. 58 (1976).

96. Comment, "An Analysis of the Citation System in Evanston," 65 *J. Crim. Law and Criminology* 75, 82 (1974). Reprinted with permission.

97. Cf. *Schilb* v. *Kuebel*, 404 U.S. 357 (1971).

98. *Matter of Floyd* (Second Judicial District Court, Washoe County, Nevada, May 1, 1975).

99. Id.

**Part II
Beginning and Operating
Citation Procedures**

PART II
Teaching and Organizing
Child-Centered
Curriculum

7 Development in New York City: An Idea Becomes a Reality

It is one thing for legal theoreticians and lawmakers to develop abstract ideas as to how things might be better. It is an altogether different thing, however, for a police agency to take these ideas and put them into effect in an operational setting, particularly if the ideas have not been widely tested.

The first large police agency to make major use of the citation procedure for criminal offenses was that in New York City. To give some sense as to how the idea became an operational reality, this chapter traces its development in New York City, focusing on its history and on problems and issues that have arisen.

Major use of the citation procedure for criminal cases began as an experiment in the Fourteenth Precinct in Manhattan in early 1964. The background of this experiment was described to the National Bail Conference by Police Commissioner Michael Murphy later in 1964. The commissioner first discussed what the department had already been doing:

> As you know, a summons [the New York term for a citation] is an order served on an individual directing and requiring him to be present in court on a specified date and time, to answer a specified charge brought against him. Last year, the Police Department issued just over two and a half million summons. . . . Almost all of them were issued for traffic offenses, but there were a considerable number—90,264—issued for other offenses such as disorderly conduct and violation of city ordinances.[1]

He then discussed some earlier but limited uses of the summons in New York:

> The number of minor offenses for which summons may be issued by the man on post has expanded rapidly. More and more of the city's ordinances and rules and regulations of the various city departments have been included. This process began in 1932 when then Governor Franklin Delano Roosevelt signed a bill declaring that "The Board of City Magistrates with the concurrence of the Police Commissioner shall adopt regulations providing for the service of a summons in lieu of arrest but not in the case of a felony."[2]

It was not until 1961, however, that the procedure was used for a nontraffic misdemeanor in New York City.

> In 1961, through an agreement with the Magistrates Courts . . . certain subdivisions of the disorderly conduct statute were included. Today, we issue summons rather than make arrests for such violations as those pertaining to animals, any misdemeanor punishable by fine not exceeding $100 or imprisonment not exceeding 60 days, or both, any violation of the labor law, vehicle and traffic law, workmen's compensation law, New York City Charter and administrative code, any violation of the rules of the Fire Department, and many violations of the multiple dwelling law, the alcohol beverage control law and the navigation law.[3]

By early 1964 these procedures had pretty well reached the limits of their natural expansion. Only two penal-law offenses qualified for the use of a summons in place of arrest—nonpayment of transportation fare by a minor and certain disorderly conduct violations, such as use of offensive language, public annoyance, congregating on the street and refusing to move, and causing a crowd to collect.[4]

Even for these offenses use was relatively slight. A survey conducted by the police department as part of the planning process for the Manhattan Summons Project disclosed that almost all arrests for disorderly conduct in the test precinct involved derelicts, and that summonses were not being issued because this group was for the most part homeless, improperly identified, liable to repeat the offenses for which they were arrested, and, as alcoholics, unreliable and unlikely to appear in court in response to a summons.[5]

Commissioner Murphy described the next step in the process:

> Until the inauguration of the current study to determine the advisability of broadening the use of summons in lieu of arrest, we had reached the limits of current summons practice. The next step, embodied in this experiment was an exceedingly important—and, I might add, bold—one. It took the use of the summons into an area which had never been penetrated, at least, in New York City. It moved it primarily from the area of regulatory law and into the area of crime per se. With the permission of the Appellate Divisions of the Supreme Court of New York State, First and Second Judicial Departments, and the Criminal Court of the City of New York, we have extended the use of the summons to the offenses of simple assault and petit larceny.

> In cooperation with the Vera Foundation, a pilot project was initiated in late March of this year in the 14th Precinct—a midtown command in the center of a large shopping and industrial area. This area was selected because of its heavy volume of arrests in these two misdemeanor categories. This precinct is not a residential area. What slums it did have, in the past twenty years, have been torn down for tunnels, highway, bus and airline terminals and office and factory buildings. The precinct, in addition to a large waterfront and warehouse area, included most of the garment area,

Pennsylvania terminal, and the city's largest and busiest shopping area, including such stores as Macy's, Gimbels, Lord and Taylor, Ohrbach's and others.[6]

Much of the impetus for the Manhattan Summons Project came from the city's experience with the earlier Manhattan Bail Project. This project began in 1961 under the sponsorship of the Vera Foundation (later the Vera Institute of Justice). It experimented with interviewing criminal defendants to determine their ties with the community and releasing on their own promise to appear those who had such ties. The project rapidly demonstrated that almost all defendants released in this manner would appear in court as promised and that this was a way of safely releasing many defendants who were not able to make bail.[7]

The Manhattan Summons Project began formally on April 12, 1964. A Vera worker, an evening law student from New York University, was positioned in the Fourteenth Precinct station house. Procedures were established for him to interview all persons brought to the station house who were accused of simple assault or petit larceny and to use telephone verification techniques that had been developed during the Manhattan Bail Project.[8] He then recommended to the desk officer that each defendant with a sufficient number of points on the objective scoring system be released on a summons instead of taken to arraignment court. The summons was returnable from five to ten days after issuance, and, as in the Manhattan Bail Project, Vera assumed responsibility for notifying the defendant of his scheduled court appearance and reminding him to be there.

The defendant also understood that failure to appear for arraignment would result in the issuance of a warrant for his arrest. A prompt appearance, on the other hand, would almost automatically result in the defendant's release on his own recognizance pending trial.

The Manhattan Summons Project was designed, as the Manhattan Bail Project had been, as an experiment—in this instance to find out whether the police would release more persons on summonses if they had verified information about their reliability and to determine if the defendants would appear in court as required.[9]

The project was an immediate success. In its first six months 346 petit larceny and assault defendants were interviewed, 231 summonses recommended, 223 summonses issued, and all but 4 of the defendants appeared as promised for arraignment.[10]

The project continued to evolve as experience was gained. According to a report by the Vera Institute:

It was found that the arresting officer was not necessary in arraignment court on the return date of a summons in a shoplifting case, as the store detective was more knowledgeable about the complaint and was quite able to prepare the complaint for arraignment purposes. This meant a saving of eight to nine hours in each case—a formidable gain in police patrol time alone.

In addition, it was possible to narrow the area of discretion exercised by the police officer in deciding on summons eligibility. The phrase "apparently respectable" was removed from the criteria the officer was to apply to the accused, as being too imprecise and allowing arbitrary application. Accused gamblers and prostitutes were taken off the list of defendants denied summonses, and addicts were put on. Also, attempts were made in the operation of the project to keep down those instances where summonses were denied to "known criminals" who were defined in the regulations as persons with prior arrest records, regardless of whether the arrests resulted in convictions.[11]

Six months after its initiation in the Fourteenth Precinct, the Manhattan Summons Project was extended to the Sixteenth Precinct to the north, covering the busy Times Square area. Six months later it was extended again, into the Thirteenth Precinct on Manhattan's Lower East Side. By 1966 the police department was administering the project throughout Manhattan, having phased the Vera workers out of the station houses, and by the summer of 1967 the summons program had been extended to all five boroughs of the city.[12]

Early Results under City-wide Operations

When the summons program was adopted on a city-wide basis in 1967, it was expanded to include almost all misdemeanors and petty violations. These included such high-volume arrest offenses as disorderly conduct, harassment, simple assault, malicious mischief, loitering, resisting arrest, petit larceny, and theft of services. In all, there were approximately 300 different charges for which a summons could be issued. Exclusions were limited to serious "fingerprintable" misdemeanors.[13]

The department policy statement issued to govern city-wide operation of the program stated:

> The basis for this program is the belief that persons with certain demonstrable roots in the community may be relied upon to appear voluntarily in compliance with a . . . [citation]. To objectively measure these factors, the defendant, with his consent, is interviewed and the information obtained subject to verification. This information is weighed by the use of a point scale developed for this purpose. Minimum standards for release on a . . . [citation] have been established and persons meeting these standards shall be considered for such release.[14]

In practice, the person to be charged was brought to the station and interviewed there by the arresting officer, following an interview form. The interviewing officer then made a name check with the Identification Section. If the desk officer requested, he also sought to verify the information supplied concerning residence, family ties, and employment.

A defendant was considered eligible for a citation if he:

1. Attained a minimum of five points on the investigation.
2. Was not incapacitated by virtue of intoxication or injury, except that an injured or hospitalized prisoner could be summonsed as authorized by paragraph 20 of the order.
3. Was not a current narcotic user.[15]

The interview investigation was mandatory for most misdemeanors except those involving public intoxication or admitted, current heroin users. In these instances the interview investigation was undertaken only "for those who reasonably stand a chance of meeting the established criteria."

The point system used is shown in table 7-1. The final decision as to the issuance of the citation rested with the desk officer. In most instances he issued the citation ("summons") if the arresting officer so recommended, but was not bound to do so.

The time-saving features of the summons procedure were further enhanced by extending the authority to issue summonses to department-store security guards and railroad, housing, transit, and Port Authority police. Each of these agencies conducted its own presummons interview and, after obtaining the telephone consent of the desk officer at the nearest precinct, issued the summons.[16]

During 1967-1968, the first year of city-wide operation, 14,232 summonses were issued; by 1970-1971, the figure had reached 31,946. Several factors contributed to the increase, including a larger percentage of defendants who consented to be interviewed for summonses, a larger percentage who were eligible for a summons recommendation, and a larger percentage for whom summonses were actually granted.[17]

From the beginning of city-wide operation the rate of release differed substantially from area to area. Thus in 1968-1969, the second year of city-wide operation, releases ranged from 16.1 percent in Manhattan to 80 percent in Queens and 87.5 percent in Richmond, as shown in table 7-2. The low rate of release in Manhattan was attributed by the department to the large number of transients arrested in that borough.[18]

During these early years of city-wide operation the jump rate—the percentage of summonsed defendants who failed to appear in court on the return date of the summons—remained fairly constant at approximately 5 percent, as shown in table 7-3 for mid-1968 to mid-1969.

Of those persons who failed to appear in 1968-1969, fifty-two appeared voluntarily at a later time and an additional sixty-two were unable to appear

Table 7-1
Manhattan Summons Project Point System

Residence	Over 1 year at current address—3 points
	6 months at current address or present and prior 1 year—2 points
	Present 4 months or present and prior 6 months—1 point
Family ties	Lives with family and has regular contact with other family members—3 points
	Lives alone but has regular contact with other relatives—1 point
	Lives with family but has no other family contacts—2 points
Employment	Current job over 1 year—3 points
	Current job over 6 months—2 points
	Present job 4-6 months, present and prior 6 months, or supported by family—1 point
Prior arrests	No previous convictions—2 points
	One misdemeanor or violation conviction—1 point
	Two misdemeanors or violation convictions or one felony conviction—0 points
	Three misdemeanors or two felony convictions—minus 1 point
	Four or more misdemeanors or three or more felony convictions—minus 2 points
Length of time in New York area	Over 10 years—1 point
Discretionary information	Favorable factors—pregnancy, old age, poor health, continuous medical treatment, gets financial aid, attends school, etc.—1 point
	Unfavorable—vague answers, lie detected, transient background—minus 1 point

Source: New York City Police Misc. Form No. 357.

Table 7-2
New York City Citation Releases
(July 1, 1968 to June 30, 1969)

	Citable Offenses	Citation Releases	Percentage of Citation Releases
Bronx	6,884	3,702	53.8
Brooklyn	11,857	7,494	63.2
Manhattan	32,830	5,273	16.1
Queens	6,759	5,410	80.0
Richmond	921	806	87.5
Total	59,251	22,685	38.3

Source: New York City Police Department, unpublished data.

for reasons such as hospitalization or confinement by another agency. If these cases are taken into account, the rate of appearance is 95.3 percent.

During its first four years, the Manhattan Summons Project was estimated to have saved New York City more than $6.7 million in police time. Each summons was calculated by the department to save the equivalent of ten hours of police patrol.

These savings are primarily based on the greater efficiency that the summons allows in scheduling the first appearance in court. In New York the arresting officer is required to attend this court appearance, and under the regular arrest procedure he often must work beyond his scheduled tour of duty in order to do so. Under the summons procedure he can schedule several appearances on the same day and conduct his business during regular working hours.[19]

Prior to 1971 the New York City Police Department received its authority for the issuance of citations by court rule. In 1971, however, the New York State legislature adopted a new Criminal Procedure Law that recognized the success of the Manhattan Summons Project and authorized the use of citations for all misdemeanor and violation arrests by any police

Table 7-3
New York City Citation Appearance Rate
(July 1, 1968 to June 30, 1969)

Arrested	59,251
Citations issued	22,685
Failures to appear	1,182
Rate of appearance	94.8%

Source: New York City Police Department, unpublished data.

agency in the state.[20] In revising its procedure to conform with the new law, the New York City Police Department renamed the Vera summons the *desk appearance ticket,* and authorized its usage for most misdemeanors, provided the defendant was not under the influence of alcohol, narcotics, or dangerous drugs. Defendants charged with possession of dangerous weapons, sex offenses, and some other serious misdemeanors were not eligible for release as the department wanted current photographs for these defendants and required borough processing in order to accomplish this.[21]

Later Developments

One major development during the 1970s has been a rapid increase in use of the desk-appearance ticket. Usage has gone from around 20,000 summonses in 1968-1969 to well over 35,000 desk-appearance tickets in 1980, as shown in table 7-4. Although there is considerable variation from year to year and borough to borough, as shown in table 7-5, the total regularly amounts to a half or more of the city's misdemeanor arrests. (In some years prior to 1980 there was a larger number of desk-appearance tickets but also a larger number of misdemeanor arrests.) In addition to the desk-appearance tickets given misdemeanor defendants, many persons charged with regulatory offenses continue to be given what amounts to a field citation. This form of release is called a *universal summons* and is also legally an appearance ticket. In 1980 there were about 7,000 violation arrests, and it is estimated that 4-5,000 of these received a universal summons.

City-wide about a third of the desk-appearance tickets are issued for theft offenses and another fifth for traffic offenses, as shown in table 7-6. Other major categories are disorderly conduct and similar offenses (10

Table 7-4
Citations Issued by Year

1964-1967	less than 1,000
1967-1968	14,232
1968-1969	22,685
1970-1971	31,946
1973	36,156
1974	44,033
1975	43,473
1976	43,513
1977	44,700
1978	48,606
1979	44,032
1980	37,739

Source: New York City Police Department, unpublished data.

Table 7-5

Desk-Appearance Tickets as a Percentage of Misdemeanor Arrests in New York City, 1980

	Desk-Appearance Tickets	Misdemeanor Arrests	DAT's as Percentage of Misdemeanor Arrests
Manhattan	16,186	30,971	52
Brooklyn	10,712	15,995	67
Bronx	5,142	9,736	53
Queens	3,677	11,007	33
Staten Island	2,022	2,223	91
City total	37,739	69,932	54

Source: New York City Police Department, unpublished data.

percent), narcotics (10 percent) and assault (8 percent). Again there is considerable variation from borough to borough.

Most misdemeanor defendants not released on desk-appearance tickets are detained because they are ineligible under departmental guidelines and not as a result of the exercise of discretion by local commands. In Brooklyn in 1978, for example, 39 percent of those not released were ineligible because they had been arrested for a photographable offense and 37 percent had a warrant outstanding. Ten percent lacked an adequate address or identification, 4 percent were from out of state, 3 percent were intoxicated or addicted, another 3 percent were thought to pose some danger of repeating the offense, and 2 percent were detained because a codefendant was ineligible.[22]

Table 7-6

Desk-Appearance Tickets Issued by Charge

(April 25 - May 1, 1977, percent of total)

	Manhattan	Brooklyn	Bronx	Queens	Staten Island	City Total
Theft	36	27	12	53	45	32
Traffic	20	26	22	16	15	21
Conduct	6	14	12	13	5	10
Narcotics	9	14	11	1	5	10
Assault	9	5	12	7	8	8
Other	20	14	31	10	19	19
Total	100	100	100	100	100	100
Number	(338)	(215)	(95)	(75)	(40)	(763)

Source: O. Ben-Ami, "The Use of Desk Appearance Tickets (DAT's) in New York City" at 5 (New York City Criminal Justice Agency) (April 1978).

Table 7-7
Desk-Appearance Tickets—Failure to Appear at Arraignment
(December 29, 1980 - February 1, 1981)

	Percentage of Defendants Failing to Appear at Arraignment
Brooklyn	32
Bronx	22
Manhattan	46
Queens	20
Staten Island	13
City-wide	36

Source: New York City Criminal Justice Agency, "Failure-to-Appear-Rates for Defendants Issued Desk Appearance Tickets," Exhibit IV (August 1981).

Defendants given desk-appearance tickets do not appear to differ greatly as to age, race, sex, or prior criminal history from those detained for similar offenses. About two-thirds have a prior arrest and one-third a prior conviction.

Sixty-nine percent of those who appear as promised have their cases disposed of at the first court appearance. Thirty percent have their cases dismissed or diverted for mediation or some similar program; 39 percent plead guilty, and 31 percent obtain continuances. Virtually none are physically detained after the appearance. Of those who plead guilty 95 percent are given a fine and most of the remainder are considered for probation or conditional discharge.[23]

As the rate of issuance of desk-appearance tickets has increased, so also has the rate of nonappearance. Nonappearance rates in the city were over 20 percent for 1975 and over 35 percent in 1980—both well above the 5 percent rate of the 1964-1969 experimental period.[24] As with the rate of issuance and the types of offense involved, the differences in the failure-to-appear rate by borough were enormous, as shown in table 7-7.

This increase appears to have come in two stages—the first in the early 1970s and the second in the period since. Knowledgeable observers both inside and outside the department attribute the early 1970s' increase primarily to the increasing rate of release. Increased pressure on precinct commanders to curtail serious crime resulted, they say, in increased emphasis on keeping officers on the street. One way of accomplishing this was by increasing use of the desk-appearance ticket. At the same time the city's budget problems put pressure on the department to control the amount of overtime, and this too served to increase the use of the desk-appearance ticket. With this kind of pressure at the precinct command level, the belief is that field and desk officers began to pay less attention to the point scale that had previously been used.

Table 7-8
Failure to Appear at Arraignment by Time from Arrest
(December 29, 1980 - February 1, 1981)

Days to Arraingment from Arrest	Percentage of Arraignments Scheduled	Percentage of Defendants Failing to Appear at Arraignment
0-6	5	12
7-13	3	22
14-20	14	32
21-27	23	38
28-34	21	38
35-41	13	34
41-55	13	38
56-181	8	48
Overall	100	36
Number of Cases	(2,239)[a]	(804)[b]

Source: New York City Criminal Justice Agency, "Failure-to-Appear-Rates for Defendants Issued Desk Appearance Tickets," Exhibit I (August 1981).

[a]There were 36 cases for which the days to arraignment could not be determined.

[b]Number of failure-to-appear cases.

The later increases are harder to explain. It seems likely, however, that these have come in large part because of increases in the time between arrest of the defendant and the scheduled date of appearance. A 1981 study by the department and the city's criminal-justice agency shows that less than 10 percent of all defendants given desk-appearance tickets are scheduled to appear in the first two weeks after arrest and that more than a third are scheduled for an appearance date a month or longer after arrest. This study also shows that defendants who are scheduled to appear quickly have a low failure-to-appear rate, while those who are given a delayed appearance date have a much higher failure-to-appear rate, as indicated in table 7-8.

The overall failure-to-appear rate indicated in this study for the city is much higher than that for most other cities. The rate for defendants scheduled to appear in the first two weeks is the same as or lower than that for most cities, however. This and the other study findings strongly suggest that the high New York rates are in large part the product of delayed appearance dates, and that the reason the failure-to-appear rate has been increasing is that the time to appearance has been increasing. The 1980 practice contrasts sharply, for example, with that during the early summons project when appearances were set for five to ten days after arrest.[25] The fact that the 1980 appearance rate for defendants scheduled to appear within five to ten days remains almost as low as it was during the experimental period provides further confirmation of the critical role played by the increasingly delayed appearance dates. This thesis is also consistent with studies from other cities which indicate that failure-to-appear rates for defendants granted bail or other forms of pretrial release by the courts increase as the time on release increases.[26]

One reason the time to appearance has been increasing is that the courts have begun to use the desk-appearance ticket as a method of calendar control, setting daily quotas on the number of appearances that may be scheduled. When the number of desk-appearance tickets issued exceeds the number of appearances that may be scheduled for a given day, the appearance must be scheduled for a later date. Changes in departmental duty schedules also have made it somewhat more difficult to schedule cases for early appearance.

Failure-to-appear rates have increased in the city for other agencies also, such as the housing police and the transit police and for private store-security personnel, who are authorized by virtue of their appointment as "special patrolmen" by the police commissioner to issue desk-appearance tickets in much the same way as the police. In some years the failure-to-appear rate for store-security personnel has been 50 percent or more. While it might be expected that this would be a source of alarm to the stores, it apparently has not been. The stores seem to think that, having been cited once, the individuals involved will not come back to their stores. To the extent that this is true, the stores calculate that they have accomplished their principal purpose at a cost saving, since their security personnel do not have to spend as much time in court.

One troubling aspect of the store cases is that a few shoplifters have apparently learned enough about how the system works to be able to beat it. For these defendants, when a police officer or the store calls to verify residence or family ties, someone at the other end of the phone makes the verification even if the defendant has given a phony name and address.

Although police department support for the use of desk-appearance tickets has remained high throughout the time they have been used, there has been concern at times about the failure-to-appear rate. In 1977 as a result of this concern the department and the criminal-justice agency began a series of studies to see if performance could be improved.

The first was a pilot study to determine whether a letter notifying defendants of the time of their appearance would reduce the failure-to-appear rate.[27] Prior research by the criminal-justice agency indicated that notification had an effect on defendants released on their own recognizance after appearance in court and gave reason to believe that this might also reduce the failure-to-appear rate for desk-appearance cases. Letters were consequently sent to 1,000 defendants released on desk-appearance tickets in Manhattan and Brooklyn, and their failure-to-appear rate was compared with that of similar defendants who did not receive letters.[28] In Manhattan the improvement was dramatic—the defendants who received letters had a failure-to-appear rate that was 12 percent less than those who did not. In

Brooklyn the improvement was only 1.5 percent but still clearly measurable. The improvement was greatest in the disorderly-conduct and non-department-store-theft cases and least in the case of department-store thefts.

Thirty-three percent of the Manhattan and 10 percent of the Brooklyn notification letters were returned as undeliverable. These defendants had failure-to-appear rates that were double those who had good addresses and who were sent notification letters. Most of the letters returned indicated that the addressee was either unknown or had moved. A few indicated that there was no such number.

A second study sought to determine whether additional address or identification information could be developed concerning the defendants denied release because of inadequate information concerning these matters.[29] The study found that this could be done for some defendants but that doing so would not greatly increase the release rate because this was a minor reason for not using the desk-appearance ticket.

The study found that the principal reason for not issuing desk-appearance tickets was the department's eligibility rules concerning warrants and photographable offenses and suggested that there should be some reexamination of these rules. According to the study nearly 40 percent of the ineligible defendants had strong community ties, many were already being recommended when they appeared in court for release-on-own-recognizance, and the failure-to-appear rate for these defendants when released at court was a very low 8.7 percent.

Based on this analysis a third study was undertaken in the Bronx.[30] In this study the criminal-justice agency conducted investigations and made recommendations as to whether misdemeanor defendants, including ineligibles, should be released on desk-appearance tickets. As a result of the project interviews, the failure-to-appear rate declined from 30 percent before the experiment to 23 percent after. Five reasons were thought to have contributed to the decline: (1) the defendants released had stronger community ties as a result of greater selectivity in determining who was released; (2) the project interviews produced verified addresses for sending notification letters; (3) the time from arrest to arraignment was shortened because a night court was opened up during the project; (4) the availability of the night court permitted defendants to appear without losing a day of work; and (5) the project provided a greater amount of explanation to defendants concerning what they were expected to do and the consequences of failing to appear. The study suggested more experimentation in order to determine which of these were the most important causes.

The study findings of the second study objective—whether more defendants could be released on desk-appearance tickets—were more equivocal. The study concluded that the project had resulted in a small increase in the release rate but also reported data that could be interpreted as showing a small decline.

Based on these studies the criminal-justice agency was asked to continue the work it had begun in the pilot studies. In June 1978 the agency began to send letters notifying defendants released on desk-appearance tickets of their appearance dates, and in 1979 it began to conduct interviews on a regular basis for misdemeanor defendants in the Bronx and Manhattan.[31]

There has been no thorough analysis of the impact of these steps. They clearly have not lowered the failure-to-appear rate to the level of the experimental period or even of the mid-1970s. It seems likely that they have helped but that they simply have not been enough to reverse the effects of the lengthening times to appearance.

In addition to the widespread increase in the number of desk-appearance tickets there have also been some changes in methods of processing since the experimental period. Defendants are now booked through central borough booking facilities and released from there rather than from neighborhood precincts. This system gives somewhat greater uniformity in decisionmaking, but because the officer must travel to the central booking facility it cuts down on the amount of officer time saved. Future changes can be expected because the department is beginning to develop a computerized booking system.[32]

In assessing the development and implementation of the citation idea in New York it seems clear that the program has been both important and beneficial. The benefits were recently summarized in one of the joint studies by the police department and the criminal-justice agency:

> Police Department overtime costs are reduced by scheduling arraignments only during an officer's regular tour of duty, and individual officers may spend less time in the courthouse by scheduling more than one DAT for the same day. Moreover, it is possible to divert suitable cases from the formal court process to mediation programs, for example, given the extra time between arrest and scheduled arraignment. Similarly, the District Attorney has a greater opportunity to assess his case, to determine whether the complaining witness will appear in court, and possibly, to decline prosecution.[33]

The factors which have led to this success also seem clear. The most important are:

The willingness of the police department to try new ideas.

The careful way in which these ideas have been tried out, generally through the use of pilot programs that were evaluated and then either dropped if unsuccessful or expanded if successful.

A concern for program monitoring and improvement that is common in business and industry but rare in the criminal-justice system.

An ability to adapt the program to new circumstances.

The fruitful collaboration between the police department and the Vera Institute and the criminal-justice agency.

The continuing interest over a substantial period of time of key personnel.[34]

Notes

1. Murphy, "Fact-Finding, Release and Summons," in *National Conference on Bail and Criminal Justice, Proceedings and Interim Report* 63-72, at 65 (April 1965).

2. Id. at 65-66. The statute was 1932 N.Y. Laws, ch. 537, §§82h, 84, at p. 1145.

3. Id. at 66.

4. Vera Institute of Justice, *Programs in Criminal Justice Reform* 48 (May 1972).

5. Id. at 49.

6. Murphy, "Fact-Finding, Release and Summons," in *National Conference on Bail and Criminal Justice, Proceedings and Interim Report* 63-72, at 67-68 (April 1965).

7. See Vera Institute of Justice, *Programs in Criminal Justice Reform* 20-50 (May 1972).

8. Id. at 50.

9. Id. at 50-51.

10. Id. at 51. See also R. Goldfarb, *Ransom* 166-172 (1965), for an early account of the New York program.

11. Vera Institute of Justice, *Programs in Criminal Justice Reform* 52 (May 1972). Reprinted with permission.

12. Id. at 52-53.

13. Id. at 55.

14. New York City Police Department T.O.P. 456 (Dec. 1968).

15. Id.

16. Vera Institute of Justice, *Programs in Criminal Justice Reform* 53 (May 1972).

17. Id. at 52-53.

18. Interviews with various department officials. See Feeney, "Citation in Lieu of Arrest: The New California Law," 25 *Vand. L. Rev.* 367, 377 (1972).

19. Vera Institute of Justice, *Programs in Criminal Justice Reform* 53 (May 1972).

20. N.Y. Crim. Proc. Law §§140.20(2), 150.10-150.70 (McKinney 1971, Cum. Supp. 1980-1981).

21. Vera Institute of Justice, *Programs in Criminal Justice Reform* 55 (May 1972).

22. O. Ben-Ami, "Desk Appearance Ticket (DAT) Issuance Practices: Brooklyn Central Booking" (New York City Criminal Justice Agency) (May 1978).

23. O. Ben-Ami, "The Use of Desk Appearance Tickets (DAT's) in New York City" at 5 (New York City Criminal Justice Agency) (April 1978).

24. The source for the 1975 rate is New York City Police Department, unpublished data. Some of the difference between the 1975 and the 1980 rates could be attributable to different methods of counting but both rates are clearly higher than the pre-1970 rates.

25. Vera Institute of Justice, *Programs in Criminal Justice Reform* 50 (May 1972).

26. Clarke, Freeman, and Koch, "Bail Risk: A Multivariate Analysis," 5 *J. Leg. Studies* 341 (1976).

27. O. Ben-Ami, "The Use of Desk Appearance Tickets," at 5.

28. The defendant groups were similar. Odd numbered cases were sent letters while even numbered cases were observed only.

29. O. Ben-Ami, "Desk Appearance Ticket (DAT) Issuance Practices: Brooklyn Central Booking" (New York City Criminal Justice Agency) (May 1978).

30. New York City Criminal Justice Agency, "DAT Policy Review: First Report on a CJA/NYPD Pilot Program in the Bronx" (March 1979).

31. New York City Criminal Justice Agency, Quarterly Report, April 2, 1979–July 1, 1979, at 30. Notification letters to Staten Island did not begin until January 1, 1979.

32. The purpose of central booking is to provide greater control over the arrest process for all offenses and to save money. It was not introduced as a result of any dissatisfaction with desk-appearance tickets.

33. O. Ben-Ami, "The Use of Desk Appearance Tickets," at 1.

34. One important reason for the success of the New York program has been the continued involvement of Michael Farrell. As a police lieutenant Mr. Farrell was involved in getting the program started. Later as a police inspector in charge of the department's criminal-justice bureau he was involved in widening and improving the program. Still later as director of the city's pretrial release agency he set in motion the studies and pilot programs of the late 1970s.

8

Some Case Examples

How citations are used obviously depends a great deal on the problems and organization of the agency involved. What works in one agency or community may be wholly inappropriate for another. To provide some idea as to how the citation procedure has been implemented in a number of different communities, this chapter describes its initiation and use in five different agencies:

Oakland, California, a city of 340,000 with a large minority population and serious crime problems, has used both field and station release for a number of years for a broad range of crimes; uses almost twice as many field as station releases.

New Haven, Connecticut, a city of 125,000 with a sizable minority population, has used both field and station releases for a number of years; station releases predominate. Police also have bail-setting authority.

District of Columbia, the nation's capital with a population over 600,000 and a considerable crime problem, makes extensive use of station releases but does not use the field citation. Release decisions are partially based on a point system administered by the D.C. Pretrial Release Agency.

Jacksonville, Florida, a city-county of 540,000 with combined police-sheriff functions, uses both station release and field citations, each developed at a separate time. Station citations predominate thus far.

Minneapolis, Minnesota, a city of 370,000 in a state that recently (1975) mandated the use of citations, uses field citations only, but the sheriff's office, which runs the jail, uses station release to some extent. Failure-to-appear rate began high, but is now declining.

Oakland, California. Oakland is a city of 340,000 with a substantial minority population. It was one of the early departments to develop a system using both field and station citations. Use began in February 1970.

At the outset the department instructed officers to issue field citations to all adults arrested for any misdemeanor offense unless the situation fell within one of the following guidelines:

1. The suspect requires medical care or is unable to care for his own safety.
2. There is a reasonable likelihood that the misconduct would resume, or that persons or property would be endangered.
3. The suspect cannot or will not offer satisfactory evidence of identity.
4. The prosecution of the offense for which the suspect was arrested or of another offense would be jeopardized.
5. A reasonable likelihood exists that the arrested person will fail to appear in court as promised (a warrant check is mandatory).
6. The misdemeanant demands to be taken before a magistrate or refuses to sign the citation.[1]

If the defendant was physically arrested his situation was again reviewed at the jail. A jail citation was then to be issued unless the circumstances met one or both of the following detention criteria:

1. A reasonable likelihood exists that the suspect will fail to appear in court as promised.
2. The evidence indicates that the suspect, if released, would commit an offense causing or threatening injury to persons or property.[2]

A point system similar to that used in New York was used for a time in determining whether jailed defendants were likely to appear in court. When a citation was not issued, either in the field or in jail, short descriptions of the reasons for nonissuance were required. While some consideration was given to forbidding citations for some offense categories, this approach was ultimately rejected, and most misdemeanor arrests were made eligible for both field and station-house release.[3]

From the beginning the procedure was widely used. In the first three months 67 percent of the eligible defendants were released.[4] Over the next year this figure dropped considerably, to around 50 percent. This decrease was caused in part by the addition of several new categories of eligible defendants and in part by an attempt to reduce the number of defendants cited who did not appear in court.

At the outset of the program the failure-to-appear rate was around 25 percent. By the end of six months it had dropped to 17 percent, and by the end of fifteen months to 7.8 percent. This rate was similar for both field and jail citations.[5]

When the citation program was first instituted, it was expected that there would be far more jail than field citations. In practice, however, the number of field citations has been about three times as great as the number of jail citations.[6]

Field citations were used for a wide variety of offenses but most heavily for petty theft and shoplifting. Few field citations were issued for emotionally charged offenses, such as disturbing the peace, battery, and resisting arrest. Many jail citations were issued for these offenses, however, and the department's October 1970 guidelines indicated that "after an enforced cooling-off period, an offender who could not be cited in the field can nonetheless constitute a good risk for citation later in the jail."[7] The primary reason given for not issuing even more field citations was identification problems.[8]

Further experience with the procedure has produced relatively few changes. There has been some tinkering resulting from subsequent legal developments but no major changes in direction or method.

The first change relaxed the prohibition on citing misdemeanor vehicle-code offenses. This exclusion had been based on legal rather than policy considerations and was removed following a legal opinion in 1970 from the city attorney indicating that these offenses were citable.[9] The second change involved another exclusion from eligibility. In the original order, as a result of judicial concerns, offenders for whom an arrest warrant existed were eligible for citation only if they turned themselves in. In July 1971, however, the judges agreed to expand eligibility to all warrant defendants who had not previously failed to appear.[10]

In 1973 the authority to cite drunks was withdrawn due to a court ruling that arrests could not be made for this offense.[11] Various legal rulings have also dictated the removal at times of the authority to cite persons arrested for prostitution. In addition, there has been some concern about the releasability of prior record information to field officers for the purpose of determining whether offenses such as petty theft are felonies or misdemeanors.[12] Marijuana possession was added as a citable category in 1976.[13]

With these exceptions the original departmental order of 1969 remained in force until September 1976. At that time a new order reflecting these technical changes was adopted.[14]

The rate of citation use continues to be heavy, generally following the patterns of offense and method of release set in the earlier years. In 1975 about 45 percent of all eligible defendants were released and about three times as many were given field citations as were given station citations, as shown in table 8-1. Since this time use has, if anything, increased.

New Haven, Connecticut. New Haven is a city of 125,000, with a considerable minority population and a large university near its core area. It utilizes both field and station-house releases. These procedures were developed at different times and in somewhat different ways.

The station-house release procedure came first.[15] It began as the result of a 1965 act by the legislature granting authority to the courts to release defendants on their own recognizance.[16] By resolution the Circuit Court

Table 8-1
Nontraffic Citations in Oakland, California

Type of Citation	Number	Percentage of Citations Issued
Field (patrol)	1339	50.8
Jail	495	18.8
On warrants (station)	573	21.8
Vice squad	96	3.6
Other	129	5.0
Total	2632	100.0

Source: Oakland Police Department, unpublished data.
Note: Eleven-month sample, 1975. Data not available for November 1975.

Judicial Council extended part of its new authority to the police, authorizing the release of misdemeanor defendants on the posting of an unsecured appearance bond. Since, in this procedure, the defendant is not required to pay a bondsman or to put up any immediate cash, it is similar in most ways to release on a simple promise to appear. Some question existed at the time as to the legality of the authority conferred by the resolution, and many Connecticut police agencies did not implement the procedure. The New Haven department did so, however. Although precise statistics are not available it appears that a sizable proportion of the misdemeanor defendants were released in this way, perhaps as many as half or more of the non-warrant misdemeanor cases.[17]

In 1967, as a result of a new act by the legislature, this function was taken over both in New Haven and statewide by a state bail commission. In 1969, however, the legislature again considered the problem. Partly as an economy move and partly for other reasons it returned this function largely to the hands of the police.[18]

The 1969 statute obligated the police to interview every defendant arrested for a bailable offense, whether a felony or a misdemeanor.[19] After the interview the chief of police or his delegate was obligated to make a decision as to release:

> After such a waiver, refusal or interview, unless such officer finds custody to be necessary to provide reasonable assurance of such person's appearance in court, he shall promptly order release of such person upon his execution of a written promise to appear or his posting of such bond as may be set by such officer.[20]

Although as a practical matter few felony defendants were released on a promise to appear, all were, in theory, eligible.

The statute did not mention field citations, but the department thought that the language was broad enough to allow the chief of police to delegate authority to interview and release defendants to each officer.[21] This was done in October 1970.

The authority granted to field officers was limited to misdemeanors, however, and persons arrested for either weapons or sex offenses were also excluded.[22] Suspects between the ages of 16 and 21 were eligible for field citation, but the signature of a parent or guardian was required as persons in this age group were not bound by their signatures under Connecticut law. Juveniles under 16 were not included in the field-citation procedure because they were handled under a separate set of procedures.[23]

During the first year of the field-citation procedure about three times as many defendants were released under the station-house citation procedure as were released under the field citation.[24] Excluding intoxication offenses, 10.8 percent of all nontraffic misdemeanor defendants were released under field citations, while over 33 percent were released at the station house, as shown in table 8-2. Unlike what happens in many cities that use both procedures, defendants charged with petty theft generally were not released through the field-citation procedure.[25]

Contrary to expectation, the creation of the field-citation procedure did not cause a decrease in the number of station releases. In the months prior

Table 8-2
Types of Releases for Misdemeanants in New Haven, Connecticut
(October 1, 1970 to September 30, 1971)

Offense[a]	Field Citations	Station Citations	Bond and Other Releases	Not Released
Cruelty to persons	1	2	1	2
Injury to public property	3	0	2	1
Breaking and entering	0	7	12	33
Injury to private building	13	20	8	14
Trespass	7	133	72	122
Injury to personal property	1	26	18	128
Breach of the peace	482	1,364	703	743
Disorderly conduct	3	104	61	59
Indecent exposure	0	12	8	9
Prostitution	10	28	32	39
Gaming and policy playing	38	14	441	28
Fraudulent check	0	25	18	10
Defrauding innkeeper	1	6	6	5
Tampering with vehicles	2	14	6	11
Possession of drugs	9	36	71	63
Other	127	475	594	451
Total	690	2,140	1,986	1,606

Source: Based on data provided in Berger, "Police Field Citations in New Haven," 1972 *Wisconsin Law Review* 382, 406.
[a]Excludes motor-vehicle misdemeanors and intoxication.

to the beginning of the field-citation, station releases amounted to 26 percent of all misdemeanor cases. During the first year of field-citation use the number of station releases increased by 5 percent.[26]

No data are available concerning the failure-to-appear rate for station releases during this period, but the rate for field citations was 14.5 percent. A considerably higher rate of nonappearance was experienced for an additional group of motor-vehicle offenses also brought under a citation policy at this time.[27]

By mid-1973 use of the field citation had picked up considerably, going from about 10 percent of all nontraffic misdemeanors to about 20 percent. Station releases declined slightly, but overall the release rate increased somewhat.[28]

The failure-to-appear rate for field citations and promise-to-appear cases taken together was about 34 percent. Over half the defendants not appearing responded to a mail notice, however. Although it is not clear how this rate of nonappearance compares with the earlier rate for promise-to-appear cases, it is clear that the failure rate for field-citation cases was higher than the previous rate for station citations. One study of this period suggests that the increase was the result of the greater number of field citations being issued.[29] Comparison of New Haven procedures with those in other cities suggests that part of the nonappearance problem is related to unusually poor record keeping by the courts.

A 1980 study for the Connecticut Justice Commission indicates that use of the two procedures remains about the same as in 1973.[30] The department continues to be satisfied with the procedure and has not experienced any major difficulties with it. Due to a change in the age of the majority in Connecticut, parent notification is no longer required for 18 to 20 year olds.

One somewhat unique feature of the citation procedures in New Haven is that the police department is authorized to release defendants arrested on a warrant unless the warrant shows a bond amount on its face. Defendants with parking and traffic warrants are regularly released on citation. There is also some use of the station citation procedure for the lesser felonies.

District of Columbia. The population of the nation's capital is over 600,000. The city is the center of a metropolitan area of over 3 million and has major crime problems. The District of Columbia police first instituted a citation procedure for nontraffic misdemeanors in 1968. Prior to that time the department did not use the procedure because of doubt as to the statutory authority to do so in the absence of specific legislation.[31] As a result of a recommendation by the President's Commission on Crime in the District of Columbia, Congress late in 1967 adopted legislation specifically authorizing the use of the citation for misdemeanors.[32]

By mid-1968 the department had begun to issue station-house citations. Misdemeanor defendants were screened by district desk officers after booking to eliminate those thought likely to cause injury to persons or damage to property, those arrested on warrants or wanted, those on pretrial release of any kind, and those not likely to appear in court. Defendants who passed this initial screening were then evaluated through a point system similar to that in use in New York.[33] This evaluation was sometimes conducted by the station officer, but more often by the D.C. bail agency with whom the department had an arrangement for this purpose.[34]

If the interview was conducted by the bail agency, the procedure after the initial screening by the desk officer was for the desk officer to call the bail agency, which then interviewed the defendant over the telephone, attempted to verify the information given, and called the desk officer back with a recommendation. In theory this process could be accomplished quickly, but often at the beginning it was not quick and it sometimes took an hour or two to get through to the bail agency.[35]

Because of such delays and because the procedure was new, use of citations was not heavy at first. From June 1, 1968, to May 31, 1969, 1,082 defendants were referred to the bail agency, 562 recommended for release, and 530 released, as shown in table 8-3. With the beginning of twenty-four-hour-a-day staffing by the bail agency on June 1, 1970, the number of citations began to increase, going from 659 in 1969 to over 9,000 in 1975.[36] Because of increasing work-load problems the procedure was changed in 1976. Referrals to the bail agency were limited to the more serious misdemeanors and the police department assumed greater responsibility for the less serious cases.[37] Statistics are not available concerning the impact of the revised procedure, but experienced observers believe that there has been no major change in citation use.

The rate of nonappearance was less than 0.5 percent in 1971 and only 2.7 percent in 1973.[38] Although specific statistics are not available, there are indications that failure-to-appear rates have since increased.[39]

Aside from a greater number of defendants failing to appear, the increased number of citations appears to have created no visible problems, and the procedure seems fully accepted as a matter of normal routine by the police, the prosecution, and the courts. The police continue to experience some difficulty in getting telephone calls through to the bail agency so that investigations may be conducted. Generally, however, this is limited to peak time periods.

All citation releases for nontraffic offenses are station releases, made after booking and fingerprinting. Defendants who are on probation or parole or who have cases pending in court are automatically refused citations.

One effect of citations everywhere is to reduce the number of pretrial release decisions that must be made in court. Because of the records maintained by the bail agency, this effect is more clearly visible in the District of

Table 8-3
District of Columbia Citation Referrals and Releases

	Referrals	Recommended	Released
June 1968-May 1969	1,082	562	530
1969	1,037	681	658
1970	1,875	1,426	1,399
1971	4,981	3,400	3,472
1972	6,892	5,068	4,976
1973	7,973	6,240	6,214
1975	11,303	9,293	9,302

Source: Reports of the District of Columbia Bail Agency.

Columbia than in most jurisdictions. It is most easily seen in the early years of the program when the number of in-court recommendations made by the bail agency actually declined.[40]

Jacksonville, Florida. Jacksonville is a unified city-county government with a population of 540,000. The sheriff's office, which performs all police functions for the jurisdiction, initiated a jail-release procedure in 1971.[41] This procedure involves the use of "signature bonds" and "release-on-own-recognizance" (OR). With the signature bond the defendant is released on money bail but without any money down and without the services of a commercial bondsman or any other surety. With release-on-own-recognizance the defendant is released on a promise to appear. Both procedures are similar to the station-house citation and were instituted as a part of a larger jail crisis-intervention program. After filling out the booking report, the jail crisis-intervention officer fills out a crisis-intervention and medical-data sheet. His goal is to release the prisoner immediately on a signature bond or an OR, if possible, thereby returning the suspect to his family and holding down the population at the jail.[42]

Available primarily for misdemeanor defendants, use of this procedure increased rapidly, going from less than 8 percent of all defendants in 1971 to over 20 percent in 1973, as shown in table 8-4.

Specific data on the number of defendants failing to appear is not available; however, the 1972 Sheriff's Annual Report indicated that the number was "extremely low."[43]

In October 1974 the office also began to use field citations for misdemeanor offenses. This move was in part an attempt to alleviate overcrowded jail conditions, which had been the subject of a federal court suit, and in part a method of implementing the new Florida statute and Supreme Court rule authorizing use of the citation procedure.[44]

Under the departmental general order the arresting officer may issue a field citation for a misdemeanor or an ordinance violation unless the of-

Table 8-4
Jail Releases—Jacksonville, Florida

	Signature Bond Releases	Total Arrests	Percent
1971	2,319	30,000	7.7
1972	3,534	28,045	12.6
1973	6,129	29,297	20.9
1974	6,419	31,301	20.5

Source: Jacksonville, Florida, Office of Criminal Justice Planning, unpublished data.

fense involves drunkenness, public affray, unlawful assembly, a habitual offender, or shoplifting. If the officer believes that booking is necessary he may transport the defendant to the jail, require him to be fingerprinted and photographed, and release him at that point. Jail personnel may also issue citations, but generally prefer to release defendants'on signature bond (jail release), as the paperwork involved is somewhat less complicated.

Use of the new field-citation procedure was at first slow. In January 1975, for example, only 22 citations were issued.[45] By September, however, the usage had gone up to 240 citations per month. During the five-month period from May to September 1975 the pattern of releases was as shown in table 8-5. The failure-to-appear rate for this period was about 18 percent.[46]

Table 8-5
Field Citations—Jacksonville, Florida
(May to September 1975)

	Number	Percent
Alcohol or related offenses	338	41.6
Drugs	47	5.8
Gambling	40	4.9
Violation city ordinance	39	4.8
Vehicle-registration violations	27	3.3
Illegal hunting and fishing	25	3.1
Trespass	23	2.8
Motor boat	22	2.7
Miscellaneous	21	2.6
Soliciting without permit	18	2.2
Fighting	19	2.3
Contributing to delinquency of a minor	17	2.1
Petit larceny	16	2.0
Loitering	16	2.0
Other	144	17.7
Total	812	100.0

Source: Jacksonville, Florida, Office of Criminal Justice Planning, unpublished data.

The overall release rate for misdemeanor offenses is reasonably high. No figures are available that show both field and jail releases. Extrapolating from available data, however, the picture for a sample week in 1976 would resemble the figures in table 8-6. A 1981 departmental study recommended even greater use of these two procedures as a method for relieving jail overcrowding.

Minneapolis, Minnesota. With a population of 370,000, Minneapolis is the largest city in Minnesota. This jurisdiction began full-scale use of the citation procedure on July 1, 1975, the effective date of the new Minnesota Rules of Criminal Procedure.[47]

In implementing the rules officers were instructed that if defendants were to be detained rather than released on citation, the officers should state the reason for the detention. These rules require use of the citation as opposed to physical arrest except where the defendant is unlikely to appear or has a bad prior record. Although these rules were adopted in February, the department was not made aware of them until much later and had little time to prepare for use of the procedure. Prior to this time the Minneapolis department had experimented with the use of the citation procedure in a model precinct, but had not used the procedure city-wide.

Because adequate time had not been provided to develop procedures or train field officers in the use of the citation, the department encountered a number of problems in the early days of use. Field officers did not understand the procedure or why it was necessary to use it. Consequently, the failure-to-appear rate was very high, 76 percent for the first ninety days.[48]

As the department gained experience, however, the problems began to be worked out. Field officers became more knowledgeable and more comfortable with the procedure. Detailed departmental guidelines were issued in

Table 8-6
Total Pretrial Releases—Jacksonville, Florida
(estimates for one week in 1976)

	Number	Percent
Field releases	50	29
Signature bond	76	43
Sentenced within two days in custody	18	10
Surety bond	12	7
Cash bond	3	2
In jail	8	5
Expiration of sentence	8	5
Total bookings	175	100

Source: Jacksonville, Florida, Office of Criminal Justice Planning, unpublished data.

October, and eventually the failure-to-appear rate began to come down. Within a few months it had dropped to the 25-30 percent range, and it has continued to hold steady at that level.[49]

To provide tighter control over use of the procedure and to ensure full use as required under the statute, the department's guidelines were amended in March 1976 to require that officers secure the permission of their supervisor before making a physical arrest for a misdemeanor.

As the police department does not have responsibility for the jail, it does not have a station-house-citation procedure. Such a procedure is used, however, by the Hennepin County Sheriff's Office.

While the Minnesota Supreme Court rule mandating the use of citations for misdemeanors also authorizes the use of citations for felonies and gross misdemeanors, the Minneapolis department has not attempted such use. In part this is due to statements by the Hennepin County Superior Court that it would prefer that the procedure not be used.

In 1975 the Minneapolis department issued around 1,000 misdemeanor citations.[50] By 1980 this figure had grown to 2,855 (not including ordinance violations).[51] Both the department and the courts seem well satisfied with the procedure.

Notes

1. Oakland, California, Police Department, General Order M-7, Citations for Adult Misdemeanants, February 18, 1970.

2. Id.

3. See Comment, "Pretrial Release under California Penal Code Section 853.6: An Examination of Citation Release," 60 *Calif. L. Rev.* 1339, 1350-1353 (1972).

4. Id., at table G, p. 1370.

5. Oakland, California, Police Department, Information Bulletin, August 20, 1971.

6. Oakland, California, Police Department, Memorandum Concerning Revision of Departmental General Order 70-1, Citations for Adult Misdemeanors (M-7), October 20, 1970.

7. Id.

8. Comment, "Pretrial Release under California Penal Code Section 853.6: An Examination of Citation Release," 60 *Calif. L. Rev.* 1339, 1355 (1972).

9. Oakland, California, Police Department, Memorandum Concerning Revision of Departmental General Order 70-1, Citations for Adult Misdemeanors (M-7), October 20, 1970.

10. Oakland, California, Police Department, Special Order, July 1, 1971. See also Comment, supra note 3, at 1362.

11. Interview with Robert Couzens, Research and Planning Bureau, Oakland Police Department. The case was *Crazyhawk* v. *Municipal Court* (Civil No. 431050, Superior Court, Alameda County, January 29 and April 13, 1973). By 1981 the department again had authority to arrest for drunkenness. While the department releases some of these defendants outright after they sober up, it no longer cites for this offense.

12. Id.

13. Id. See Oakland, California, Police Department Special Orders No. 2948, December 26, 1975, and No. 2962, February 26, 1976. The California law mandating this took effect January 1, 1976. Cal. Health & Safety Code §§11,357 and 11,360 (West Cum. Supp. 1981).

14. Interview with Robert Couzens, Research and Planning Bureau, Oakland Police Department.

15. This procedure is known in Connecticut as *notice to appear* and is not called a citation procedure.

16. See Berger, "The New Haven Misdemeanor Citation Program," *Police Chief* 46 (January 1972); Berger, "Police Field Citations in New Haven," 1972 *Wisc. L. Rev.* 382, 391-394. See also O'Rourke and Carter, "The Connecticut Bail Commission," 79 *Yale L. J.* 513 (1970).

17. O'Rourke and Carter, supra note 16, at 516 n. 11. See also O'Rourke and Salem, "A Comparative Analysis of Pretrial Release Procedures," 14 *Crime and Delinquency* 367 (1968). The initial New Haven program had some aspects of a court OR program and some of a police citation program.

18. Berger, "Police Field Citations in New Haven," 1972 *Wisc. L. Rev.* 382, 392.

19. Conn. Gen. Stat. Ann. §54-63c (West Cum. Supp. 1977). See also chapter 12.

20. Id.

21. Berger, "Police Field Citations in New Haven," 1972 *Wisc. L. Rev.* 382, 393.

22. Id. at 399-400.

23. Id. at 399.

24. Id. at 405.

25. Some now are, but most still are not. Among other things the department is concerned with merchant reaction in this kind of case.

26. Id. at 407.

27. Id.

28. M. Feeley and J. McNaughton, "The Pretrial Process in the Sixth Circuit: A Quantitative and Legal Analysis" 52 (1974) (unpublished paper, Yale Law School).

29. Id. at 31, 33, and 52.

30. The general order currently covering both procedures was issued April 22, 1971.

31. President's Commission on Crime in the District of Columbia, *Report* 512 (1967).

32. D.C. Crime Reduction Act of 1967, Pub. L. No. 90-226, 89th Congress, 2d. sess. See Report of the Judicial Council Committee to Study the Operation of the Bail Reform Act in the District of Columbia (May 1968), reprinted in Hearings Before the Subcomm. on Constitutional Rights of the Senate Comm. on the Judiciary, 91st Congress, 1st Sess. 507, 514 (1969).

33. See chapter 7 and table 7-1. The procedure also involves verification, as does the New York procedure.

34. See District of Columbia Bail Agency, *1969 Report.* See also *Third Annual Report, 1968-69.*

35. Interview with Nick Gedney, District of Columbia Bail Agency, 1970 (Unpublished memorandum, Center on Administration of Criminal Justice, University of California, Davis).

36. District of Columbia Bail Agency, Reports.

37. The number of citation interviews conducted by the District of Columbia Pretrial Release Agency (the successor to the bail agency) declined substantially. Police interviews, however, presumably increased.

38. District of Columbia Bail Agency, *1971 Report,* at p. I-2; 1973 Report, at p. D-2. The failure-to-appear rate is based on the number of appearances rather than the number of defendants.

39. A small sample of 1976 cases studied by the author showed a considerably higher rate of nonappearance.

40. See, for example, District of Columbia Bail Agency, *1972 Report*, at p. B-3

41. Office of the Sheriff, Jacksonville, Florida, *Annual Report 1971.*

42. Office of the Sheriff, Jacksonville, Florida, *Annual Report 1972*, at 19.

43. Id.

44. See Office of the Sheriff, Jacksonville, Florida, *Annual Report 1974-1975*, at 8, 21. The Florida Supreme Court Rule is Fla. R. Crim. P. 3.125. The statute is Fla. Stat. §901.28 (West Cum. Supp. 1977). The history of the federal court suit is given in *Miller* v. *Carson,* 401 F. Supp. 835 (M.D. Fla. 1975).

45. Information supplied by the Office of Criminal Justice Planning, Jacksonville Region.

46. Id.

47. Minn. R. Crim. P. 6.01.

48. Minneapolis Police Department, unpublished data.

49. See Serstock, "Tag or Arrest in Pigtales," Minneapolis Police Department Newsletter, at 3 (Aug. 1976).

50. Unpublished information, Office of the Administrator, Hennepin County Court.

51. St. Paul Police Department, *Annual Report 1975*, at 32. These figures are based on only six months of use of the citation procedure.

9

Implementing the Citation Procedure

Agencies not only use the citation procedure to different extents and for differing offenses, but they also have vastly different internal procedures as to who may authorize issuance of the citation, at what stage in the processing it may be issued, and according to what criteria.

Many agencies use both field and station-house citations, but some use only field citations and some use only station-house citations.

Many agencies have written procedures, but others do not.

Some agencies have release criteria based on point systems that take a multitude of factors into account; other agencies either use very simple systems or leave the issue wholly to the discretion of the individual officer.

Some agencies keep careful tabs on the number of citations and the operation of the procedure; others have only a general idea of what is going on.

Field versus Jail Citations

There are two major methods for issuing citations for misdemeanor offenses. *Field citations* are issued by officers in the field in much the same way as traffic tickets. *Station-house* or *jail citations*, on the other hand, are generally issued at the station house or jail after the defendant has been booked and identified.

The station-house-release procedure does not require a sharp departure from standard operating techniques in the early processing of a misdemeanor suspect. Each suspect may be brought to the station or jail, booked, photographed, fingerprinted, and checked through both the outstanding-warrant and prior-arrest files before a release decision is made by the officer. Under the field-citation procedure the officer must decide at the point of arrest whether a field citation should be issued.

Among the departments using the citation procedure, over half use both field and station-house releases. About two-fifths use only the field citations, and less than one-tenth use only the station-house release, as shown in table 9-1.

Table 9-1
Method of Citation Release
(percent of agencies responding)

	Field Only	Station-house Only	Both
Cities over 100,000	49	7	44
Cities under 100,000	33	10	58
State police agencies	21	0	79
Sheriff's offices	27	0	73
All agencies	39	7	54
Number of agencies responding	(62)	(11)	(84)

Source: Police Foundation–Center on Administration of Criminal Justice survey, 1976.

Approaches to the Release Decision

There are three major approaches to the release decision: the departmental-policy approach; the point-system approach, and the discretion-of-the-individual-officer approach.

Departmental-Policy Approach

A typical department using the departmental-policy approach for station releases is Richmond, California, a San Francisco Bay area city of around 75,000 with a large minority population. Richmond has a set of departmental policy guidelines that make each misdemeanant eligible for release except where there is:

1. No permanent address in California.
2. A record of failure to appear.
3. Further investigation concerning the misdemeanor required.
4. A vice arrest, until release has been cleared through the vice division.
5. An intoxication arrest, in which case the person "should be sober before being released."
6. An outstanding warrant.
7. An arrest on a warrant.
8. A hold for another jurisdiction.[1]

If these criteria are met the decision as to whether to release is that of the shift commander. He is to use his "good judgment," but make releases "as often as possible." When a defendant is not released, a "brief notation" as to the reasons for nonrelease is made.

The Contra Costa County sheriff's office uses the departmental-policy approach for field citations. The criteria by which an arresting officer in this agency decides whether or not to issue a field citation are similar to those used by Richmond for jail release. The arresting officer is instructed to determine first whether or not the defendant has a permanent local address. Such a determination is derived from the information that the defendant supplies to the officer on the scene. The arresting officer next considers the prior criminal record of the defendant. Then the arresting officer determines whether there are any outstanding warrants for the arrest of the defendant, as this would disqualify him for release. Both the prior-arrest record and the outstanding warrants are checked by the officer on his radio with the sheriff's office. If the suspect clears both checks and release is considered appropriate by the arresting officer, the suspect is given a field citation.[2]

This office also uses a jail-release procedure for suspects not released on field citation and for suspects placed in the county jail by other police agencies.

The Point System

Several versions of this kind of system exist; almost all are variations of the system used by the New York Police Department, in which a misdemeanant's ties to his community, family, employment, and other factors are evaluated on the basis of a point scale. This system attempts to develop objective tests that reduce the discretionary factor to a minimum.

Citations in the New York City department are basically station-house citations. The program has been in use in some precincts since 1964 and city-wide since 1967. It is one of the most extensive systems in use anywhere.

In practice, the person to be charged is brought to the station house or the central booking facility, where he is interviewed by the arresting officer. An interview form is used. The officer makes a name check with the Identification Section. If the desk officer so requests, he also seeks to verify the information supplied concerning residence, family ties, and employment. The point system used is shown in table 7-1.

A defendant is considered eligible for citation if he:

1. Attains a minimum of five points on the investigation.
2. Is not incapacitated by virtue of intoxication or injury.
3. Is not a current narcotic user.[3]

The interview investigation is mandatory for all misdemeanants except in cases of public intoxication or admitted current heroin users. In these instances the interview investigation is undertaken only for those who reasonably may qualify under the established criteria.

The final decision as to the issuance of the citation rests with the desk officer. In most instances he issues the citation, but he is not bound to do so.

Other jurisdictions that use point systems include Cincinnati and Washington, D.C.

The Individual-Discretion Approach

Some agencies leave the question of whether a defendant is to be released on citation largely up to the individual officer. These agencies often have no written policy or a policy that essentially repeats the language of the statute authorizing use of the procedure.

Comparing the Approaches

Each of these approaches has its uses. The point system is a useful way of standardizing decision making and reducing discretion. If the point scale is well chosen, it can also help maintain a low failure-to-appear rate. It is somewhat cumbersome, however, and is probably more time-consuming than the other approaches.

The departmental-guidelines approach generally provides useful guidance as to when citations may be issued without adding a lot of complexity. It is almost always simpler than the point system, although probably somewhat less accurate in its ability to pinpoint individuals who are likely to fail to appear.

The individual-discretion approach, in which the officer is essentially on his own, is useful primarily in smaller communities where officers have a great deal of personal knowledge of the local citizenry. Most larger departments find that it provides too little uniformity and too little help to the officer.

Any of the three approaches—departmental guidelines, the point system, or individual discretion—can be used for field as well as station citations if the officer is able to check the accuracy of the arrestee's statements by radio.

At least half the agencies now using the citation procedure seem to have adopted some form of the departmental-guideline approach. About two-thirds, for example, currently have a set of general orders regarding use, as shown in table 9-2. As might be expected, the percentage of large departments that have such orders is greater than the percentage of small departments with such orders. Although some of the general orders are simply repeats of the statute and not really specific enough to be guidelines, most contain at least enough detail to provide some guidance.

Table 9-2
Agencies with Citation General Orders
(percent of agencies responding)

	Have General Orders	Do Not Have General Orders
Cities over 100,000	83	17
Cities under 100,000	46	54
State police agencies	50	50
Sheriff's offices	50	50
All agencies	65	35
Number of agencies responding	(100)	(53)

Source: Police Foundation–Center on Administration of Criminal Justice survey, 1976.

Fewer than 5 percent of the agencies responding used any kind of point system in determining whether to release on citation.

Criteria for Release

Residence

Roughly three-fourths of all agencies using the citation procedure indicated some willingness to release on citations persons living outside their immediate jurisdictions. A few departments indicated that residence was a minor factor and said that they had no residence restrictions of any kind. Nearly one-tenth of the agencies overall indicated that they would release statewide, and almost a fifth were willing to release throughout their metropolitan area, as shown in table 9-3.

Criteria for Release: Other Factors

In addition to residence, the most important considerations involved in deciding whether a citation should be used in a given case were the nature of the offense, the existence of a valid identification, and the existence of an outstanding warrant. Although most departments considered place of residence important, only one-third or so considered length of residence or employment status a factor. Even fewer considered marital or family status important, as shown in table 9-4.

Table 9-3
Residence Requirements for Citation
(percent of agencies responding)

	Agencies Issuing Citations for:	
	Misdemeanors and Ordinance or Regulatory Violations	Ordinance or Regulatory Violations Only
Immediate jurisdiction only (city, etc.)	16	50
County-wide[a]	17	21
Metropolitan area[a]	25	14
Set radius or area (that is, within 5-county area, adjoining county)	9	0
Statewide	13	7
Other[a]	21	7
Residence not a factor or minor factor only	10	0
Number of agencies responding	(135)	(14)

Source: Police Foundation–Center on Administration of Criminal Justice survey, 1976.
[a]Includes ten agencies checking both county and metropolitan area and one agency checking both county and other.

Identification

The kind of identification procedures used depends in large part on whether the citation is a field citation, as opposed to a station-house or jail citation.

If the citation is issued at the station or jail the defendant will generally be asked to show his driver's license or other identification, or, if these items have been taken into custody, they will be checked. Usually the defendant will also be required to go through the normal booking process, including fingerprinting and, in most departments, photographing as well. The defendant may or may not be required to wait until his fingerprints have been checked against the department's fingerprint files. Generally this process makes full use or nearly full use of whatever identification information and techniques the department has available. In this respect it resembles the process involved in releasing a defendant on bail in most jurisdictions and poses roughly the same problems.

If the defendant is to be released in the field, however, identification is trickier. Outstanding warrants can generally be checked by radio, but the check is accurate only if the name given is correct. To provide as much name integrity as possible, the arresting or citing officer normally checks the defendant's driver's license and often checks other information, such as credit cards or car registration, as well. The officer may also check for outstanding warrants on the name in which the car is registered.

If these checks prove positive, the officer may go ahead with the citation. If they do not, however, or if he is suspicious, he may bring the defendant in either on a full arrest or for booking and possible release on a jail citation.

Yet another identification procedure is followed in some states. In these states, either by law or by policy, defendants may be required to undergo the regular booking process for fingerprinting and photographing when they appear for court. In some states the defendant is required to undergo this process before going to court, and in others, after court or only if he is found guilty. In some jurisdictions the procedure is required of all defendants falling within some established requirement; in other jurisdictions the procedure is optional with the judge.

An increasing number of departments also require the defendant to give a thumbprint on the citation. This provides little help in ensuring the accuracy of the field identification, but it does prevent the defendant from claiming in court that he is not the person who was given the citation. This practice also provides some identification to be used in the event of non-appearance or to check against existing records, and some assurance that the person who ultimately appears is the same person as the one given the citation. This also prevents persons on probation or parole from sending someone else to be fingerprinted or booked when appearing for court.

Field Citations and Identification

Two concerns sometimes expressed about the use of field citations are how to identify defendants and how to maintain adequate records. To determine to what extent these concerns are problems, agencies using the field-citation procedure were asked whether they considered the absence of fingerprinting,

Table 9-4
Factors Involved in Decision to Issue Citations
(percent of agencies responding)

	Agencies Issuing Citations for:	
	Misdemeanors and Ordinance or Regulatory Violations	*Ordinance or Regulatory Violations Only*
Valid identification	94	67
Must reside in or near jurisdiction	71	50
Length of residence in jurisdiction	36	17
Employment status	37	0
Marital or family status	23	0
Nature of offense	94	100
Outstanding warrants	77	50
Prior record	61	33
Need for additional investigation	48	8
Other	19	0
Number of agencies responding	(137)	(12)

Source: Police Foundation–Center on Administration of Criminal Justice survey, 1976.

photographing, and other identification procedures associated with booking a problem. Over 80 percent of the agencies currently using the field-citation procedure said that they did not consider these matters to be a problem in their jurisdictions. Even among the agencies that did consider these concerns to be a problem, they were generally thought to be minor rather than major difficulties, as shown in table 9-5.

In line with the general perception among agencies using the field-citation procedure that there is no great problem involved in the absence of booking for the kind of case cited, about half the agencies now using the procedure do not book, fingerprint, or photograph, even after the defendant has been to court. The other half does so—some agencies booking almost every case going to court, while a sizable number book only those who are convicted, as shown in table 9-6.

Integrity, Ticket Fixing, and Corruption

One problem in the traffic field encountered by many police agencies over the years is the need to ensure the integrity of the citation system used. All too often citizens seek to escape the consequences of a ticket, either by paying off the ticketing officer or through the use of political influence. To combat this practice, many agencies have created strong systems of control, including numbered citations, no-alteration forms, and other similar procedures.[4]

Given the greater penalties generally involved for criminal offenses, similar problems of citizen pressure for leniency could be expected to exist in connection with the use of citations for criminal offenses.

No instances were encountered in the course of the study in which this had been a major problem. A few departments, however, had given the issue careful attention. Generally these agencies had been careful in setting

Table 9-5
Is Lack of Booking for Field Citations a Problem
(percent of agencies responding)

	Agencies Issuing Citations for:	
	Misdemeanors and Ordinance or Regulatory Violations	*Ordinance or Regulatory Violations Only*
Yes	21	93
No	79	7
Number of agencies responding	(126)	(15)

Source: Police Foundation–Center on Administration of Criminal Justice survey, 1976.

Table 9-6
Later Booking—Field Citations
(percent of agencies responding)

	Agencies Issuing Citations for:	
	Misdemeanors and Ordinance or Regulatory Violations	Ordinance or Regulatory Violations Only
Book before initial appearance	7	0
Book if sentenced to jail	32	13
Book as condition of probation	4	0
Book if court orders it	14	7
Other	18	0
Never book	38	80
Number of agencies responding	(131)	(15)

Source: Police Foundation–Center on Administration of Criminal Justice survey, 1976.
Note: Multiple responses given.

up their criminal-citation procedures to include the same kinds of controls that existed for their traffic citations. The agencies involved felt that these measures were fully adequate to control whatever problem might exist.

Mandatory versus Discretionary Use

Most agencies using the procedure do not require its use by individual officers. Over a third of the agencies using the procedure do require the use of citations in some situations, however, as shown in table 9-7. The most frequent situation in which use is required is for marijuana possession. Other instances of required use include city ordinances and violations and shoplifting. At least one department requires use of the procedure for all minor misdemeanors.

Table 9-7
Required Use of Citations
(percent of agencies responding)

	Agencies Issuing Citations for:	
	Misdemeanors and Ordinance or Regulatory Violations	Ordinance or Regulatory Violations Only
Some required use	37	33
No required use	63	66
Number of agencies responding	(140)	(15)

Source: Police Foundation–Center on Administration of Criminal Justice survey, 1976.

Although no agency mandates exclusive use of the citation procedure for misdemeanors, many strongly encourage its use. Thus the Oakland guidelines say:

> Members SHALL issue citation to all adults (persons eighteen years and older) arrested for any misdemeanor offense or taken into custody after a citizen's arrest for a misdemeanor offense, UNLESS the attendant circumstances come within one or more of the physical arrest criteria which follow.[5]

The Minneapolis, San Francisco, and other guidelines are equally strong.

Mechanics of the Citation Procedure

The mechanics of the citation procedure differ greatly from agency to agency, both in method and in efficiency. Although it must be remembered that the citation procedure is not an island unto itself and that it must necessarily relate to other departmental procedures, the differences are nonetheless striking.

Aside from such questions as fingerprinting and booking, the citation form itself, the criteria for release, and identification procedures, which are discussed elsewhere, some of the more important differences are:

> In some jurisdictions the citation is the only departmental form that the arresting officer must complete. In most jurisdictions, however, the officer must also complete an arrest report, and in some he must also complete an offense report.

> In some jurisdictions the defendant is cited to appear in court on a specific day; in others, to appear before the district attorney; in others, to appear at the police department for booking; and in others, to appear at the court clerk's office, which then sets the day to appear in court.

> In some jurisdictions the defendant is released on citations only if he is willing to sign the citation promising to appear; in others the officer may release without a signature.

> In some jurisdictions the citation form can be filed directly in court as a complaint; in others a separate complaint form must be completed and filed.

> In some jurisdictions a personal appearance in court is mandatory; in others the defendant may sign a waiver in front of a clerk and pay a prescribed fine.

Notes

1. Richmond Police Department General Order No.70 (Apr. 23, 1964); Richmond Police Department General Order No.36 (Feb. 29, 1960).

2. Contra Costa County Sheriff's Department, General Orders, app. R (undated).

3. New York City Police Department T.O.P. 456, at 3 (Dec. 1968).

4. See, for example, G. Warren, *Traffic Courts* 121-133 (1942).

5. Oakland, California Police Department, General Order M-7, Citations for Adult Misdemeanors, Oct. 20, 1970.

10 The Citation Form

Although it may seem one of the more mundane aspects of the citation procedure, the form used is a matter of some importance. It is the record retained by the defendant of what he is supposed to do and of what he is to be charged with. It is also an important police record, in some jurisdictions serving as the only record of the offense and the arrest. Lastly, in those jurisdictions which allow direct filing, it is an important document for the prosecution and the court, both as a pleading and as a record of what transpired.

What the citation form should contain and how it should be processed depends in part on whether it is to be used primarily as a notice to the defendant that he must appear in court or in some other way respond to the charges against him or whether it is to serve other purposes as well, such as those of police record keeping or of the court complaint, the document that initiates formal judicial proceedings. The principal alternatives are:

A citation form that takes the place of both the offense and arrest reports and that also serves as a formal complaint, which can be filed directly into court.

A citation form that takes the place of the police arrest report but not of the offense report or the court complaint.

A citation form that serves solely as a notice to appear to the defendant, without replacing any other reports or forms, but is in addition to standard procedures.

The first alternative has great advantages with respect to streamlining the processing of citation cases; however, it also requires that the citation form include more information than required by the other alternatives and may therefore make it more difficult to obtain a clear, simple form.

General Requirements for a Citation Form

It seems likely that a well-constructed citation form can assist in ensuring the defendant's appearance in court (or response in other appropriate

127

fashion) and in reducing the failure-to-appear rate. If the citation is to serve this function, it should presumably do the following:

1. Clearly notify the defendant what kind of response is required.
2. State the time and place that the defendant is to appear.
3. Notify the defendant what he is to be charged with.
4. Provide a place for the defendant to promise to appear.
5. Notify the defendant what will happen if he fails to appear or to respond as required.
6. Provide instructions in an appropriate language.
7. Inform the defendant of his legal rights.

1. The form should *clearly notify the defendant what kind of response is required*. If a court appearance is mandatory, the citation form should clearly notify the defendant that he must appear in person. This is particularly important in that many people are familiar with the traffic ticket, which permits the forfeiture of bond by mail, and they may not realize that the citation involves a mandatory personal appearance.

If a personal appearance is not mandatory, then the form should clearly notify the defendant of his alternatives. Some jurisdictions permit the defendant to appear before a clerk of the court to sign a waiver that stipulates that he enter a plea of guilty, waive his right to a hearing before the court, and agree to pay the prescribed penalty. Other jurisdictions permit the defendant to sign a waiver and mail it to the court.

While there may be a need to use some legal terminology in these forms, the notification should be written clearly so that the defendant will not be confused as to what is expected of him.

2. The citation form should *state the time and place that the defendant is to appear* (or whom to notify by what date) in clear and unmistakable fashion. The address should be stated boldly, and if the defendant is to go to a particular courtroom or office, that should also be stated. The street address should also be given, rather than just a more general address, such as "county courthouse."

Whenever possible, the address should be preprinted on the form so that it is clearly readable. If there are only two or three possible addresses, one of which is applicable depending on the defendant's status (adult or juvenile, for example) or on the location of the offense, then all should be preprinted with a box that can be checked to show which address applies. Only as a last resort should the officer be responsible for writing the address on the form. The major reason for this is that carbon copies are difficult to read, and sometimes the copy given the defendant will be unreadable. Officers in these instances should be instructed to check that the defendant's copy is in fact readable and to rewrite the address if necessary. An additional problem with hand-written instructions is, of course, the age-old problem that not everyone's writing is readable.

3. The form should also *notify the defendant what he is to be charged with* in terms that he can understand (for example, shoplifting, rather than just a code section for petty theft generally). This notification is even more important when the citation form also serves as a complaint. Aside from making sure that the defendant knows why he is being summoned to court, a defendant who is not incarcerated and consults an attorney before appearing at his arraignment will need to rely on the citation form to provide his attorney with some idea of the nature of the case. When an attorney consults his client in a jail setting, the booking officer or desk sergeant presumably has the arrest report available, but an attorney in a nonjail setting has to rely on other information.

4. The form should *provide a place for the defendant to promise to appear* or to respond in some other way. The defendant's signature promising that he will appear requires a physical act and should help impress the defendant that he is being given a conditional release and not just a warning. It also provides a check on a later claim that he did not receive adequate notice or that he is not the person to whom the citation was issued. (As noted in chapter 9, some departments also use thumbprints for the same purpose.) Also, a signature may be required to make subsequent charges of failure to appear (failure to keep a promise to appear) prosecutable.

5. It is important that the form should *notify the defendant what will happen if he fails to appear* or to respond in an appropriate way. This gives him adequate notice as to what additional penalties he may face if he does not take the citation seriously and also helps impress him with his obligation to appear.

6. In a jurisdiction in which a large minority population speaks a language other than English, *instructions should also be given in the appropriate language*. This requirement would apply to some eastern cities that have large Puerto Rican populations and parts of the southwestern United States that have large Spanish-speaking populations.

7. The form should *inform the defendant of his legal rights*, such as the rights to consult an attorney and to have a hearing before a judge or jury. This information is particularly important if the defendant is given the option of waiving a personal appearance in court. In addition to the general statement of rights, the form should let the defendant know what the effect of a guilty plea will be, such as the recording of a prior, which could affect any future court action (raising a future misdemeanor shoplifting charge to a felony, for example). In this instance the same type of information should be provided that would be provided in a courtroom before a judge accepted a plea of guilty.

Although the seven requirements indicated above may seem simple and obvious, few citations now in use meet them fully. Approximately seventy departments provided copies of their citation forms in response to the Police Foundation-Center survey. An examination of these forms revealed the following types of problems:

Most forms do not indicate clearly if the defendant *must* appear in court in person. Most do notify the defendant that he is to appear on *x* date at *y* location. Although this is not a problem in jurisdictions that do not require a personal appearance, it is crucial in jurisdictions that do require a personal appearance. Without clear, bold instructions, however, many citizens are likely to confuse the misdemeanor citation with traffic tickets, which look similar but do not generally require a personal appearance.

Many forms give no idea what the penalties are for failure to appear (either that a warrant might be issued or that a charge with penalties in addition to the initial charge could subsequently be added).

Many forms do not clearly show the address where the defendant is to appear, or the instructions are difficult to understand or find. Even in large jurisdictions some forms simply direct the defendant to the county courthouse or the city hall without giving its address. Other forms bury the address in the midst of other instructions or in very fine print.

Many forms apparently list only the code section of the charge, without any additional information about the nature of the offense.

Few forms make it clear that the defendant is entitled to an attorney or might be advised (indeed encouraged) to consult an attorney prior to appearance in court for arraignment. Again, because of their familiarity with traffic tickets, there is a tendency on the part of some defendants to assume that the issuance of a citation means that the misdemeanors for which they have been arrested may not be any more serious than a traffic violation.

Some forms are written in a language that is difficult to understand (that is, "in the event I fail to appear, I hereby consent to the entry of an ex parte judgment against me," "when you appear, you may stipulate, waiving your right to a trial," and so on).

Use of the Citation Form as Court Complaint

If the citation is to serve as a court complaint as well as a notice to the defendant to appear in court, the citation must contain more information and meet the statutory requirements for a complaint. These requirements vary from jurisdiction to jurisdiction, but typically include:

The court in which the charge is filed.

Date and time of the offense.

Name of the defendant.

Description of the offense.

Signature of the complainant.

Verification of certification.

Use of the Citation Form for Police Records

As already indicated, the citation form may be used as the sole police record for the offense, or the agency may require the completion of its normal arrest and offense reports as well. Even if arrest and offense reports are completed, however, the citation remains an important police record and should include certain basic information, such as the date, time, and place of issuance and the name of the issuing officer.

If an arrest or offense report is required in addition to the citation form, then the citation need not contain a detailed description of the offense or much information about the defendant. Some linking number will be necessary to readily tie the citation form to the appropriate offense and/or arrest reports. On the other hand, if the citation is the only report required, it needs space for more information.

If the defendant is released after booking at the station house or after being jailed, there will probably be a separate arrest form (or at least some type of booking form) completed in addition to the citation. Where the citation is issued in the field, however, an additional arrest report is generally not essential and would in fact appear to involve an unwarranted amount of extra paperwork on the part of the patrol officer. The citation form in this instance should therefore contain personal data on the defendant, both for general departmental record-keeping purposes and to assist in locating the defendant should he fail to appear in court as required. This information would generally be similar to that included on an arrest report:

Defendant's home address and telephone number.

Address and telephone number of defendant's place of employment (or school, if student).

Date of birth.

Race.

Weight and height, color of hair and eyes, and other personal descriptive information.

Driver's license number or other identification used to establish identity before issuance of the citation.

Evidence or contraband seized and retained by the arresting officer.

In addition, when a citation is issued in the field and no booking has as yet taken place, the form might contain a box to be checked indicating whether or not the defendant is to be booked. This practice varies from jurisdiction to jurisdiction, depending on the policy of the court. In San Francisco the defendant is automatically required to report to the police department on his arraignment date to be booked before going to court, and the clerk of the court instructs him to be booked before he is arraigned if he somehow gets to court without a certification from the booking officer. In other jurisdictions booking takes place only on specific orders from the judge, sometimes only after adjudication.

Additionally, as noted elsewhere, some departments include a space on the form for a thumbprint, which is imprinted in the field by the arresting officer. In Minneapolis taking a thumbprint was once a standard part of the procedure, and the department experimented for a time with a special impregnated paper that made thumbprints possible without using an ink pad. The experiment was not wholly successful, however, and use of the thumbprint is now optional with the arresting officer.

When the citation form serves as the offense report as well, the following information is also needed:

Name and address of complainant if other than the arresting officer.

Sufficient information about the offense to substantiate the charge in court (essential facts of the offense).

Location of the offense.

Names and addresses of witnesses.

Other special information, such as type and value of loss, statements made by the defendant, and so on.

Any additional information that the arresting officer deems appropriate, such as attitude of the defendant.

Examination of police misdemeanor offense reports would probably indicate that the essential offense information could easily be noted on a citation form, using both the front and back of the police department's copy, and that a separate offense report is not needed in the majority of the cases. A procedure might be established in which the citation form usually serves as the offense report but, when necessary, a supplementary offense report could be completed and attached. This would also save a considerable amount of paperwork.

Other Considerations

Additional Information. In addition to information needed by the defendant, the police, the prosecutor, and the court about the offense and the "arrest," there can be a provision for additional information to be added during processing. Many jurisdictions use the original (court) copy of the citation form as an official court record or docket and preprint (usually on the back of the form) appropriate lines for docket number, dates of court appearances, disposition, and sentence.

Number of Copies. How many copies of the form are needed depends on the various functions served by the form and on its distribution. The number of copies made from carbons as the officer fills out the citation form in the field should not exceed the number that can be made legibly. Additional copies can be made from the original before it is distributed if necessary.

Instructions to Officers. In addition to the general orders and other information given to the officers about the citation procedure and the completion of the form, a number of jurisdictions have also printed instructions on the citation book cover. The New Mexico State Police, for example, have provided such instructions, which remind the officer:

That he has a choice of using the citation form or of making a physical arrest.

That the form may be used for nontraffic petty misdemeanors only.

What he should explain to the defendant.

When to set the appearance date.

Requirements pertaining to the use of the form as a lawful complaint.

A reminder to add appropriate additional identification information.

These instructions would vary according to the procedures in effect in a given jurisdiction, but they can provide a ready reference for the field officer and a reminder of the provisions of the department's general orders.

Statutory Requirements. Many states spell out specific requirements or wording that must be included on the citation form or the complaint.[1] When designing forms, departments should be sure to meet all the statutory requirements.

In some states the statutory requirements are a problem because they contain stilted or unclear language.[2] In a few states authority to issue uniform forms is given to the state supreme court or judicial council.[3] This procedure has the advantage of providing a uniform statewide form, and it allows more flexibility than the statutorily prescribed formats. A few states have made the Uniform Traffic Citation and Complaint usable for misdemeanor citations as well.[4] This practice has certain obvious advantages in reducing the number of forms that police officers must keep up with, but does sacrifice some space on the face of the citation.

Some Examples of Good Forms

One particularly impressive citation form is that of the Jacksonville, Florida, sheriff's office (see figures 10-1, 10-2, and 10-3). It is the only form that the arresting officer must complete, contains full information about the offense, and can be filed directly into court. It is made out in five copies: the first is for the court, the second for the state's attorney, the third for the defendant, the fourth for the arresting officer, and the fifth is an already prepared warrant in the event of nonappearance by the defendant. The copies have varying types of information printed on the backs of them, depending on whose copy each is. The face of each copy is the same. The form is approximately 5½ by 10½ inches and contains space for a thumbprint, although the thumbprint is not generally used.

Another impressive citation form is that formerly used in New Haven, Connecticut, as shown in figure 10-4.[5] It is a four-copy form, approximately 4½ by 7½ inches. The first copy is the court copy, the second copy is given to the defendant, the third copy is retained by the police department, and the fourth copy goes to the bail commissioner (a position that does not exist in most states). The face of the citation states in large print "THIS IS AN ARREST—COURT APPEARANCE REQUIRED," and on the lower portion, again in large print, "YOU MUST APPEAR AT," and in large letters gives the court's address. There is also space for the date and time. Instructions are also given in Spanish. On the reverse side of the defendant's copy, in both English and Spanish, is a section entitled "Notice of Rights," which spells out a defendant's right to remain silent, to have an attorney, and to be presented before the next session of the court (and explains that signing the citation is a waiver of this last right). Under the section on rights, the penalties for failure to appear are given.

Figure 10-1. Front of Citation Form Used in Jacksonville, Florida

WAIVER INFORMATION

If you desire to plead Guilty or Nolo Contendere and you need not appear in court as indicated on the face of this notice, you may present this notice at the CLERK OF THE COUNTY COURT'S OFFICE, located in the DUVAL COUNTY COURT HOUSE, ROOM 100, within FIVE working days, between the hours of 8:00 A.M. and 5:00 P.M., MONDAY through FRIDAY and pay a fine of _____ dollars; or mail _____ dollars in CASHIER'S CHECK or MONEY ORDER to: CLERK OF THE COUNTY COURT, ROOM 100, COUNTY COURT HOUSE, 330 EAST BAY STREET, JACKSONVILLE, FLORIDA 32202.

The waiver below must be completed. Read carefully.

Your failure to answer this summons in the manner prescribed will result in a warrant being issued on a separate and additional charge.

In consideration of my not appearing in court, I the undersigned, do hereby enter my appearance on the affadavit for the offense charged on the other side of this notice and waive the reading of the affadavit in the above named cause and the right to be present at the trial of said action. I hereby enter the plea of ☐ Guilty or ☐ Nolo Contendere, and waive the right to prosecute, appeal, or error proceedings.

I understand the nature of the charge against me; I understand my right to have counsel and I waive this right and the right to a continuance. I waive my right to trial before a Judge or Jury. I hereby enter the plea of ☐ Guilty or ☐ Nolo Contendere to the charge being fully aware that my signature to this plea will have the same effect as a judgement of this court.

Total Fine and Cost: _____

Defendant: _____
                        (Signature)

Address: _____

Figure 10-2. Back of Citation Form Used in Jacksonville, Florida

CAPIAS

CITATION FOR MISDEMEANOR OR ORDINANCE VIOLATION

STATE OF FLORIDA,
CITY OF JACKSONVILLE > VS.

FOR CLERK'S USE ONLY

CCR #

_____ DEFENDANT, AGE _____

(LAST NAME)   (FIRST)   (MIDDLE)

_____ FLORIDA, PHONE _____

(PRESENT HOME ADDRESS)   (CITY)

_____ PHONE _____

(PLACE OF EMPLOYMENT)   (ADDRESS)

SEX	RACE	DATE OF BIRTH	HEIGHT	WEIGHT	COLOR HAIR	COLOR EYES	SOCIAL SECURITY NUMBER	

MAKE VEHICLE	YEAR	STYLE	COLOR	TAG NUMBER	YEAR	STATE	DRIVERS LICENSE NUMBER	TYPE

IN THE NAME OF AND BY THE AUTHORITY OF THE CITY OF JACKSONVILLE COMES THE UNDERSIGNED AND SAYS:

ON THE _____ DAY OF _____, 19 ___ , THE ABOVE NAMED PERSON DID

UNLAWFULLY COMMIT THE FOLLOWING OFFENSE IN VIOLATION OF

STATE STATUTE	
LOCAL ORD.	

SECTION _____, PROVIDING AGAINST _____

AT THE FOLLOWING LOCATION WITHIN THE CITY OF JACKSONVILLE, FLORIDA:

_____

IN THAT THE DEFENDANT DID: _____

(NARRATIVE OF THE OFFENSE)

_____

_____

_____

_____

AND FAILED TO APPEAR OR PRESENT THE NOTICE AS REQUIRED BY RULE 3.125, FLORIDA

RULES OF CRIMINAL PROCEDURE.

To all and Singular the Sheriffs of the State of Florida, Greetings:

You are hereby Commanded to take _____

if he be found in your County, and him safely keep so that you have his body before the Judge of our COUNTY COURT, in and for the County of Duval and State of Florida, at the Courthouse in Jacksonville, Florida, instanter, to answer unto the State of Florida for failure to comply with the notice to appear previously executed by the aforementioned individual.

And have you then and there this writ.

WITNESS, the Honorable _____
Judge, of the County Court, as also
S. MORGAN SLAUGHTER, Clerk of said Court,
at the Courthouse at Jacksonville aforesaid,

this _____ day of _____ A. D. 19 _____

S. MORGAN SLAUGHTER
Clerk

By: _____
Deputy Clerk

DEFENDANT'S
FINGER PRINT
RIGHT INDEX
FINGER

CLERK'S COPY

Figure 10-3. Fifth Copy of Citation Form Used in Jacksonville, Florida— Warrant Form to Be Used in Event of Nonappearance by Defendant

THIS IS AN ARREST – COURT APPEARANCE REQUIRED

| NEW HAVEN MISDEMEANOR CITATION - NOTICE TO APPEAR | DOCKET NO CR-6- |

| LAST NAME | FIRST | MIDDLE | COMPLAINT NO. |

| ADDRESS | CITY | STATE | DATE OF BIRTH | MONTH | DAY | YEAR |

| PLACE OF BIRTH | SEX | RACE | EYES | HAIR | HEIGHT | WEIGHT | SOCIAL SECURITY NO. |

| DRIVER'S LICENSE AND STATE | LOCATION OF ARREST | DATE OF ARREST | MONTH | DAY | YEAR | TIME |

| CHARGES | NO. 23082 |

I have been informed of my constitutional rights and of the penalties for failure to appear in Court as indicated on the form I have received. Without making any plea, I waive my right to appear before the next Circuit Court. I promise to appear, to answer the charge made against me, at Sixth Circuit Court in New Haven, on the date below and on any date to which my case is continued.

Se me ha informado de mis derechos constitucionales y también de las penalidades si no comparezco en la Corte Circuito en la fecha indicada en esta citación. Sin hacer ninguna declaración, renuncio a mi derecho de comparecer ante la próxima sesión de la Corte Circuito de New Haven. Prometo comparecer, para contestar el cargo que se me ha hecho, en la fecha indicada abajo y en cualquier otra fecha durante mi juicio

| YOU MUST APPEAR AT | SIXTH CIRCUIT COURT | MONTH | DAY | YEAR | AT |
| DEBE COMPARECER A | 169 CHURCH STREET NEW HAVEN, CONN. | ON: | / | / | 10 A.M. |

X _____
SIGNATURE OF ARRESTEE
OR GUARDIAN IF UNDER AGE

X _____
SIGNATURE OF OFFICER

SHIELD NO.

Side column (vertical): COURT COPY — CONFIDENTIAL INFORMATION - NOT SUBJECT TO SUBPOENA — FAMILY STATUS — HOME PHONE — EMPLOYER'S ADDRESS — EMPLOYER — REFERENCE — DURATION AT HOME ADDRESS / IN NEW HAVEN AREA — ADDRESS AT JOB — DURATION AT JOB — EMPLOYER PHONE — CITY — STATE

(Front of Form)

NOTICE OF RIGHTS

1. You have a right to remain silent. Anything you say may be used against you. If you do answer questions, you have a right to stop answering at any time.

2. You have a right to a lawyer before answering any question and at any time during questioning. If you cannot afford one, the court may appoint one for you.

3. You have a right to be presented before the next Circuit Court session in New Haven. By signing this citation, you waive that right and agree to appear in Court on the date shown on the reverse side of this form.

PENALTIES FOR FAILURE TO APPEAR

You are charged with a misdemeanor. If you fail to appear in Court on the date indicated on the reverse, or on any date to which your case is continued, you may be charged with an additional misdemeanor, rearrested, and fined up to $500.00 or imprisoned up to one year.

NOTICIA DE DERECHOS

1. Usted tiene derecho de no hablar. Cualquier cosa que usted diga puede ser usada en contra suya. Si usted contesta a las preguntas usted tiene derecho a quedarse callado en cualquier momento durante el período interrogatorio.

2. Usted tiene derecho a un abogado antes de contestar cualquier pregunta y en cualquier momento durante su interrogatorio. Si usted no puede pagar un abogado la corte podría asignarle uno.

3. Usted tiene derecho de ser presentado ante la próxima sesión de la Corte Circuito en New Haven. Al firmar usted esta citación, renuncia a ese derecho y debe comparecer a la Corte Circuito de New Haven, en la fecha indicada al dorso.

ADVERTENCIA

Se le ha acusado de un delito. Si usted no comparece a la Corte en la fecha indicada al dorso, o en cualquier otra fecha durante su juicio, puede ser acusado de delitos adicionales, puede ser arrestado de nuevo y puede ser multado hasta $500.00 dólares o hasta un año de cárcel.

(Back of Form)

Figure 10-4. Citation Form Formerly Used in New Haven, Connecticut

Notes

1. See, for example Del. Code tit.11, §1907 (1979); R.I. Gen. Laws §12-7-11 (Cum. Supp. 1980).

2. See, for example, Del. Code tit.11, §1907 (1979). The old Rhode Island statutory form was worse but was changed in 1977.

3. See, for example, Cal. Penal Code §853.9 (West Cum. Supp. 1981) (Judicial Council); Neb. Rev. Stat. §29-423 (1979) (Supreme Court); N.C. Gen. Stat. §15A-302 (1978) (Administrative Office of the Courts).

4. See, for example, the forms prescribed by the California Judicial Council, Cal. Penal Code §853.7 (West Cum. Supp. 1981).

5. The New Haven form has since been replaced by a state-mandated form.

11

Relationship to Other Agencies: The Courts, Prosecutors, and OR Programs

Attitudes of Prosecutors and Courts

Both courts and prosecutors have played an important role in developing the citation procedure. One of the earliest jurisdictions after New York to implement the procedure on any large scale was Contra Costa County, California. In this county the district attorney, John Nejedly, first suggested in 1963 that the procedure be tried and provided leadership in calling the police agencies, the courts, and others in the community together to develop plans for testing the procedure.[1]

The courts have also taken a strong interest in the procedure in a number of states. In Alaska, Arkansas, New Jersey, Pennsylvania, Tennessee, Vermont, and Washington the procedure was first authorized, and in Minnesota it was mandated, by court rule.[2] Court rules are also in effect in Florida and Ohio, although the procedure was first authorized by statute in these states.[3] In California the state judicial council has assisted in the development of a uniform citation form and in meshing court and police procedures,[4] and in other states individual judges have played an influential role in bringing about or expediting use of the procedure.

Although, on the whole, the attitude of courts and prosecutors has been highly favorable, a few jurisdictions indicated court mistrust or doubt as a major reason for not using the procedure. Concerns in these jurisdictions usually focused on an anticipation that defendants would fail to appear as promised.

Even if not specifically unfavorable, however, court and prosecutor attitudes and procedures can sometimes unwittingly have an adverse impact on the use of citations. Illinois, for example, was one of the earlier states to adopt a statute authorizing the use of citations.[5] In order to implement other provisions of the same statute, however, the Illinois Supreme Court issued rules mandating the use of preset bail schedules for cases in which the judge was not available.[6] While not intended to do so, these rules had the effect of inhibiting implementation of the citation provisions of the statute.

The Chicago police in 1966 and the Evanston police in 1969 nonetheless undertook use of citations to a limited extent.[7] Major use did not begin, however, until 1973 when the circuit court for Chicago issued an order directing the use of citations for nontraffic offenses punishable by fine when a judge was unavailable and the defendant was unable to post bail.[8]

141

Subsequent court orders in 1974 and 1976 extended this procedure to misdemeanors and ordinance violations for which the preset bail was $1,000 or less and to many new traffic offenses.[9] Under these new procedures the number of citations issued by the Chicago police increased from 2,021 in 1973 to 29,239 in 1976.[10] Although traffic citations accounted for most of this increase, use for criminal offenses also increased considerably. In 1977 the Illinois Supreme Court amended its rules to make it clear that the preset bail schedule and the citation were alternative procedures and that the rules were not "intended to limit a peace officer's discretion to issue a Notice to Appear in an appropriate case."[11]

Prosecutors in a number of jurisdictions are able to file the citation directly as a complaint, and some see this as a definite benefit in the efficiency of the office.[12] Even in jurisdictions that do not provide for direct filing of the citation, either as a matter of policy or of law, there is a general perception that the citation procedure is useful. In many states the fact that there is a delay of several days between the time the citation is issued and the time the defendant appears in court makes it possible for the prosecutor to review cases prior to filing, thus enabling the prosecutor to eliminate weak cases and reduce his work load. This is often not possible with cases in which there is an arrest, because these generally go to court promptly, either on the day of the arrest or the next day.

In addition to planning or initiating citation procedures, courts and prosecutors are heavily involved in day-to-day administration. To determine how the procedure has worked in practice, prosecutors and court officials in ten widely scattered jurisdictions were contacted for their views. In general, the response was highly positive and supportive of the use of the procedure.

Court clerks and administrators generally find no particular problem with the citation procedure. They are, for the most part, used to handling other kinds of citations and find that administration of the misdemeanor citation is not that different. Failure-to-appear cases create a problem, but one that is similar to that encountered in traffic and other citation cases.

Trial-court judges also seem to be pleased with the citation procedure. In a few jurisdictions, however, judges have found the number of defendants failing to appear to be too high and have ordered the citation procedure discontinued.[13]

The Mechanics of Prosecution

In some states a citation may be filed directly in court as the charging document for misdemeanor offenses. This procedure allows charging without the preparation of a new document and can result in a considerable saving of clerical time and some saving of prosecutorial time. The procedure need not interfere with any need for screening cases by the prosecutor or any other necessary precourt processing.

The California statute provides for this kind of processing; it says:

> [W]henever the written notice to appear has been prepared on a form approved by the Judicial Council, an exact and legible duplicate copy of the notice when filed with the magistrate shall constitute a complaint to which the defendant may enter a plea and, if the notice to appear is verified, upon which a warrant may be issued. If the notice to appear is not verified, the defendant may, at the time of arraignment, request that a verified complaint be filed.[14]

Practices under this statute vary a great deal. The Alameda County district attorney's office does not make use of the statute, preferring instead to draw up its own complaint in each case on which it decides to file. Other offices, however, do make full use of the statute, believing that it saves both time and money. In some of these offices, complaints are regularly issued on all citations issued. In some counties in which all citations are charged the filing of the citation is handled by the district attorney's office, but in others the citations go directly to court from the police. In still others the district attorney's office prefers to screen the citations and issue charges only on the better cases. In the offices that screen before charging all citations go initially to the district attorney. That office then reviews the citations, filing those on which it wishes to issue charges and not filing the others.

Another jurisdiction that allows the citation to be filed directly is Jacksonville, Florida. In this jurisdiction all citations are signed by the officer and notarized. Thus the citation not only satisfies the documentary requirements for charging, but also supplies a verified statement that is sufficient, under local interpretation, to allow the magistrate to make a determination of whether there is probable cause in the case.[15]

Relationship with Pretrial-Release Programs

In recent years many localities around the country have established organized programs for releasing defendants on their own recognizance rather than through the use of money bail. In some localities these programs have been funded through local sources and have developed strong organizational and financial roots in local government. In many other jurisdictions, however, these programs have no clear organizational home and have been funded largely from grant funds that will eventually run out.

An issue that has already emerged and that is likely to grow larger as more and more local jurisdictions are asked to take over funding of local

OR programs is that of rationalizing, or in some instances replacing, these programs with police-release procedures. Most local governments are already hard pressed financially and are looking for ways to eliminate or cut down the costs of pretrial-release processing. The expansion of police-release programs is an obvious answer, particularly in jurisdictions where the OR program is heavily involved with misdemeanors.

To a large extent this kind of transition has already occurred in Minneapolis. Here a large, well-financed, and well-managed OR program was established in the early 1970s. When grant funds ran out, the county cut the program back and transferred the jail interviewing and release function for misdemeanants to the sheriff's office. Consideration was given to maintaining the OR project for felony cases and providing information and backup for misdemeanor cases. In the end, however, local funds were not available even for these limited functions.

It seems undesirable to cut programs back to this extent. There is a limit to the work load that police and sheriff's offices can absorb without additional staff, and there is a clear need for OR personnel to assist with the more serious cases.

No other jurisdictions were identified in which this kind of total shift has taken place, but the connection between the scope of police release and the level of OR-program effort needed seems obvious. In Washington, D.C., for example, as the number of police releases between 1969 and 1975 went up, the number of court OR releases went down.[16] Two other jurisdictions in which police or jail personnel make OR-type investigations are Albuquerque, New Mexico, and the Sacramento County, California, sheriff's office.[17]

While situations in individual localities vary, it seems clear that in any well-designed system of pretrial release the police will play a major part—through both field and station-house citations. Use of these procedures will ensure that the great number of defendants whose arrests are routine, who are likely to appear in court, and who are not thought to be dangerous will be released speedily and cheaply. Release-on-own-recognizance programs and the courts will then be free to devote their time and attention to the more serious and difficult cases.

Notes

1. *Bail and Summons: 1965*, at 146-150 (August 1966).
2. Ark. R. Crim. P. 5.2; Alaska R. Crim. P. 4(a)(2); Minn. R. Crim. P. 601; New Jersey Rules Governing Criminal Practice 3:3-1; Pa. R. Crim. P. 51 through 56; Vt. R. Crim. P. 3; Tenn. R. Crim. P. 3.5; Wash. Just. Ct. Crim. R. 2.01.

3. Fla. R. Crim. P. 3.125 and Ohio R. Crim. P. 4(F) and 4.1.

4. See Cal. Penal Code §853.9 (West Cum. Supp. 1981).

5. Ill. Ann. Stat. ch. 38, §107-112 (Smith-Hurd 1980).

6. Illinois Sup. Ct. R. 528.

7. See S. Schiller, *The American Bar Association Standards for the Administration of Criminal Justice: Illinois Compliance* 30-34 (1974); Comment, "An Analysis of the Citation System in Evanston, Illinois: Its Value, Constitutionality and Viability," 65 *J. Crim. L. and Criminology* 75 (1974).

8. Circuit Court of Cook County, Illinois, First Municipal District, General Order No. 73-1, January 4, 1973.

9. Circuit Court of Cook County, Illinois, First Municipal District, General Order No. 74-5, June 7, 1974; No. 76-19, December 13, 1976.

10. Study Committee on Bail Procedures of the Illinois Judicial Conference, *Report* 9 (March 1978).

11. Order Revising Illinois Supreme Court Rules 501 through 556, 66 Ill. 2d R. 26 (Feb. 17, 1977). See also *Naperville* v. *Lawrentz*, 51 Ill. App. 3d 798, 367 N.E. 230 (1977).

12. California, Florida, and Nevada, for example, permit direct filing of the complaint under some circumstances. See Cal. Penal Code §853.9 (West Cum. Supp. 1981); Fla. R. Crim. 3.125; Nev. Rev. Stat. §171.1778 (1975).

13. In general, the concern here was the number of failure-to-appear cases.

14. See, for example, Cal. Penal Code §853.9(b) (West Cum. Supp. 1981).

15. *Gerstein* v. *Pugh*, 420 U.S. 103 (1975).

16. See chapter 8, note 40.

17. See 2 J. Galvin, W. Busher, et al., *Instead of Jail: Pre- and Post-Trial Alternatives to Jail Incarceration* 47-48 (October 1977) (U.S. Government Printing Office).

Part III
The Future and
Some Other Issues

12 Some Other Uses of Citations: Felonies, Juveniles, and Warrants

Felony Citations

Statutes or court rules in five states authorize the use of the citation procedure for felonies as well as misdemeanors. Little information is available, however, as to whether this authority is actually used and whether it is considered useful or not.

The states that formally authorize use of citations for felonies are Connecticut, Illinois, Minnesota, Montana, and Vermont.[1] Most of the statutes or court rules are clearly simply authorizations if the police agencies in the state choose to use the procedure. Thus according to the Vermont Rules of Criminal Procedure:

> A law enforcement officer acting without warrant may issue a citation to appear in lieu of arrest or continued custody to a person charged with any felony where arrest or continued custody is not patently necessary for the public safety and such facts as the officer is reasonably able to ascertain as to the person's place and length of residence, family relationships, references, past and present employment, his criminal record, and other relevant matters satisfy the officer that the person will appear in response to a citation.[2]

The only statute relating to the release of felony defendants on citations that is at all directory is that of Connecticut, and it is only mildly obligatory. It requires that the police chief or his designate shall interview suspects arrested without a warrant and, unless the suspect waives his right to be interviewed, "promptly order release of such person upon his execution of a written promise to appear or his posting of such bond as may be set" by the police officer.[3]

As a practical matter this statute is, like the other provisions, treated as discretionary. In New Haven, for example, pursuant to an understanding between the police and the courts, relatively few felony defendants are released on a promise to appear. In Illinois the authority to cite felony defendants has been even further curtailed. There the court rules are interpreted to prohibit entirely the release of felony defendants through the citation procedure.[4]

Overall, only 13 of the 157 departments reporting use of citations use them for felony offenses, and only half of these appear to use the procedure on anything other than an occasional basis. As might be expected use is greater for property felonies than for offenses involving assaultive behavior.

About three-fifths of the departments that use the citation procedure for felony crimes favor this use in appropriate cases. Among departments that do not currently use the procedure, however, 85 percent are opposed to having this kind of authority, as shown in table 12-1.

Juveniles

About half the agencies using the citation procedure for adults use some form of citation for juveniles as well. Almost none, however, use the same procedure for juvenile citations as for adults.

Where a citation procedure is used for juveniles, the juvenile is most commonly cited to the juvenile court, rather than to the probation department or to the police department, as shown in table 12-2.

Those departments which do use citations or some other form of non-custody referral for juveniles show enormous differences in the extent to which the procedure is used for misdemeanor offenses, as shown in table 12-3. The percentage of juveniles referred in the different departments ranges from 1 to 98 percent.

Warrants

Traffic and parking warrants generally result from some failure on the part of the person named to respond to the citation originally issued. Misdemeanor warrants generally result from some failure to appear in court or from the swearing out of a complaint by a citizen or a police officer.

Table 12-1
Attitudes toward Felony Citations
(percent of agencies responding)

	Favor Police Authority of This Kind	Oppose Police Authority of This Kind
Agencies using felony citations	60	40
Agencies not using felony citations	15	85
All agencies	18	82
Number of agencies responding	(25)	(116)

Source: Police Foundation–Center on Administration of Criminal Justice survey, 1976.

Table 12-2
Citations for Juveniles
(percent of agencies responding)

	Agencies Issuing Citations for:	
	Misdemeanors and Ordinance or Regulatory Violations	Ordinance or Regulatory Violations Only
Cited to juvenile court	29	33
Cited to probation department	4	0
Cited to police department	7	7
Cited to juvenile court and probation department	4	0
Cited to juvenile court and police department	2	7
Cited to probation department and police department	2	0
Cited other places (magistrate, etc.)	4	0
Not cited at all	47	53
Number of agencies responding	(130)	(15)

Source: Police Foundation–Center on Administration of Criminal Justice survey, 1976.

In theory, once a warrant is issued the police should send out an officer, arrest the person named, and bring him before the court that issued the warrant as soon as possible. This series of events may well have happened in an earlier era, particularly when the constable worked more or less directly for the magistrate. As a practical matter today, however, this situation does not usually occur in most larger jurisdictions. The number of warrants is simply too great to permit such individualized service.

Most agencies do, of course, take felony warrants seriously and attempt to provide the manpower for individualized attention. For other offenses, however, many agencies have developed a system in which they attempt to secure voluntary compliance through mail or telephone contact. To supplement this system almost all of these agencies routinely check persons stopped for traffic offenses or arrested on some other charge to see if they have any outstanding warrants. Although this procedure does not ensure that any particular person wanted on a warrant will be quickly apprehended, it does provide some level of enforcement of the warrants involved.

One question this procedure raises which has already been discussed is whether persons arrested in this manner should be eligible for a police citation. Another question raised is whether the basic concept should be regularized in some way. Many jurisdictions have no real legal authorization for the mail or telephone notice procedure, and the notice sent therefore has no legal effect. In one sense this is not particularly important, as it is doubtful

Table 12-3
Percent of Juvenile Misdemeanants Cited
(percent of agencies responding)

	Agencies Issuing Citations for:	
Percentage *Cited*	*Misdemeanors and Ordinance or Regulatory Violations*	*Ordinance or Regulatory Violations Only*
1–10	20	20
11–20	10	0
21–40	10	0
41–60	12	0
61–80	20	20
81–100	28	60
Number of agencies responding	(50)	(5)

Source: Police Foundation–Center on Administration of Criminal Justice survey, 1976.

that the creation of specific authority would increase the response rate much or even at all. On the other hand, it seems desirable that there be some penalty for continued failure to respond, and it would generally seem both easier and fairer to impose a penalty if the present procedures were sanctioned by specific law. One way of achieving this goal would be to authorize the police to issue citations or summonses on the warrants.

In order to determine the extent to which the practice of writing or telephoning persons wanted on warrants is now used, the Police Foundation-Center on Administration of Criminal Justice survey asked agencies how they sought to bring persons named in parking, traffic, and misdemeanor warrants to justice. As indicated in table 12-4, fewer than half of the agencies responding viewed arrest or personal contact as the primary method for handling parking warrants, but over three-fourths saw arrest or personal contact as the primary method for handling misdemeanor warrants.

In large part the practice of writing or telephoning persons wanted on warrants has evolved as a response to the work-load burden of attempting apprehensions for all warrants, rather than out of concern for defendants or for the other reasons more typically given for development of the citation procedure. In part, however, these practices are the result of these concerns and of the fact that the overwhelming majority of defendants in these categories will respond to noncustody methods of handling. No statistics are available, but in some agencies it is common practice to delay arrest to allow deserving defendants time to clear up warrants. This situation sometimes happens even when personal contact is made for the purpose of apprehension.

Table 12-4
Primary Method Used for Serving Warrants
(percent of agencies responding)

	Type of Warrant		
	Parking	*Traffic*	*Misdemeanor*
Attempt to serve each warrant	40	56	68
Personally serve after an attempt has been made to contact the defendant by telephone or mail	21	21	15
Try to contact by mail or telephone but attempt no personal service other than warrant checks on traffic and street stops and jail bookings	19	11	6
Rely entirely on warrant checks on traffic and street stops and jail bookings	8	4	4
Other	5	3	2
Do not handle these types of warrants	7	5	5
Number of agencies responding	(177)	(187)	(195)

Source: Police Foundation–Center on Administration of Criminal Justice survey, 1976.

To some extent the existence of these informal practices indicates that there is no pressing need for formal citation authority for warrant cases. On the other hand, the successful use of these practices also indicates that there is little reason for not making such authority explicit. Doing so would assist those departments and agencies which feel that they are legally bound to make arrests in every case and would allow the decision of whether to arrest to be made in each case on the basis of need for custody.

The argument for this kind of authority and procedure is strengthened by the fact that a number of important jurisdictions have abandoned arrest and the warrant procedure as a method for handling most traffic and parking matters. In New York, for example, except for serious offenses, such as drunk driving and hit and run, these matters are handled entirely by the Department of Motor Vehicles.[5] Drivers failing to respond to citations are not given warrants, but are instead denied licensing and other driving privileges. This practice relieves the police of the necessity of including traffic and parking warrants in their warrant files and of checking on the existence of warrants at the time defendants are stopped or booked. In addition, defendants who have outstanding traffic or parking obligations are not thereby precluded from being released on a citation for a misdemeanor offense. Similar systems are also in effect in Minneapolis, Minnesota, and in Florida.[6]

Notes

1. Ill. Rev. Stat. ch. 38, §107-112 (Smith-Hurd 1980); Minn. R. Crim. P. 6.01 (1981); Mont. Rev. Codes Ann. §95-614 (1969); Conn. Gen. Stat. Ann. §54-63c (West Cum. Supp. 1980); Vt. R. Crim. P. 3(c)(3) (1974). In addition to these five states, in Arkansas the ranking station officer may issue a citation to a defendant arrested for a felony if this is recommended by a prosecutor. Rules of Crim. P. 5.2(c) (1977).

2. Vt. R. Crim. P. 3(c)(3) (1974).

3. Conn. Gen Stat. Ann. §54-63c (West Cum. Supp. 1980).

4. See S. Schiller, *The American Bar Association Standards for the Administration of Criminal Justice: Illinois Compliance* 30 (1974).

5. The New York procedure is discussed in detail in A. Halper, and J. McDonnell, *New York State Department of Motor Vehicles Administrative Adjudication Bureau* (1975) (U.S. Department of Justice).

6. Interviews in Minneapolis, Minnesota, and Jacksonville, Florida.

13 The Role of the Individual Officer

Officer attitudes are important in virtually every police activity. They are particularly important in activities that involve the use of judgment and discretion. As most agencies expect officers to exercise judgment and discretion in the use of citations, the extent to which citations are actually used generally depends on the attitude toward citations of the officers within the department.

Given the diversity of agencies involved in the use of citations and the variety of procedures and policies used, there is obviously some question about the extent to which information from one department is applicable to other agencies. What information there is, however, about officer attitudes toward citations generally indicates a positive approach toward the use of citations. Interviews with officers at both the policy and the street level in a dozen widely scattered communities throughout the country that use the procedure brought forward few negative comments about the procedure. Although some officers did not have much to say about the procedure one way or another—finding it essentially a routine operation—virtually none were hostile or even critical of it. Many, on the other hand, were quite positive.

It seems clear from discussions with agency officials, however, that officer attitudes are not always uniformly positive. Introducing the procedure without proper training and familiarization seems particularly likely to produce negative attitudes. One agency indicated that, because of changes in the law in its state, it had been forced to begin an extensive citation program on short notice and with no training at all. As might be expected, this resulted in considerable confusion and a great deal of resentment in the beginning. Later, after the department had had an opportunity to develop the procedure and officers had used it in practice, attitudes began to change.

In a number of other departments the beginning of the use of citations was also an important period, during which there was considerable skepticism and doubt concerning the procedure. In Evanston, Illinois, a city of about 80,000 just outside Chicago, a citation-release procedure was adopted in August 1971 as a result of action by the city council.[1] The procedure authorized the release of persons arrested for simple assault, disorderly conduct, solicitation of alcoholic beverages, ticket scalping, and municipal-code violations other than those involving deadly weapons, juveniles, prostitution, lewdness, sex offenses, or traffic offenses.[2]

Under the procedures adopted officers were authorized to issue field citations if they were satisfied that the offender had given authentic identification, was not wanted on an outstanding warrant, was a temporary or permanent Illinois resident, would appear in court, and would desist in the conduct that provoked the citation.

Interviews with sixty-one of the seventy-three street patrolmen about a year after the procedure was instituted indicated that the police officers had a basically negative attitude about the procedure[3] and had used it relatively little. Three primary reasons were cited for the negative feelings:

1. The persons cited would not appear as promised.
2. Offenders would be given the impression that the crime was not taken seriously.
3. The citation would not result in any convictions.

One officer felt that "the offenders will take it as a joke," and another remarked that "no one will honor a mere piece of paper which is issued at the scene of the incident."[4]

Officers also complained of a number of procedural problems. The most frequently mentioned problem concerned the crowds that gathered at the scene of an incident. Fifty-two percent of the officers interviewed said that crowds interfered with the citation procedure:

> These officers maintained that it was necessary to remove the offender from the scene of his misdemeanor. According to some officers, the practice of completing the citation in the field kept them in the vicinity of the incident longer than usual.[5]

Twenty-five percent of the officers, however, observed that the citation procedure could be followed by merely taking the alleged offender into the squad car and driving out of the neighborhood. These officers thought that a citation could be issued with greater ease at a less volatile location.

About 30 percent of the officers interviewed indicated that it was difficult to complete a citation in the field because they needed information about the offender and the charge that was available only at headquarters.[6] Air time apparently was often too limited to permit obtaining this information by radio.

Athough the data available indicate that convictions ran about the same for citation cases as for arrested cases and that the failure-to-appear rates were at least arguably similar for both arrested and cited cases,[7] the skepticism felt at the outset of the program did not go away easily. The data also indicate rather clearly that the general negative attitude about the procedure had some impact on its use—only 25 percent of the defendants eligible for citation release were released under the procedure. Twelve percent of the officers interviewed indicated that at one time or another during the year they had failed to issue a citation simply because they had forgotten that it was available.[8]

Not all departments have experienced this kind of problem at the outset of the procedure, however. Through the use of limited experiments or through training and familiarization, many departments appear to have had high acceptance from the beginning. Moreover, even in departments that experienced some initial doubt, a more positive attitude generally seemed to develop after the procedure had been in use for a period of time.

Individual officer attitudes in a department that has had the procedure in effect for a considerable period of time are illustrated to some degree by a survey of the Sacramento police department conducted in April 1976 by a member of the department.

The procedure was first adopted by the Sacramento department in 1970 and is used extensively, as shown in table 13-1. Over 20 percent of all misdemeanants excluding public drunkenness are cited.

Generally, any misdemeanant is citable if the conditions indicated in table 13-2 are met.

With 70 of 180 officers contacted responding, the attitudes of this department were much more positive than those at the outset of the Evanston pro-

Table 13-1
Sacramento Police Department Citation Statistics, 1975, Adults Only

Crime	Total Arrests	Booked	Cited
Assault and battery	291	274	17
Petty theft	1,087	517	570
Prostitution	336	287	49
Liquor laws	77	20	57
Marijuana possession	239	227	12
Other drug	62	61	1
Indecent exposure	39	38	1
Lewd act	3	2	1
Weapons (misdemeanor)	101	93	8
Disturbing the peace	162	155	7
Vandalism	81	72	9
Resisting arrest	143	142	1
Beg, prowl, peep	202	201	1
Drunkenness	7,307	7,277	30
Deadly weapon	15	14	1
Miscellaneous misdemeanors	294	236	58
Traffic, other than DUI	472	471	1
Total	10,913	10,087	826

Source: Gillis, "Citations and Summons: A Comparative Analysis" (Master's Thesis, California State University, Sacramento, 1977). Reprinted with permission.

Note: Only those offenses for which at least one citation was issued during the year are included.

Table 13-2

Conditions Required by Sacramento Police Department for Issuance of a Misdemeanor Citation

The offender must:
  establish his identity beyond a reasonable doubt
  reside in the City of Sacramento or within a 20-mile radius of Sacramento for at least one
    year and preferably two or more years
  be locally employed for one year or more or be a student in lieu of employment
  waive his right to be taken immediately before a magistrate
  sign the citation
  have no facts that indicate to the officer there is a need to book him instead

An arrest is mandatory if:
  he has a prior felony conviction or more than one misdemeanor conviction
  he has a prior failure to appear
  he is intoxicated
  he was arrested for a vice violation, has an outstanding warrant, or is wanted by another
    jurisdiction
  there is need for further follow-up of the crime (it may become a felony, for example)
  there is a threat of immediate danger to the public, or to law enforcement personnel, by
    reason of the offender's mental attitude
  the offender is charged with a crime that, if convicted, would require his registration as a sex
    offender

Source: Gillis, "Citations and Summons: A Comparative Analysis" (Master's Thesis, California
State University, Sacramento, 1977). Reprinted with permission.

cedure. When asked whether they would use a misdemeanor citation release as an alternative to arrest for a person with no prior arrests, over two-thirds of the officers responding said "always" or "usually," and only 5 percent said "never" or "undecided."[9]

Even in this department, however, attitudes began to vary if the person arrested was one with a few arrests. For this kind of defendant only 18 percent said "always" or "usually," while 35 percent said "never" or "undecided." The largest group (40 percent) said "occasionally."

When given a list of misdemeanor offenses and asked which they felt were the most appropriate for citation release, virtually all the officers responding indicated that they felt such release was appropriate for use with petty theft cases. Very few felt that citation release was appropriate for loaded-gun or indecent-exposure cases, and fewer than 20 percent felt that the procedure would be appropriate for use in felony crimes. (California does not permit such use.) If a felony citation program were instituted, however, the offenses felt to be the most appropriate were embezzlement and dangerous drugs. (Earlier, Sacramento had had a felony-drug citation program, which was discontinued when marijuana possession was reduced to a misdemeanor.)

About 60 percent of the officers responding indicated that they had in the past booked offenders to whom they would have issued citations had they been permitted to do so by department policy.

Notes

1. Comment, "An Analysis of the Citation System in Evanston, Illinois: Its Value, Constitutionality and Viability," 65 *J. Crim. L. and Criminology* 75, 78 (1974).

2. Id. at 75-76 and n. 51.

3. Id. at 83.

4. Id. at 84.

5. Id. at 85.

6. Id.

7. The conviction rate for citation cases was 44 percent; for arrest cases 45 percent. The failure-to-appear rate for citation cases was 22 percent, against 15 percent for arrest cases. See id. at 84-85.

8. Id. at 83 and n. 87.

9. R.J. Gillis, "Citations and Summons: A Comparative Analysis" (1977) (Master's Thesis, California State University, Sacramento).

14 Police Bail-Setting Authority

The role played by the police in handling arrestees during the pretrial and precourt period differs considerably from city to city and state to state. In some jurisdictions police have a relatively limited role. When an arrest is made, the defendant is brought to court almost immediately. Neither the police nor the prosecutor screen cases, and because there is no delay the decision about pretrial release is made largely by the judge. The citation procedure may still be used, but there is no need for bail to be set prior to appearance in court because appearance in court occurs almost instantaneously, at virtually the same time as booking.

In other jurisdictions, however, the appearance in court is often not until the next day. The police, the prosecutor, or both screen the arrests to determine which cases they will prosecute, and the first court appearance is often a day or two later or, if the suspect is arrested over the weekend, perhaps three days later. In these jurisdictions there often is some kind of procedure for allowing pretrial release to defendants prior to their first appearance in court.

One such procedure obviously is out-of-court contact with the judge so that he may set bail. In many jurisdictions, however, there is a more regular procedure for minor offenses, such as a bail schedule, in which a specific bail amount is indicated as the bail necessary for a specified charge. Bail for petty theft, for example, might be set at $500, and that for obstructing the sidewalk at $200.

Under this kind of arrangement the jailer is obligated to make the bail amount known to the defendant and is authorized to accept bail prior to the defendant's appearance in court.[1] When the case goes to court the judge may decide to raise or lower the bond amount, but the defendant will have already had the opportunity to secure release if he had the necessary funds.

This kind of bail schedule is less common for felonies and more serious crimes, but is employed in such cases to some extent.[2] Generally, when used for felonies and, in some jurisdictions, for misdemeanors as well, the jailer or the arresting officer is given the option of saying that he does not want the schedule used with respect to a particular defendant. This gives most defendants the benefit of the general schedule but also makes it possible for the officer on duty to hold for a more careful determination those defendants for whom he feels it is necessary.

Bail schedules of the kind described are normally set by the local judiciary, sometimes pursuant to statutory authority, and sometimes simply by local court rule. The California statute, for example, states:

> It is the duty of the . . . judges in each county to prepare and adopt by a majority vote, at a meeting called by the presiding judge . . . a uniform schedule of bail for all bailable . . . offenses.[3]

In a few jurisdictions the police have been given authority beyond that of administering a schedule set by the local judiciary. In Connecticut, for example, the police are directed to interview defendants, and, unless they find custody necessary to ensure appearance in court, they are directed to release the defendant on citation or the "posting of such bond as may be set by such officer."[4]

In formal terms this authority clearly exceeds that of the police in jurisdictions operating under bail schedules, but the difference in practice may be considerably less. In New Haven, Connecticut, for example, an informal schedule for felony crimes is set by the judges and honored by the police.

There is also considerable doubt as to whether this kind of authority is desirable. In England and Australia, where authority of this kind also exists, there is some tendency for police to use their authority to set a low bail as a bargaining tool to obtain confessions or other information.[5] Similar bargaining also appears to take place in some agencies in Connecticut.[6]

This situation seems clearly undesirable, both from the defendant's perspective and from that of the police. If the defendant ought to be released, he should be released. If the defendant ought to have a high bail set to keep him in custody, he should not be released because he gives a confession or other information. To do otherwise perverts the pretrial-decision process.

Notes

1. See W. Thomas, *Bail Reform in America* 211 (1976).
2. See, for example, Cal. Penal Code §1269b (West Cum. Supp. 1981).
3. Id.
4. Conn. Gen. Stat. Ann. §54-63c (West Cum. Supp. 1980). This kind of authority once existed in West Virginia also. It has been repealed, however. See chapter 3, note 58.
5. M. King, *Bail or Custody* 6 (1973); Vickery, "The Police Bail Power in Victoria," 50 *Law Institute Journal* 523 (1976).
6. See Epps, "The Use of Bail Schedules" (1976) (unpublished paper, Yale School of Law).

15

A Constitutional Right to Citation Release?

The use of citations in the United States today is the result of actions by police administrators, reformers, and legislators. Litigation has not played a major role, and there has been virtually no litigation contending that there is a constitutional right to citation release for minor crimes.

While there is a whole host of problems involved in dealing with the pretrial release of minor offenders as a matter of constitutional law, there are at least six theories on which such a right might be claimed: (1) the Fourth Amendment, (2) due process of law, (3) equal protection of the law, (4) the right to bail, (5) cruel and unusual punishment, and (6) state constitutional provisions. This chapter explores these possibilities.

The Fourth Amendment

The provision of the federal Constitution most directly concerned with the law of arrest is the Fourth Amendment. Since 1949, as a consequence of the Fourteenth Amendment, this amendment has been held applicable to the states as well as to the federal government.[1] It provides that:

> The right of the people to be secure in their persons, houses, papers, and effects, against unreasonable searches and seizures, shall not be violated, and no warrants shall issue but upon probable cause, supported by oath or affirmation and particularly describing the place to be searched and the persons or things to be seized.

In this language an arrest is a seizure, and the basic command of the Fourth Amendment insofar as arrests are concerned is that arrests be "reasonable." Principally this means that arrests must be based on probable cause to believe that a crime has been committed and that this suspect is the person who has committed the crime.

To date there has been virtually no litigation concerning the need to take the suspect into custody. The question arises therefore as to whether it is reasonable to physically arrest a suspect for a minor crime, when a citation would accomplish the law's purpose just as well.

163

Reasons for Thinking There May Be
Some Constitutional Limitations

One reason for thinking that there may be some constitutional limitations in this area is that at least two justices of the Supreme Court have indicated that there may be. In his concurring opinion in *Robinson* v. *United States*, a 1973 case dealing with the legitimacy of searching a suspect who had been arrested for a minor traffic offense, Justice Stewart said:

> It seems to me that a persuasive claim might have been made in this case that the custodial arrest of the petitioner for a minor traffic offense violated his rights under the Fourth and Fourteenth Amendments.[2]

Because the suspect had not raised the question the other justices did not comment. In a 1977 case, however, Justice Stevens alluded to the issue while commenting on another traffic situation:

> In this case, there was no custodial arrest, and I assume (perhaps somewhat naively) that the offense which gave rise to the stop of Mimms' car would not have warranted a full custodial arrest without some additional justification.[3]

Several recent lower-court cases have imposed constitutional limitations in related areas. A 1971 District of Columbia case concerned arrests of material witnesses. The court concluded that the normal requirement of probable cause had to be met by proving that there was reason to believe that the testimony of the witness was material. The court also concluded, partly on statutory and partly on constitutional grounds, that the government had in addition to show that there was some impracticability involved in obtaining the presence of the witness by subpoena.[4]

A 1975 Washington state case involving a civil statute that permitted the arrest of fathers who failed to support their illegitimate children was even more explicit. It found the statute unconstitutional because it allowed the defendant to be arrested "without adequate justification." The court said:

> The ultimate protection of the Fourth Amendment is against "unreasonable searches and seizures." For an arrest to be "reasonable" it must serve some governmental interest which is adequate to justify the imposition on the liberty of the individual.[5]

The court indicated that the government interest in ensuring the support of illegitimate children is "substantial," but, the court said,

> [It] does not require their arrest. Arrest is justified when a person may flee from legal process, or where he may constitute a danger to the public if

allowed to remain at large. . . . It is not justified simply by the fact that it is necessary to bring him into court for trial."[6]

No cases have been found that specifically rule on the question of arrest for traffic or minor offenses. A number of lower courts have raised questions about the constitutionality of the practice, however.[7]

Several commentators have also discussed the issue recently. Professor LaFave, in his treatise on search and seizure, concludes that "it is difficult to see how a physical taking of custody can be accepted as an inherently reasonable means for invoking the criminal process even in the instance of petty violations."[8]

He concedes that the Fourth Amendment should not be read "as requiring every police officer to conduct a bail-type hearing on the street corner in order to determine on a case-by-case basis, whether a citation will suffice." He suggests, however, that legislation or regulations governing the procedure might somehow be required under the Fourth Amendment.

Reasons for Doubting the Applicability of the Fourth Amendment

While there are persuasive reasons for finding Fourth Amendment limitations requiring the use of citations rather than physical arrest for minor offenses, there are also reasons for thinking that the Supreme Court might be hesitant to adopt such limitations.

In two related areas of the law the Supreme Court has recently refused to adopt somewhat similar limitations. In one case the Court was asked to limit the right to search incident to arrest in minor traffic situations, in which, ordinarily, no specific need for a search arises out of the arrest. The Court declined to adopt this kind of limitation, however, choosing instead to keep a simple rule that allows searches incident to any custodial arrest.[9]

In another case the Stanford University student newspaper had taken photographs of a demonstration in the early 1970s. Seeking to investigate the disturbance, the local police obtained a search warrant and searched the offices of the newspaper. The newspaper sued, claiming that the police ought to be required to seek the information through the use of a subpoena before being allowed to search for it. Again, however, the Court refused to accept the limitation. If there was probable cause to believe that the newspaper had the pictures and that they related to a crime, this was enough, said the Court, to authorize the search. There was no need to go into the question as to whether the pictures could be obtained in some less drastic way.[10]

The Fourth Amendment cases as a whole show some tendency to require more justification as state intrusion becomes greater. Body-cavity searches, at least in some contexts, require greater justification than normal searches of persons, which in turn require greater justification than pat downs. The cases just discussed, however, indicate that there are severe limits on the extent to which the Supreme Court is willing to extend this principle.

The Past a Guide to the Future?

In the past one guide as to whether a particular practice is found reasonable or unreasonable by the Court in the Fourth Amendment area is in the practices observed in England at the time the Fourth Amendment was adopted. Do these suggest anything with respect to a constitutional right for citation release?

There were in fact at the time the Fourth Amendment was adopted two significant limitations on the use of arrest for minor offenses. One was that arrests for misdemeanors could be made without a warrant only if for a breach of the peace committed in the presence of the officer. A less well known but even more relevant limitation was that for the most minor offenses arrest could not be made at all, whether with or without a warrant.[11]

On several occasions in the past the Supreme Court has acknowledged the common-law rule limiting misdemeanor arrests to breaches of the peace committed in the presence of the officer.[12] The Court has never considered, however, whether this limitation is required by the Constitution. This issue is important because many states have, by statute, extended the right to arrest to all cases in which the offense is committed in the presence of the officer and some states have extended this right to all offenses for which there is probable cause to arrest.[13]

The few modern cases that have considered this question and the most recent commentary have concluded that the limitation is not of constitutional dimensions and that statutes allowing the use of the broader arrest powers are valid.[14] A number of older state cases, however, did find the limitation to be of constitutional magnitude.[15] Most of these have been overturned, but a few have not.[16]

For reasons that are not altogether clear the limitation on the use of arrest for summary offenses is not as well known as the other common-law rules concerning arrest. The legislation that has broadened or eliminated these rules has consequently never been subjected to a constitutional test.[17]

The framers of the Fourth Amendment would probably be surprised to find constables arresting persons for petty offenses, particularly those not involving breaches of the peace. Modern commentators have almost universally found such practices equally unreasonable.[18] In these circumstances it seems at least possible that the Supreme Court might overcome its reluctance to impose additional complexity on the law of arrest and insist that minor offenses be handled, where possible, through the use of a means less drastic than arrest. To do so, however, the court would have to face the difficult question of how to enforce the rule and would probably have to adopt a constitutional definition of minor offenses as well.

Due Process of Law

A second theory upon which a constitutional right to citation treatment for minor crimes might be based is that an arrest is a deprivation of liberty without the hearing or the procedural protections required by due process of law.

The Supreme Court has held in a number of situations that it is unconstitutional to deprive an individual of a substantial right without an opportunity to contest the deprivation in advance. Welfare benefits, for example, may not be terminated without an opportunity for a hearing.[19] In other instances, however, such as the revocation of parole, the Court has said that a hearing in advance is not essential provided that there is an opportunity for a hearing promptly after the deprivation occurs.[20]

In some situations, of course, the courts do rule in advance before an arrest is made. This is one of the major purposes of the warrant. However, the Supreme Court has refused to require that warrants be obtained for arrests even when it is feasible to do so.[21] Rather, the Court has provided that there must be a prompt hearing after arrest for those defendants who continue to be held in custody.[22] These rulings were made in response to Fourth Amendment claims, and the Court did not consider whether the due-process clause itself might require some kind of procedural protection before detention is undertaken.

A recent California case involved a somewhat related issue. In this case the California Supreme Court held that, when a defendant has been arrested and brought to court, both state and federal due process require that the state bear the burden of demonstrating that he is not likely to appear if released on his own recognizance.[23]

The analogy between this case and the defendant who might be released on either a field or a station-house citation is far from complete. If it is correct, however, that the government bears some responsibility for showing why the court should not use the least onerous alternative for release, then it does not seem unreasonable to require the government to make the same kind of showing with respect to the initial decision to detain as well.

A second due-process argument is that, since there is no necessity for detention in the case of minor offenders, there is a violation of substantive due-process concepts. One New York case, later reversed on other grounds, held that there was.[24] In another case a federal district court found it to be fundamentally unfair to detain before trial defendants whose maximum punishment was a fine.[25]

Equal Protection of the Law

Under present U.S. law many defendants are unable to raise the bail necessary to be released pending trial. It can be argued that those who are detained are denied equal protection of the law.

Several claims of this kind have been made by defendants seeking to be released on their own recognizance. Asserting that they were discriminated against by having bail set in amounts that they were unable to post, indigent defendants sought to establish a presumption in favor of release on own recognizance. The courts have thus far been unwilling to establish such a presumption.

In one case the United States Fifth Circuit Court of Appeals said that "the argument favoring a specified priority sequence for the various forms of release overlooks the fact that its impact may vary under varying conditions."[26] "Utilization of a master bond schedule," the court pointed out, "provides speedy and convenient release for those who have no difficulty in meeting its requirements." The court indicated that money bail has its limits, however:

> The incarceration of those who cannot [take advantage of the master bail schedule], without meaningful consideration of other possible alternatives, infringes on both due process and equal protection requirements. . . . We have no doubt that in the case of an indigent, whose appearance at trial could reasonably be assured by one of the alternate forms of release, pretrial confinement for inability to post money bail would constitute imposition of excessive restraint.[27]

Other courts have been unwilling to go even this far,[28] and it seems clear that there are many problems involved in asserting a successful equal-protection claim. Citation releases, like releases on the defendant's own recognizance, do provide an alternative to money bail that does not discriminate against indigents. Field citations also avoid the sharp disparity between arrested and cited defendants that persuaded one lower court to declare the arrest of traffic offenders unconstitutional.[29]

Even if adopted these arguments would probably not mean that every defendant would be entitled to a citation release. They would more likely require that citation release would have to be seriously considered in each case.

Right to Bail

The Eighth Amendment prohibits the imposition of "excessive bail." Another possible theory for requiring the use of citations is that the imposition of any bail is excessive for defendants who could reasonably be released on citation.

One problem with this theory is that there is some uncertainty as to whether this portion of the Eighth Amendment applies to the states.[30] A more serious problem is that the courts have generally interpreted excessive bail to mean "greater than what is customary in the community" rather than "greater than what this defendant can pay" or "greater than what is necessary to have this defendant appear in court."[31]

Cruel and Unusual Punishment

The other part of the Eighth Amendment prohibits the imposition of "cruel and unusual punishment." Another theory that might be advanced is that pretrial detention is cruel and unusual punishment when the defendant could safely be released on citation.

It is clear that this portion of the Eighth Amendment applies to the states,[32] but the courts have generally been unwilling to find that pretrial detention is punishment or to examine the necessity for the detention.[33]

State Constitutional Provisions

Although states may not provide less protection to citizens than that required by the United States Constitution, they are free to provide more. Most states have provisions in their own constitutions that guarantee due process, equal protection of the law, the right to bail, freedom from cruel and unusual punishment, and other rights. All the arguments discussed above and others could also be made on state constitutional grounds.

One provision that may have particular importance is the right of privacy, which is guaranteed by many state constitutions. The Illinois courts have found that this right prohibits strip searches for minor offenses,[34] and it is possible that such provisions might also be interpreted to prohibit arrests for minor offenses.

Summary

There has been no litigation thus far seeking to establish a constitutional duty to use citations for minor crimes. Despite the many problems involved in declaring and enforcing such a duty, it would be in keeping with the values contained in the Fourth Amendment and the due-process and equal-protection clauses.

Notes

1. *Wolf* v. *Colorado*, 338 U.S. 25 (1949).
2. 414 U.S. 218, 266-267 (1973).
3. *Pennsylvania* v. *Mimms*, 434 U.S. 106, 122 n.11 (1977). See also *Robbins* v. *California*, 101 S.Ct. 2841, 2858 n. 11 (1981).
4. *Bacon* v. *United States*, 448 F.2d 162 (9th Cir. 1973).
5. *State* v. *Klinkner*, 85 Wash.2d 509, 537 P.2d 268, 277 (1975).
6. Id.
7. *People* v. *Troiano*, 35 N.Y.2d 476, 323 N.E.2d 183, 363 N.Y.S.2d 943 (1974); *State* v. *Martin*, 253 N.W.2d 404 (Minn. 1977). See also *People* v. *Copeland*, 77 Misc. 2d 649, 354 N.Y.S.2d 399 (1974), rev'd on other grounds, 82 Misc. 2d 12, 370 N.Y.S.2d 775 (1975), aff'd mem., 39 N.Y.2d 986 355 N.E.2d 288, 387 N.Y.S.2d 234 (1976); Shea, "Cars, Cops and Custody—Stopping and Searching Motorists in New York," 24 *N.Y.L.Sch.L. Rev.* 405, 434-437 (1978).
8. 2 W. LaFave, *Search and Seizure* 256-260, 288-291 (1978). The quotation is at 260. See also Amsterdam, "Perspectives on the Fourth Amendment," 58 *Minn.L. Rev.* 349, 415-429 (1974).
9. *Robinson* v. *United States*, 414 U.S. 218 (1973).
10. *Zurcher* v. *Stanford Daily*, 436 U.S. 547 (1978).
11. See chapter 3.
12. *United States* v. *Watson*, 423 U.S. 411 (1976); *Carroll* v. *United States*, 267 U.S. 132 (1925); *Bad Elk* v. *United States*, 177 U.S. 529 (1900); *Kurtz* v. *Moffitt*, 115 U.S. 487 (1885). See also *Street* v. *Surdyka*, 492 F.2d 368, 372 n. 3 (4th Cir. 1974).
13. *Model Code of Pre-Arraignment Procedure* app. X (1975).
14. See chapter 6, note 36.
15. See *United States* v. *Watson*, 423 U.S. 411, 455 n. 21 (1976).
16. See, for example, *In re Kellam*, 55 Kan. 700, 37 N.W. 960 (1895); *Polk* v. *State*, 167 Miss. 506, 142 So. 480 (1932).
17. Many of the statutes involved have been reviewed on other points.
18. See, for example, note 8 supra.
19. *Goldberg* v. *Kelly*, 397 U.S. 254 (1970).
20. *Wolff* v. *McDonnell*, 418 U.S. 539 (1974).
21. *United States* v. *Watson*, 423 U.S. 411 (1976).
22. *Gerstein* v. *Pugh*, 420 U.S. 103 (1975).
23. *Van Atta* v. *Scott*, 27 Cal.3d 424, 613 P.2d 210, 166 Cal.Rptr. 149 (1980).
24. *People* v. *Copeland*, 77 Misc. 2d 649, 354 N.Y.S.2d 399 (1974), rev'd on other grounds, 82 Misc. 2d 12, 370 N.Y.S.2d 775 (1975), aff'd mem., 39 N.Y.2d 986, 355 N.E.2d 288, 387 N.Y.S.2d 234 (1976).
25. *Allen* v. *Burke*, 29 Crim. L. Rep. 2297 (E.D. Va. 1981).

26. *Pugh* v. *Rainwater*, 572 F.2d 1053, 1057 (5th Cir. 1978) (en banc).

27. Id. at 1057-1058.

28. See Comment, "Challenging Bail Laws: Bellamy, Henson and Van Atta—Background and Strategy," 13 *U.C.D.L. Rev.* 300 (1980).

29. See note 24 supra.

30. Comment, "Challenging Bail Laws: Bellamy, Henson and Van Atta—Background and Strategy," 13 *U.C.D.L. Rev.* 300, 312 (1980).

31. Id. at 313.

32. *Robinson* v. *California*, 370 U.S. 660 (1962).

33. *Bell* v. *Wolfish*, 441 U.S. 520 (1980).

34. *People* v. *Seymour*, 80 Ill. App. 3d 221, 398 N.E.2d 1191 (1979).

16 Use in Other Countries

Many other countries have also recognized that arrest and detention until trial is not necessary in every case and that in many instances it is not the best way to initiate criminal proceedings against a suspect. In 1964 the laws of many of these countries were reviewed by the Commission on Human Rights of the United Nations. Recognizing that *arrest* and *detention* had different technical meanings in each country, the commission nonetheless found a great deal of similarity in the underlying concepts and considerable concern for maintaining alternatives to arrest or detention:

> Involving as they do a total deprivation of liberty, arrest and detention are properly regarded as serious measures and the codes of many countries reflect a desire to avoid their employment where this is reasonably possible. This may be shown by restrictions which the law has placed on the number of cases in which arrest is mandatory, and by provisions for the use of summons and other less drastic measures to ensure the availability of the suspect or accused for investigation or trial.[1]

The commission described the use of the promise to appear:

> In some countries, the accused may be released on his promise or whenever required to do so. Such release, however, is usually allowed in limited situations. For example, in one country [Mexico], release on recognizance (*bajo protesta*) is allowed, provided the following prerequisites are fulfilled: (a) the accused has fixed and known domicile at the place of the proceedings and has maintained residence therein for at least two years under common court procedure and one year under federal procedure; (b) the accused has a profession or occupation to secure him a decent way of living; (c) the offence is punishable with less than two years' imprisonment under federal procedure or less than six months' imprisonment under common court procedure; (d) that the accused is a first offender; (e) the court believes that there is no fear that the accused will attempt to escape or evade penal action; and (f) the accused declares under oath that he will appear in court whenever requested to do so. In certain other jurisdictions, such release is permitted whenever in view of the personal circumstances of the accused and the facts of the case a suspended sentence is likely to be imposed and his record is such that there is no reason to believe that he may attempt to frustrate the ends of justice, or if the authority ruling on the detention regards the written declaration of the accused to appear when summoned as sufficient, having regard to the character of such accused and the nature of the offence.[2]

The commission also described the use of the judicial summons as an alternative to arrest:

> The appearance of the suspect or accused before a judge or other competent authority conducting the preliminary investigation or trial may be secured through the use of a summons or order to appear. The issuance of a summons, instead of a warrant of arrest or other warrants involving the use of compulsion, may be discretionary upon the authority concerned. In some countries the appearance of the suspect before a court is generally secured by means of a summons rather than arrest.[3]

In other countries the summons is used less but nonetheless available:

> The issuance of a summons may be discretionary in less serious cases only, or in all or most cases. In many countries the use of a summons is mandatory in cases involving less serious offences unless the accused has absconded, or he has no fixed dwelling or known residence, or he is a recidivist, a fugitive from justice or accused of certain specified offences, or arrest is deemed essential to protect the safety of the injured party or prevent frustration of the investigation. For the purpose of determining what constitutes a less serious offence involving such mandatory use of the summons, the law may specify the maximum penalty involved, e.g., imprisonment for not more than three years, or 341 days, or thirty days.[4]

England

The police role in pretrial release is quite different in England than in the United States. Three English police practices greatly reduce the number of defendants held in custody:

1. Many minor offenders cannot be arrested at all. While statutes do allow arrests for many petty offenses, England has no general statute allowing arrest for all ordinance and misdemeanor violations. The general rule is therefore the same as at common law—no arrests for petty offenses and warrantless arrests for misdemeanors only for breach of the peace.[5]
2. Both felony and misdemeanor cases may be, and often are, started by summons instead of warrant.[6]
3. The police have statutory authority to release arrestees at the police station pending appearance in court.[7]

Police Release

The current English statute concerning the third of these practices, police release pending appearance in court, authorizes the police to grant bail either with or without security in cases that are not "serious." Granting bail with security is different from United States practice, because commercial bondsmen are illegal in England and the security must be provided by the defendant or his family and friends. Granting bail without security is roughly equivalent to a station-house release:

> On a person's being taken into custody for an offence without a warrant, a police officer not below the rank of inspector, or the police officer in charge of the police station . . . may, and, if it will not be practicable to bring him before a magistrates' court within twenty-four hours after his being taken into custody, shall, inquire into the case and, unless the offence appears to the officer to be a serious one, grant him bail [with or without security].[8]

Neither the statute nor the courts have defined what constitutes a "serious" case. In the early 1970s, however, most drug arrests appear to have been treated as serious cases.[9] A study by the British Home Office indicated that the police set bail in over 40 percent of the cases in 1969, as shown in table 16-1.[10]

Two American observers described the procedure at the station as follows:

> When the officer in charge decides the offense is not serious and release is indicated he will say to an accused person: "we are going to release you on your own recognizance of [blank] pounds to attend court—and if you fail to appear in court you will be liable to forfeit some or all of that [blank] pounds."[11]

Table 16-1
Bail by Police—England

	1966	1969
Bail on arrest	37.4	46.0
Custody on arrest	54.5	48.4
Not applicable[a]	7.8	4.8
Don't know	0.3	0.8
Total	100.0	100.0

Source: F. Simon and M. Weatheritt, *The Use of Bail and Custody By London Magistrates' Courts Before and After the Criminal Justice Act 1967*, at 64 (1974) (Home Office Research Studies No. 20). Reprinted with permission of the Controller of Her Britannic Majesty's Stationery Office.

[a]*Not applicable*-was recorded if the defendant had been arrested such a short time before his appearance in court that bail was not practicable.

Generally, according to these observers, the police verify the defendant's residence and set bail without sureties; this practice is similar to a station-house release. Only if the bail exceeds fifty pounds are sureties usually required.[12]

Although it does not deal specifically with the issue, the Home Office report tends to confirm these observations. It shows the percentage of all releases, both court and police, as to which sureties were required. For minor offenses—the kind most likely to be released by the police—sureties were required in less than 5 percent of the cases. For indictable offenses, however, where the release is probably made by the courts, sureties were required in 80 percent of the cases, as shown in table 16-2.

The failure-to-appear rate for defendants released by the courts appears to be generally low. One study showed a rate in 1969 in London of about 5 percent, if drunks are excluded.[13] The rate including drunks was much higher in inner London (9.6 percent) than outer London (1.4 percent).

Data maintained by the Metropolitan Police Department (London) also tend to show that the rate of re-arrest for crime while on release is also quite low.[14]

As in Connecticut, police authority to set bail has led to some tendency on the part of the police to use the promise of bail as an inducement to give a statement concerning the offense.[15] This practice does not seem to be limited to bail with sureties, however. One such case of bail bargaining reached the Court of Appeal. In this case the defendant asked a police officer, "If I make a statement will you give me bail now?" The police officer replied, "yes," and the defendant made a statement. Later, the defendant appealed his conviction, claiming that the statement was induced by the promise of bail. The Court of Appeal agreed that the offer to grant bail was an improper inducement and allowed the appeal.[16]

Table 16-2
Bailed Defendants Required to Obtain Sureties, 1969

	Percentage
Summary offenses	3
Summary or indictable	34
Summary or indictable tried summarily[a]	24
Summary or indictable committed for trial	37
Indictable only	80
Indictable only committed for trial	83

Source: F. Simon and M. Weatheritt, *The Use of Bail and Custody By London Magistrates' Courts Before and After the Criminal Justice Act 1967,* at 66 (1974) (Home Office Research Studies No. 20). Reprinted with permission of the Controller of Her Britannic Majesty's Stationery Office.

[a]Preconviction only.

Summons

As previously mentioned, English courts have long had the authority to begin criminal cases by use of the summons instead of arrest with or without warrant. Much of the initiative, however, as to whether to use this procedure lies with the police.

Two observers reported in 1964 that:

> In metropolitan areas the summons is seldom used in police prosecutions in cases other than minor traffic offenses. Occasionally an exception is made when an offense such as minor assault or petty larceny comes to light—considerably after the crime is alleged to have been committed. . . . Apart from traffic offenses and a few violations of the administrative code metropolitan police are directed to arrest whenever they have the power to do so. It is our understanding that the summons is used more extensively in rural areas for two reasons: courts do not sit continuously and the accused is generally quite familiar to the police.[17]

The report of the metropolitan police commissioner for 1968, for example, indicates that in London serious offenders are generally arrested rather than brought to court by judicial summons.[18] Court statistics for the country as a whole, however, indicate much greater use. In 1971, for example, about a quarter of all persons proceeded against for indictable offenses and nearly 60 percent of those proceeded against for all other nontraffic offenses were summoned to court rather than arrested. These figures include over three-fourths of all drunk-driving charges and, as shown in table 16-3, charges for many relatively serious offenses.

Table 16-3
Use of Judicial Summons and Arrest—Adult Males Proceeded against in England and Wales, 1971

	Arrest	*Summons*	*Total*
Murder	216	0	216
Wounding or other act endangering life	1,228	56	1,284
Other wounding	11,088	4,400	15,488
Indecent assault	1,483	809	2,292
Burglary of dwelling	6,914	314	7,228
Burglary of other building	15,472	932	16,404
Robbery	1,532	21	1,553
Shoplifting	12,164	2,282	14,446
Auto theft	7,610	1,628	9,238

Source: Great Britain, Home Department, Statistical Branch, *Criminal Statistics, England and Wales, 1971,* at 22–26.

The Home Office stopped collecting these statistics in 1973, indicating in its commentary that the figures shown in past years were "probably inaccurate."[19] A 1981 study for the Royal Commission on Criminal Procedure, however, indicated that the summons was used to begin 87 percent of all nonindictable and 24 percent of all indictable cases.[20]

Citation to the Police Station

A wholly separate facet of British police practice that is quite different from any that exists in the United States is that the British police also have statutory authority to release defendants on condition that they return to the police station. This enables the station authorities to even out their work load to some extent and to look further into cases in which detention is not necessary but for which they have not yet decided whether a charge is necessary. The statute provides that:

> Where, on a person's being taken into custody for an offence without a warrant, it appears to any such officer . . . that the inquiry into the case cannot be completed forthwith, he may grant him bail . . . subject to a duty to appear at such a police station and at such a time as the officer appoints unless he previously receives a notice in writing . . . that his attendance is not required. . . .[21]

Until recently the criminal-justice literature in England has if anything given even less attention to the police decision to arrest, release or detain than the literature in the United States. The 1981 report of the Royal Commission on Criminal Procedure and the research undertaken for the commission is a conspicuous exception to this situation, providing a wealth of valuable information.[22]

The commission has also proposed major changes in the English law of arrest. Under these proposals police authority to arrest would be extended to all offenses punishable with imprisonment. At the same time, however, all powers to arrest would be restricted by a "necessity principle," which would allow a defendant who had been delivered to the police station to be detained only if the station officer finds and records one of the following:

> The defendant is unwilling to identify himself so that a summons may be served upon him.
>
> A need to detain to prevent continuation or repetition of the offense.
>
> A need to detain to protect the arrested person or other persons or property.
>
> A need to detain to secure, preserve, or obtain by questioning evidence of the offense.

A likelihood that the defendant will fail to appear in court.[23]

These proposals are similar in some respects to those made in the United States by the Uniform Commissioners on State Laws. If adopted, the mechanisms for arrest would change but English police would continue to release before trial many more defendants than their American counterparts.

Canada

Concerned about the large number of defendants held in custody prior to trial, Canada adopted a major revision of its laws concerning pretrial release in 1971.[24] Like the Uniform Rules of Criminal Procedure, the new law operates in part by limiting the situations in which a physical arrest may be made.

Three kinds of offenses are covered by these new limitations: minor offenses that are punishable by summary conviction; offenses that may be prosecuted either summarily or by indictment; and some indictable offenses, including thefts under $200, obstructing a police officer, keeping a common gaming house, bookmaking, and keeping a common bawdy house.[25]

For these offenses the officer may make a physical arrest without a warrant only if he first determines that the "public interest" cannot be satisfied without an arrest. Among the factors to be taken into account in making this determination are the need to establish the identity of the person, the need to secure evidence of the offense, the need to prevent continuation of the offense or the commission of another offense, and whether the accused "will fail to attend in court."

The police officer is authorized to issue an "appearance notice" (citation) for these offenses or, if he so chooses, to seek a judicial summons. For the indictable offenses included he may, and normally does, require the accused to appear to be photographed and fingerprinted. If the officer arrests a suspect, the law requires that he consider release as soon as possible.

If the suspect is brought into the jail, the officer in charge must release the accused as soon as possible unless he finds detention necessary for identification, the preservation of evidence, the prevention or continuation of the offense, or to ensure appearance in court. The officer in charge may make the release by issuing a station-house citation ("promise to appear"), seeking a judicial summons, or setting bail not to exceed $500.[26]

The officer in charge is also expected to use these procedures for dealing with two additional groups of suspects: those who have been arrested for offenses punishable by less than five years imprisonment and those arrested under warrants that have been endorsed by the magistrate.

The general way in which the law is expected to work was described by John Turner, the minister of justice and attorney general of Canada, to a meeting of the Canadian Association of Chiefs of Police in 1970, just before the law was adopted:

> The Bail Reform Bill imposes a duty on the police NOT TO ARREST without a warrant in those circumstances where he has reasonable and probable grounds to believe that the public interest may be secured by some other means. However, even though there is a responsibility upon an officer to consider the other means of procuring an accused's attendance at trial, if he reasonably believes that no other course of action will secure the public interest, he is at liberty to place a suspect under arrest. Arresting a suspect will continue to be a perfectly justifiable course of action provided the officer has directed his mind to the alternatives available to him. There is no intent in the Bill to . . . dissuade police forces from effective law enforcement.[27]

The effect of the act appears to have been substantial. A survey by Statistics Canada indicated that approximately one-third of all defendants coming to court in 1973 had been given appearance notices rather than arrested.[28] Other forms of release or alternatives to arrest, including stationhouse promises to appear and judicial summonses, were also widely used. Overall, only 17 percent of all defendants came to court in custody.

As might be expected, the use of appearance notices and promises to appear has been more frequent for minor offenses than for more serious offenses. Nevertheless, there is considerable use of police release for criminal-code offenses as well as for municipal and provincial statutory offenses. The Statistics Canada survey indicated that only 26 percent of those charged with criminal-code offenses came to court in police custody. A study in the Ottawa-Carleton area indicated that 11 percent of defendants charged with criminal-code offenses in 1974 were given appearance notices, 19 percent station-house promises to appear, and 21 percent judicial summonses.[29]

According to the Statistics Canada survey implementation of the act has varied considerably by province. The use of appearance notices, for example, ranged from 67 percent of all defendants in Saskatchewan to 12 percent in Quebec.[30]

The information available indicates that failure-to-appear rates are generally similar to or lower than those in U.S. departments. The Statistics Canada survey showed a failure-to-appear rate for all forms of release of 6.3 percent. In the Ottawa-Carleton area the failure-to-appear rate for appearance notices was 3.5 percent, and that for station-house promises to appear, 7.3 percent.[31]

The 1971 law was controversial and was amended in a number of important ways in 1975.[32] The police were among the more important critics of the act, but were more concerned about the approach it specified for the courts than any problems related to the police. The amendments to the act consequently did not appreciably alter the police-release provisions.[33]

The appearance notice appears to have been particularly well accepted by the police. A mail survey of ninety-two line police officers in metropolitan Toronto in 1974 indicated that over 90 percent were quite satisfied or moderately satisfied with the use of the appearance notice for minor offenses.[34] Over three-fourths were quite satisfied or moderately satisfied with all the expanded police powers or release under the act, and over 60 percent thought the police should be required or should probably be required to justify detention in all cases.

About 40 percent of the officers indicated that the act had led them to take a more liberal personal attitude toward release, but 14 percent said the act had led them to take a more conservative personal attitude. Nearly 80 percent found the act clear and the statutory criteria generally adequate.

The Canadian act contains one important feature not found in the U.S. statutes: it provides that a peace officer who makes an arrest when he should have issued an appearance notice or taken some other release action is "deemed to be acting lawfully."[35] This feature is designed to prevent civil suits against officers except in situations in which they did not have reasonable cause to take any action.[36] That this is a concern of police officers is illustrated by the fact that about a third of the Toronto officers indicated that, when deciding whether to release a defendant under the act, they sometimes consider whether they might be sued.[37]

The Canadian courts have been somewhat grudging in their treatment of the appearance notice, requiring that it be confirmed by the magistrate before the defendant can be held responsible for failing to appear in court. This attitude seems something like a throwback to the earlier attitudes that viewed the citation procedure as a judicial process.[38]

Denmark

Another system that operates quite differently from that in general use in the United States is that of Denmark. Although the laws of arrest and detention in Denmark are not greatly different from those in the United States, the administrative practice is quite different. Perhaps the most important difference is the extensive use by the Danish police of the judicial summons to originate criminal cases. According to observations made by Bernard Botein and Herbert Sturz for the National Conference on Bail and Criminal Justice:

> Danish authorities estimate that about two-thirds of all prosecutions originate with a summons. In these cases, it is not uncommon for a person

to be charged, to be indicted, to stand trial, and, if found guilty, to await sentencing, all while at liberty. It may happen that a person will run the gamut of these procedures and then be sentenced to prison. Charges such as simple theft, burglary, embezzlement, simple assault, and forgery may originate with the summons. The summons may be by telephone or letter. Generally first offenders will not be seized or spend any time in custody prior to trial unless charged with a very serious crime. Danish authorities feel that seizure is "very upsetting" to persons accused of a crime for the first time. The Danes are concerned with keeping the accused person's record free from the stigma of arrest, as well as giving him an opportunity to keep his job and life intact.[39]

The Danish police also have long had authority to release defendants arrested on any charge. According to Botein and Sturz:

In 1961, 6,600 persons were seized by the police; of these 5,000 were released—generally covering those charged with misdemeanors—within 24 hours. If the police detain a person, it is rare for the court, composed of one career judge, to release him at the detention hearing.[40]

More recent statistics indicate that in 1975, 68,876 persons were arrested throughout Denmark and 60,561 were released within twenty-four hours. In Copenhagen there were 26,123 arrests and 24,381 releases within this time period.[41]

One area in which the Danish law does differ from that of the United States concerns police investigation. In Denmark the police have what amounts to the power of subpoena. They may order any citizen to come to the police station to explain any situation in which the person is suspected of a crime.[42] The person brought in for questioning in this way is not required to give answers to police questions, may bring an attorney, and may be detained for no longer than six hours. Whether there is any relationship between the existence of this authority and the ability of the Danish police to institute so many proceedings without detention is unclear. The existence of this kind of authority does, however, clearly eliminate the need for any detention based on the need for further questioning of a suspect, and it is likely that it has at least some impact on the overall use of arrest and detention by the police.

Notes

1. United Nations, *Study of the Right of Everyone to Be Free from Arbitrary Arrest, Detention and Exile* 59-60 (1964). Reprinted with permission.
2. Id. at 68.
3. Id. at 59.

4. Id. at 59.

5. See L. Leigh, *Police Powers in England and Wales* 60-103 (1975).

6. Id. at 73-75. See also Indictable Offenses Act of 1848, 11 & 12 Vict. c. 42, §1.

7. This authority has existed since 1879. Summary Jurisdiction Act, 1879, 42 & 43 Vict., c. 49, §38.

8. Magistrates' Courts Act, 1952, 15 & 16 Geo. 6 & 1 Eliz. 2, c. 55, §38(1), as amended Bail Act, 1976, c. 63.

9. M. King, *Bail or Custody* 5-7 (1973). See also L. Leigh, *Police Powers in England and Wales* 56-59 (1975).

10. Lower figures are estimated in at least one other study. See L. Leigh, *Police Powers in England and Wales* 22-23 (1975).

11. B. Botein and H. Sturz, "Pre-trial Release Practices in Sweden, Denmark, England, and Italy," in *National Conference on Bail and Criminal Justice, Proceedings and Interim Report* 319, 342 (April 1965).

12. Id.

13. F. Simon and M. Weatheritt, *The Use of Bail and Custody By London Magistrates' Courts Before and After the Criminal Justice Act 1967,* at 31-32 (1974) (Home Office Research Studies No. 20).

14. United Kingdom Home Office Working Party, *Bail Procedures in Magistrates' Courts* 11-12 (1974).

15. M. King, *Bail or Custody* 6-7 (1973).

16. *Regina* v. *Zaveckas,* [1970] W.L.R. 516 (C.A.).

17. B. Botein and H. Sturz, "Pre-trial Release Practices in Sweden, Denmark, England and Italy," in *National Conference on Bail and Criminal Justice, Proceedings and Interim Report* 319, 344-345 (April 1965). See also M. Friedland, *Detention Before Trial* 9-44 (1965).

18. Commissioner of Police of the Metropolis (London), *Report, 1968,* at 59 (Cmnd. 4060).

19. *Criminal Statistics, England and Wales 1973,* at 7 (1974) (Cmnd. 5677).

20. Royal Commission on Criminal Procedure, *Arrest, Charge and Summons, Research Study No. 9,* App. A (1981). This is discussed in Lidstone, "Investigative Powers and the Rights of the Citizen," 1981 *Crim. L. Rev.* 454, 461.

21. Magistrates' Courts Act, 1952, 15 & 16 Geo. 6 & 1 Eliz. 2, c. 55, §38(2), as amended Bail Act, 1976, c. 63.

22. Royal Commission on Criminal Procedure, *Report* (1981) (Cmnd. 8092).

23. "Royal Commission on Criminal Procedure," 1981 *Crim. L. Rev.* 441, 442.

24. See generally C. Powell, *Arrest and Bail in Canada* 1-20 (1972).

25. Can. Rev. Stat., c. C-34, §3 450-452 (1970 and 2d Supp.).

26. Can. Rev. Stat., c. C-34, §§453-453.1 (1970 and 2d Supp.).

27. C. Powell, *Arrest and Bail in Canada* 3 (1972). Reprinted with permission of Butterworth's, Toronto.

28. Coordinated Law Enforcement Unit, British Columbia Attorney General, "Bail Reform Act Report" 64-68 (Oct. 1975).

29. G. Ferguson and F. Bobiasz, "A Study of the Bail Reform Act in the Ottawa-Carleton Region" 74 (1974).

30. Coordinated Law Enforcement Unit, British Columbia Attorney General, "Bail Reform Act Report" 64-68 (Oct. 1975).

31. G. Ferguson and F. Bobiasz, "A Study of the Bail Reform Act in the Ottawa-Carleton Region" 74 (1974).

32. See C. Powell, *Arrest and Bail in Canada* 1-2 (2d ed. 1976).

33. See, for example, Coordinated Law Enforcement Unit, British Columbia Attorney General, "Bail Reform Act Report" 3-8, 28-35 (Oct. 1975). See also Criminal Law Amendment Act, 1975, 1974-75-76 Can. Stat., c. 93.

34. Koza and Doob, "Police Attitudes toward the Bail Reform Act," 19 *Crim. L.Q.* 405 (1977).

35. Can. Rev. Stat. c. C-34, §§450(3), 452(3), 453(3).

36. See J. Scollin, *Pre-trial Release* 23-24 (1977).

37. Koza and Doob, "Police Attitudes Toward the Bail Reform Act," 19 *Crim. L.Q.* 405 (1977).

38. See James, "Appearance Notices and Confirmation Thereof," 22 *Crim. L.Q. 344 (1979-1980).*

39. B. Botein and H. Sturz, "Pretrial Release Practices in Sweden, Denmark, England, and Italy," in *National Conference on Bail and Criminal Justice* 319, 331 (April 1965).

40. Id. at 332.

41. *Poliets Arsberetning 1975* (Police Yearbook), at 73-74, 81-83 (1976).

42. *Bekendtgorelse af lov om rettens pleje 1975* (Text of Law on Administration of Justice), §807.

17 The Need for More Research and Statistics

Although it is clear that citations fill an important need, much more must be known before they reach their full potential.

Research

Much more needs to be known about the failure-to-appear problem, for example. In a number of jurisdictions failure-to-appear rates have risen sharply as the number of citations issued has increased. Normally the rate has stabilized somewhere between 15 and 20 percent, near the rate of nonappearance for traffic citations.

There has been almost no research into this problem, however. The little information available suggests that many of the people involved eventually appear voluntarily and were simply confused or lost. Is this information correct? Assuming that many defendants who initially fail to appear are in this category, would they respond in a more timely fashion if given clearer instructions at the time the citation is issued? Would more written information on the citation itself be helpful? If so, what kind of information? Does the form of the citation matter? Should a telephone number or an address be given so that defendants with emergencies could notify the court in advance of their problem and reschedule their appearance? Would this serve to reduce the no-show problem or to encourage dilatoriness?

What about those who are not simply lost or confused; who are they? What consequences do they now suffer when they finally do appear or are identified to the court? Some information suggests that they appear primarily because they are picked up on traffic stops or when arrested for some other crime. They seem almost never to be prosecuted or to suffer any penalty whatever for their flouting of the appearance requirement. Do those who fail to appear assume that there is no penalty for doing so, or do they believe that they will be penalized and simply fail to show up anyway? Are they repeaters who have failed to appear previously?

Would active prosecution make any difference with respect to these defendants? Suppose, for example, that there was a mandatory $100 fine or five days in jail for anyone who failed to appear without having rescheduled his appearance in advance. It might be assumed that really stiff mandatory penalties would have no greater impact here than in other areas of the law where they have been tried without conspicuous success.[1] But what about a relatively light, but nonetheless clearly labeled penalty defined in such a way that it would be easy to prove, perhaps even created as a strict-liability crime for which there is no defense?

Given the much larger number of citations issued and a failure-to-appear rate of 15 to 20 percent, it might be thought that many of these questions would already have been answered with respect to the traffic citation and that, while the answers might not be fully applicable to the misdemeanor citation, some analogies could be drawn. Despite 30 million traffic citations a year and perhaps 6 million nonappearances, however, there is even less information available about the traffic citation than about the misdemeanor citation.[2] Although some information exists about failure-to-appear rates, there is virtually none as to who fails to show, why, and whether some procedures are better than others in ensuring appearance in court. What little information there is is tantalizing, though, and suggests the enormous potential for further research. Administrative adjudication appears to have reduced the rate of nonappearance in New York from 50 to 25 percent.[3] It is not clear, however, why this occurred, whether the effect elsewhere has been similar, or whether the process has been carried to its logical conclusion. An apparently tremendous technological breakthrough has clearly not been exploited. Nor has there been any research into the enormous disparity between the New York rates and those in some other states that show only 10 percent failures to appear.[4]

It might also be supposed that some of the questions would have been answered in the context of the warrant process. Millions of dollars have been spent in recent years developing automated warrant systems to increase the capacity of the police and others to apprehend persons for whom a warrant, often a traffic or parking warrant, has been issued.[5] Almost no systematic information is available, however, as to the effects of present police procedures in many jurisdictions that leave enforcement on minor warrants up to traffic stops and arrests for other offenses. In some ways the decision not to pursue minor offenders but to assume that they will eventually be caught through this process is a highly rational choice and a wise allocation of scarce manpower. There would be more confidence about the wisdom of the decision, however, if more were known about the effects of such a policy on the persons for whom the warrants were issued. Is this a case in which a little enforcement would induce a lot of compliance, or would more enforcement simply go unnoticed like a rock thrown into the ocean?

There is also considerable uncertainty about the need for detaining persons arrested with a warrant and probationers and parolees who are arrested for minor offenses. In many jurisdictions all three groups are automatically incarcerated, even for minor offenses. Although physical arrest is clearly needed in some warrant situations, in many situations a citation or summons would work just as well. The major concern in the case of probationers and parolees is the possibility of revocation. It is not clear, however, how often revocations occur for minor offenses, and there has been virtually no study of the costs and benefits of present policies.

What is needed is some ongoing research into these problems. Many of the most obvious questions could be answered through a series of inexpensive and easy-to-conduct experiments. Some of the questions are clearly more difficult and perhaps even unanswerable. Even as to these, however, better guesses could be made if more information were available.

Many other serious questions about the citation process could be answered through relatively simple empirical inquiries. How often does the field-citation process let someone wanted for a serious crime slip through?[6] Are methods available for field or station-house release that could be used to provide positive identification? Could full fingerprints, for example, be taken more often in the field? Do voiceprints hold a hope for remote identification checks for the future? Is there a difference in failure to appear between the field-citation cases and the jail or station releases? What is the appearance rate for persons from outside the immediate community? Are there mechanisms, such as required telephone contacts, that would reduce the failure-to-appear rate, and, if so, what are the best ways to organize and administer these mechanisms?

The use of citations also raises some broader system issues. Do speedy releases increase court delay, and if so, by how much and can this easily be reduced? How much crime is committed by offenders on citation release? Because use of the citation is easier than arrest, do police bring people into the system whom they would have released previously? (Of the departments contacted in the 1976 study survey, 60 percent said that this never happened or happened only rarely, 32 percent said that citations sometimes had this effect, and 4 percent said that this often happened. The data are very soft, however, and changes are possible in any event as the citation procedure becomes more extensive.)[7]

Another issue of great possible importance is the extent to which the citation procedure could be combined with a bail-forfeiture system, such as that used for traffic and parking offenses, as a method for disposing of minor criminal matters. The merits and demerits of such a combination are totally unexplored in the literature, despite the obvious attractiveness of such a procedure for saving court time and cost.

Statistics

One reason so little is known about the use of the citation procedure is that so little statistical information is available. Careful data was maintained by the Manhattan Summons Project and a number of other experimental programs, such as those in Oakland, California, New Haven, Connecticut, and Cincinnati, Ohio.[8] Some of these departments and some other cities have continued to collect data, but most communities have virtually no information available on a regular basis, either as to the total number of citations issued or as to the particular offenses for which citations were issued. A few special studies, such as those made in Contra Costa County, add some information to this general picture but are not adequate to provide the kind of consistent, ongoing information needed.[9]

In 1969 the Uniform Crime Reports attempted to fill this gap with a new reporting format that distinguished between persons charged through the use of a summons and those charged on the basis of a physical arrest. The format chosen, however, did not distinguish between defendants summoned by order of a court and those cited or summoned by the police on their own authority.[10] It is therefore not possible to tell how many cases are based on police citations and how many are based on court action.

In addition, relatively few departments supplied the new information. The number of agencies participating was low at the beginning and did not increase, and the percent of the population covered decreased, as shown in table 17-1. As a result of these and other problems this information was dropped from the reporting format in 1978.

Because of the state's early involvement and interest in citations, the California Bureau of Criminal Statistics in 1969 developed a reporting format aimed at developing reliable statistical information on the use of citations. This information has been supplied for over ten years but has never been published. The information also contains a serious definitional problem. Unlike the Uniform Crime Reports it does not combine police

Table 17-1
Uniform Crime Reports—Persons Summoned

Year	Agencies Reporting	Population Served	Total Arrestees Summoned
1969	1,284	29,838,000	11.7%
1970	1,223	31,200,000	13.1
1971	1,056	24,956,000	15.1
1972	1,094	17,911,000	20.1
1973	1,284	22,151,000	15.4
1974	1,170	18,696,000	20.2
1975	1,330	17,474,000	22.0
1976	1,544	18,366,000	29.8
1977	1,380	17,979,000	30.1

Source: *Crime in the United States,* 1969, p. 103; 1970, p. 115; 1971, p. 111; 1972, p. 114; 1973, p. 117; 1974, p. 175; 1975, p. 175; 1976, p. 218; 1977, p. 217.

and court-ordered summonses in the same category. It does, however, attempt to distinguish between arrests and citations. The instructions issued are clear enough for cases in which the defendant is given a field citation or in which the defendant is arrested and never released. The first is clearly a citation, and the second clearly an arrest. The instructions are hopelessly ambiguous, however, as to whether a defendant who is booked and then released should be classified as an arrest or a citation. Discussions with staff in a number of departments indicated that some classify this kind of case as an arrest and others classify it as a citation.

This information and that which the Uniform Crime Reports attempted to collect is important, and if compiled in a clear fashion could add greatly to our knowledge about the extent of citation use and the kinds of problems that need to be solved. As the citation procedure becomes more important, the need for reliable data will grow as well.

Notes

1. Harsh mandatory penalties generally do not work because prosecutors are reluctant to charge them and judges reluctant to impose the sentences required.

2. The number of citations is estimated from California filings (3,612,500 in 1973-74). See Cal. Department of Motor Vehicles, "Administrative Adjudication of Traffic Offenses in California" 127 n. 82 (April 1976). Nonappearances are also estimated. See, for example, A. Halper and J. McDonnell, *New York State Department of Motor Vehicles Administrative Adjudication Bureau* 55 (1975) (U.S. Dept. of Justice).

3. Halper and McDonnell, note 2 supra, at 55.

4. Cal. Department of Motor Vehicles, "Administrative Adjudication of Traffic Offenses in California" (April 1976), estimated a failure-to-appear rate of 11.6 percent for 1973-74 for California. A 1969 study indicated a failure-to-appear rate of only 4 percent. Research and Statistics Section, Cal. Department of Motor Vehicles, "Conviction Rate for a Sample of Citations Issued by the California Highway Patrol" (December 1969) (unpublished study). No definition of failure to appear is given in any of these studies, however, and it is difficult to know whether there is a true difference.

5. See, for example, California State Sheriff's Association, "Statewide Warrant Processing and Service System Study" (1974).

6. One government report suggests that many fugitives and serious criminals use falsified identification information to escape apprehension. The report recommends that the identity of persons arrested be verified prior to their release. To meet this requirement without endangering the

rights of arrestees the report recommends use of high-speed equipment to transmit fingerprints and other identifying data between local and federal agencies. Federal Advisory Committee on False Identification, United States Department of Justice, *The Criminal Use of False Identification* xxi-xxii, 35-36 (1976). The report does not contain significant information about the extent of the problems involved or how much, if any, the remedies proposed would assist in its solution.

Some methods currently in use for checking identities and problems associated with these methods are discussed in J. Murphy, *Arrest by Police Computer* (1975).

7. Comment, "An Analysis of the Citation System in Evanston, Illinois: Its Value, Constitutionality and Viability," 65 *J. Crim. Law and Criminology* 75, 84 (1974).

8. All of these programs were initially assisted with external grants either from foundations or LEAA.

9. See Feeney, "Citation in Lieu of Arrest: The New California Law," 25 *Vand. L. J.* 367 (1972).

10. The UCR instructions established two categories: persons "arrested" and persons "summoned, notified, or cited." (Form 12-92). Persons "arrested" included "persons arrested by police for violations that happen in the reporting jurisdiction and turned over to the courts for prosecution." Persons "summoned" included "persons served with court summonses or police notices, citations and the like, excluding traffic violation notices. All summonses, whether served by the police or not, are included." FBI, *Uniform Crime Reporting Handbook* 77 (Jan. 1976).

18 Findings and Recommendations

The following are the most important findings of this analysis.

Over three-fourths of the nation's police agencies are now using some form of the citation procedure for misdemeanors, regulatory violations, or both.

Over half the agencies using some form of the citation procedure use both the field and the station-house citation.

Most departments now using these procedures are satisfied with them and are not having any serious problems in their use.

In particular, most departments report no serious problems with defendants failing to appear. A few departments, however, are having problems of this kind, and, where careful procedures are not followed, failure-to-appear rates may go to 20 percent or higher.

Use of the procedures is growing rapidly.

Most departments find that the procedures save forty to sixty minutes per arrest.

One-third or more of the 7 million misdemeanor offenders arrested annually are already being released on some form of police citation.

Within five to ten years this use is likely to increase to 75 percent of all misdemeanor arrests.

Citations are replacing bail and release on own recognizance as the primary method of pretrial release for misdemeanor crimes in many jurisdictions. The procedure is also being used by some jurisdictions as a way of relieving overcrowded jails and of complying with court orders concerning jail conditions.

Thirty-eight states now have statutes or court rules that authorize the use of citations, and citations are used to some extent in at least forty-five of the fifty states.

Statutes or court rules in eight states mandate the use of citations to some extent.

191

There is a growing trend toward more mandatory legislation and a strong possibility that arrest laws will eventually prohibit the physical detention beyond booking of minor offenders without specific justification.

Although experience is limited and more research is needed concerning the effects of mandatory legislation, agencies in jurisdictions with such provisions do not appear to be encountering any significant problems.

The long-range historical trend is clearly toward less use of arrest as a means of starting cases.

While once frequent, arrest is rarely used today for civil cases or for detaining witnesses.

Despite this trend, however, there is more use of arrest for very minor offenses today than there was 200 years ago. This suggests a particular need for considering use of the citation for these offenses.

Five states now permit use of citations for felony cases.

There is no evidence at this point to indicate that, because the citation procedures are easier than making an arrest, they are being used to bring additional defendants into court.

Legal rules often preclude the use of police release on a promise to appear in warrant cases.

Based on these findings and on those of other study groups this study has six major recommendations:

1. Each police agency, large or small, which does not now use citations, should immediately begin to do so. The practice has proved effective under almost every conceivable circumstance, and there is no reason to believe that it will not work in the agencies not now using it.
2. Each police agency now using the procedures should review its policies to determine whether it is making maximum effective use of citations. In particular, agencies should review the list of excluded offenses to determine if the exclusions in force are necessary. As a general rule, if an agency is releasing less than 50 percent of its misdemeanor arrestees under some form of police citation, its use is low.
3. Police agencies should begin to experiment with use of the citation for minor felonies. Fifty percent or more of the defendants in these cases are ultimately released on bail or OR, and many could be released as easily and as safely by the police as by the courts.

4. Jurisdictions with release-on-own-recognizance programs for misdemeanor defendants should encourage the use of police citations as the primary method of pretrial release, leaving the OR program free to concentrate on felony cases and other cases in which more extensive pretrial-release services are necessary.

5. Each state that does not now have a statute or court rule mandating use of the procedures should promptly adopt such a statute or court rule.

6. States that do have statutes or court rules authorizing use of the procedures should assess the desirability of more mandatory legislation or rules.

The study also recommends that:

Agencies beginning use of citations should be careful to provide adequate training and familiarity to officers in the department before implementing the procedure.

All agencies should have written policies governing the use of citations.

The citation form itself should be simple and should clearly indicate where the defendant is to appear.

In warrant cases involving misdemeanors police should be given statutory authority to release defendants on a promise to appear.

Agencies should keep track of failure-to-appear cases and make changes in procedures as necessary to ensure high rates of appearance.

More innovation and research is necessary to improve procedures and eliminate problems.

Failure to appear should be taken seriously—prosecutors should charge failures to appear, and judges should impose separate, short sentences or fines as penalties.

19 Some Concluding Thoughts

The citation proved its usefulness for traffic offenses years ago. Today it has also clearly proved its usefulness for criminal offenses—both from the point of view of defendants charged with crimes and from that of the agencies entrusted with administering the criminal justice system. Used properly it adds a considerable measure of efficiency and fairness to a criminal justice system that has all too often lacked both these highly necessary qualities.

Endorsed by every major commission and group that has studied the criminal justice system in the past two decades, the use of citations for criminal offenses is already substantial and is growing. Many jurisdictions have not yet adopted the citation for criminal offenses, however, and many others still make only minor use of the procedure. Thus much remains to be done.

Police administrators in particular need to examine practices in their jurisdictions to determine whether they are making maximum use of the procedure. Does the agency have a workable set of guidelines? Do these guidelines clearly indicate when citation use is mandatory and when it is discretionary? Do these guidelines exclude offenses that could be handled by citations? Are the exclusions clearly necessary or justifiable? Does the department regularly monitor the number of citations issued and the results of these citations? Do all officers in the agency use citations when they should and refrain from using citations when they should not? Does the agency use both field and jail citations? Does the citation form clearly indicate what the defendant is expected to do?

Judges, prosecutors, and others concerned with criminal justice also need to examine their actions. Can they do anything to further the process? Have they encouraged it as far as possible? Are they complying with any rules for requiring booking or criminal identification? Do prosecutors regularly charge defendants with failure to appear when they are apprehended, or do they take the easier course and charge only the principal offense? If convicted, do judges sentence on the failure-to-appear charge, or do they simply deal with the principal charge?

Legislators also have a continuing role. Much of the progress thus far has been made because legislators have been interested in the problem and have created incentives and authorization for the use of citations. This process is not complete, however, and nearly one-third of the states still do

195

not have rudimentary legislation authorizing the use of citations. Even in those states which have legislation governing citations, there is room for further study and improvement. The area has thus far been very active and fertile, and legislatures should continue the work that they have so well begun.

State planning agencies and research staffs also have major tasks. Because the early work of the Vera Institute was one of the prime generators of the whole movement toward the use of citations and clearly demonstrated the payoff of research and study in this area, even minimal thought would seem to have dictated the need for further research and demonstration projects. This has not occurred, however, and much more research is now needed to gain the maximum benefits that the procedure can bestow. The failure-to-appear problem must be tackled and won, and there are a great many details of technique which can be improved far beyond the horse-and-buggy stages of today.

As the use of the citation grows in the years ahead, the citation will ultimately become the rule rather than the exception as the method for charging minor crimes. This is already nearly the case in Minnesota, and by some accounts at least is the case in Denmark.

Citations, probably of the jail-release variety, are also likely to come into much greater use for felony crimes. No doubt this will take longer, but the logic of the procedure is compelling for many felonies and will eventually prevail.

The atom that once compelled the police to take a defendant into physical custody whenever they wanted to accuse him of a crime has been split. From here on the trend will be toward requiring a separate justification for each action. The decision to accuse will continue to require probable cause to believe that a crime has been committed and that this is the person who did it. The decision to take into physical custody will require justification in the first instance, and the decision to continue to detain past the booking process will require a separate justification.

How soon the procedure reaches its full potential depends in large part on the extent to which the police are willing to examine seriously their current practices and procedures and to ask realistically in each case whether custody serves any useful purpose.

Appendix A:
Statutes and Court Rules Relating to Nontraffic Citations

Alaska Rules of Criminal Procedure Rule 4 (a)(2) (1975)

Arizona Revised Statutes, §13-3903 (1978)

Arkansas Rules of Criminal Procedure Rule 5.2 (1977)

California Penal Code §853.6 (West Cum. Supp. 1980)

Colorado Revised Statutes §16-3-105(b)&(c) (1978)

Connecticut General Statutes Annotated §54-63c (West Cum. Supp. 1980)

Delaware Code tit.11, §§1907-1908 (1979)

District of Columbia Code §23-1110 (1973)

Florida Rules of Criminal Procedure Rule 3.125 (West Cum. Supp. 1981)
(See also Florida Statutes Annotated §§901.28-901.30.)

Hawaii Revised Statutes §803-6 (1976 and Supp. 1980)

Illinois Annotated Statutes ch. 38, §107-12 (Smith-Hurd 1980)

Indiana Code §35-1-17-7 (Burns Cum. Supp. 1980) (infractions only)

Iowa Code Annotated §§804.1, 805.1-805.5 (West 1979)

Kansas Statutes §22-2408 (Cum. Supp. 1980)

Kentucky Revised Statutes §431.015 (Cum. Supp. 1980)

Louisiana Code of Criminal Procedure art. 208 (West 1967)

Maine Revised Statutes tit. 14, §5544 (West Cum. Supp. 1980)

Michigan Statutes Annotated §§28.868 (1)-(7) (1978)

Minnesota Rules of Criminal Procedure Rule 6.01 (1981)

Montana Revised Codes Annotated §95-614 (1969)

Nebraska Revised Statutes §§29-422 through 29-435 (1979)

Nevada Revised Statutes §§171.177 through 171.1779 (1975)

New Hampshire Revised Statutes Annotated §594:14 (1975)

New Jersey Rules Governing Criminal Practice Rules 3.3-1 and 3.4-1 (1981)

New Mexico Statutes Annotated §31-1-6 (1978)

New York Criminal Procedure Law §§140.20, 140.27, 150.10-15.75 160.10-160.40 (McKinney 1971 and Cum. Supp. 1980)

North Carolina General Statutes §15A-302 (1978)

Ohio Revised Code Annotated §2935.10 (Page 1975) and Rules of Criminal Procedure Rules 4(F) and 4.1 (1980)

Oklahoma Statutes Annotated tit. 22, §209 (West 1969)

Oregon Revised Statutes §§133.045-133.100 (1979)

Pennsylvania Rules of Criminal Procedure Rules 51 through 56 (1980) (summary offenses only)

Rhode Island General Laws §§12-7-11 through 12-7-12 (1970 and Cum. Supp. 1980)

Tennessee Rules of Criminal Procedure Rule 3.5 (Supp. 1980)

Utah Code Annotated, Code of Criminal Procedure §§77-7-18 through 77-7-22 (Special Supp. 1980)

Vermont Rules of Criminal Procedure Rule 3 (1974)

Virginia Code §§19.2-74 and 19.2-74.1 (Cum. Supp. 1980)

Washington Justice Court Criminal Rules Rule 2.01 (1980)

Wisconsin Statutes Annotated §66.119 (West Cum. Supp. 1981) (ordinance violations only)

Appendix B: Guidelines for Initiating a Citation Procedure

Virtually all the information in this volume is intended to be of assistance to agencies interested in developing citation procedures. In this connection, chapter 9, on implementation, and chapters 7 and 8, which discuss how programs have been initiated in some selected jurisdictions, should be particularly helpful.

The purpose of this appendix is to set forth in summary, checklist form the major steps that should be taken in initiating a citation procedure. These include:

Planning.

Consultation.

Training.

Implementation.

Monitoring and Evaluation.

Planning

I. Establish policies and procedures.
    A. Substantive issues.
        1. Scope of the program—should criteria be general or tied to specific offenses? Should domestic disputes, resisting arrest, minor sex offenses constitute specific exceptions, for example? Should citations be mandatory for very minor offenses or minor municipal ordinances, for a contrasting example?
        2. Deciding type of program to be used: field, jail, or combination.
        3. Method of release—should criteria differ by type of citation (jail versus field)? Should criteria be general or based on a point system?
        4. Mandatory, discretionary or presumption in favor of release (will officer be required to state reasons for nonrelease)?
        5. Should warrants other than for failure to appear be treated differently or entail special criteria?

6. Should a citation be issued after a citizen's arrest?
7. Will juveniles and adults be handled in the same way?
B. Procedural issues.
   1. Will booking be mandatory? If so, when?
   2. Will a court appearance be required? If not, what alternatives will be followed?
   3. What types of identification will be considered satisfactory before issuance of a citation?
   4. Will the district attorney's office review the citation before filing, or will the case be filed directly into court?
   5. Calendaring—how many days delay should there be? Who will decide at what date and time the defendant should appear?

II. Draft written guidelines (general orders).
A. Include statement of rationale behind program.
B. Spell out criteria for release.
C. Spell out procedures to be followed.
III. Design citation form.
A. Will it replace arrest/offense reports?
B. Will it include a formal court complaint?
IV. Check statutory requirements and guidelines.
V. Determine whether outside resources are needed to begin program (usually not).

Consultation

I. Review policy and procedure, citation form, and written guidelines with appropriate persons.
A. Departmental personnel with responsibility for carrying out program—administrative, jail personnel, patrol, warrant division, records.
B. Judges.
C. District attorney's office.
D. Public defender's office.
E. Court clerk's office.
F. Other law-enforcement agencies (state police, sheriff's office, etc.).
G. City or county officials.
II. Revise policies as needed.

Training

I. Should be directed at developing understanding of rationale behind program and benefits to accrue to the department and patrol officers specifically and establishing positive attitudes.

II. Review procedures to be followed and make sure all officers understand criteria for release and nonrelease.

III. Review citation form and proper completion of all parts.

Implementation

Will program be implemented as a special project or not? Initiating as an experiment with a special project title helps call attention to the new procedure and get officers involved in making needed changes.

Monitoring and Evaluation

I. In the initial stages of implementation citation forms should be checked to see that they are being correctly filled in, officers should be spot-checked to be sure that they understand and are following correct procedures, and feedback should be encouraged to iron out any problems that arise.

II. Adequate records should be maintained and reviewed on an ongoing basis.
  A. Number of misdemeanor arrests effected should be tabulated monthly by specific offense categories.
    1. Number of field releases should be tabulated monthly by specific offense categories and by division.
    2. Number of jail releases should be tabulated monthly by specific offense categories.
    3. Percentages of those eligible and actually released should be tabulated.
  B. Court failure-to-appear data should be matched to citations and arrest/release reports, tabulated by method of release (bail, OR, etc.), and monitored to determine whether criteria should be tightened or broadened.
  C. Summary of reasons for use of physical arrest in lieu of citation release should be monitored at least in initial stages of program to determine whether program is being utilized as designed.
  D. Number of persons for whom warrants are issued for failure to appear who voluntarily surrender to the jurisdiction of the court within thirty days of court appearance date should be determined so that realistic failure-to-appear figure can be assessed.

III. Periodic review of program should be undertaken with appropriate persons (within the department and court and other personnel) to improve procedures or substance of program and to spot problems that need to be addressed. Monitoring and evaluation is valuable even when programs are statutorily mandated or spelled out. Statutory revisions can be made if appropriate data is available to indicate needed revisions.

Appendix C:
Checklist for a Good
Citation Procedure

There is probably no such thing as an ideal citation program. What works well in one community may not work as well in another. There are many common features, however, among the better functioning citation procedures. This appendix attempts to identify these features in checklist form.

The major characteristics of a model procedure are:

Written procedures.

Use of both field and station-house/jail citations.

Careful screening of defendants.

A high level of release.

A carefully designed citation form.

Efficient processing of defendants and documents.

A locus of responsibility for monitoring, evaluation, and improvement.

Prosecution of failure-to-appear cases.

Written Procedures

However small the agency it is important to have the basic guidelines set forth in writing. The written guidelines should cover:

1. The criteria for release.
2. Procedures to be followed in making a release.
3. Processing of defendants and documents.

Use of Both Field and Station-House/Jail Citations

A well-designed program will use both field and station-house citations. Field citations, where they can be used, save much more time and are more efficient than station-house citations.

1. Make maximum use of field citations.
2. Make citation and other forms available to store personnel and train them to have the forms completed when officers arrive in shoplifting cases.

3. Use station-house citations for defendants who are too angry or intoxicated to be released immediately.
4. Use station-house citations for defendants for whom identification is in doubt.

Careful Screening of Defendants

1. Defendants should be carefully screened for identification.
2. Defendants should be evaluated in terms of the likelihood that they will appear in court.
   a. Residence—generally defendants can be expected to appear from a fairly wide area, some go statewide or broader.
   b. Other criteria—other criteria often used include job and family ties, prior record, nature of the offense.

A High Level of Release

1. Release should not be wholly discretionary. Personnel should be instructed to release if the criteria are met.
2. Officers should be asked to identify the reasons for nonrelease.

A Carefully Designed Citation Form

1. The form should be clear and simple.
2. The place and time to appear should be clearly indicated.
3. The form should be capable of serving as a complaint for court purposes.
4. The form should be a substitute for some or all other police records.

Efficient Processing of Defendants and Documents

1. Officers should appear in court only if the defendant contests the charge.
2. The prosecutor should have an opportunity to screen the complaints prior to filing. (Routing should be to the prosecutor and then to the court.)

Clearly Assigned Responsibilities

1. The procedure should be monitored, evaluated, and improved.
2. Responsibilities for monitoring, evaluation, and improvement of the procedure should be placed with a single individual.
3. Statistics should be maintained regularly as to the number of releases and how this compares with the number of physical arrests by offense.
4. Statistics should be compiled periodically as to the reasons for nonrelease and for failures to appear.

Prosecution of Failure-to-Appear Cases

Although not strictly a matter of police procedure, prosecution of failure-to-appear cases is an important aspect of a well-run citation procedure.

1. Warrants should be processed to the extent possible.
2. Failures to appear should be charged and proved even if more serious charges are involved in the case.
3. Judges should be requested to impose a separate sentence on the failure-to-appear charge. These sentences can be fines or extremely short confinements (a few days). They should be additional rather than concurrent, and stated to be for failure to appear.

Index

Index

About the Author

Floyd Feeney is professor of law and executive director of the Center on Administration of Criminal Justice at the University of California, Davis. He formerly served as assistant director for the President's Commission on Law Enforcement and Administration of Justice and as law clerk to Justice Hugo Black of the United States Supreme Court.

DATE DUE
